Frontispiece. The General Grant Tree, Grant Grove, Kings Canyon National Park. This tree, second only to the General Sherman in volume size, is regarded by many visitors as the more beautiful of the two. Its location is optimal for rapid growth; estimates based on increment borings suggest that this tree is less than 2000 years old. *Photo by* National Park Service.

THE GIANT SEQUOIA
OF THE SIERRA NEVADA

Richard J. Hartesveldt
H. Thomas Harvey
Howard S. Shellhammer
Ronald E. Stecker
San José State University, California

V

U. S. Department of the Interior
National Park Service
Washington, D. C.
1975

As the Nation's principal conservation agency, the Department of the Interior has basic responsibilities for water, fish, wildlife, mineral, land, park, and recreational resources. Indian and Territorial affairs are other major concerns of America's "Department of Natural Resources." The Department works to assure the wisest choice in managing all our resources so each will make its full contribution to a better United States—now and in the future.

This publication is one in a series of research studies devoted to special topics which have been explored in connection with the various areas in the National Park System. It is printed at the Government Printing Office and may be purchased from the Superintendent of Documents, Government Printing Office, Washington, D.C. 20402.

Library of Congress Cataloging in Publication Data
Main entry under title:

The Giant sequoias of the Sierra Nevada.

"NPS 120."
Supt. of Docs. no.: I29.2:Se6/7
1. Sequoia gigantea.   2. Forest ecology—Sierra Nevada Mountains.   I. Hartesveldt, Richard.
QK494.5.T3G5   585'.2   74-26690

For sale by the Superintendent of Documents, U.S. Government Printing Office
Washington, D.C. 20402 - Price $2.40
Stock Number 024-005-00618-4

Contents

PREFACE   xiii

Chapter 1

INTRODUCTION   1
  Discovery   2
  Human interest   4
  Sequoia lumbering operations   9
  Public reservation of sequoia lands   12
  Significance of the giant sequoia   15
  Sequoia varietal forms   18
  Nomenclature   19
  Origin of the name sequoia   25

Chapter 2

THE TREE AS AN INDIVIDUAL   29
  Description   29
  Seedling stage   30
  Sapling stage   40
  The bark   40
  Maturity   41
  Maximum size at maturity   43
  Fused trees and grafted roots   47
  Old age   47

Cones and seeds   48
Nature of the wood   55
Longevity   57
Sequoia burls   62
Other large trees   62

Chapter 3

DISTRIBUTION OF THE GIANT SEQUOIA AND ITS RELATIVES   66
Origin   66
Present distribution   68
Soil moisture availability   77
Senescence   78
Stability of groves   79
Sequoia elsewhere   79

Chapter 4

ECOLOGICAL CONCEPTS   82

Chapter 5

LIFE HISTORY   87
Reproduction   87
    Cone and seed production   88
    Beginning age of cone production   90
Cone abundance   91
Seed viability   94
Seed dispersal and code fall   95
Seed viability loss after dissemination   99
Effects of animals on seeds upon the ground   100
Conditions for germination   100
Conditions for seedling survival   103
Seedling density   106
The sapling stage   107
Maturity   108
Old age   108
Death   116
Decay   119

Chapter 6

SEQUOIA COMMUNITY INTERRELATIONSHIPS   121
Structure of sequoia communities   121
Plant and animal relationships   123
Vertebrates   124
The food chain   126

The role of the chickeree   128
Invertebrate relationships   132
Competition within communities   137
Plant succession   137
Human impact   142

Chapter 7

MAN, FIRE, AND THE FUTURE   146

APPENDIXES

    I   Sequoia relatives   151
   II   Common and scientific names of plants   152
  III   Common and scientific names of animals   154
   IV   Common and scientific names of insects and other arthropods   156
    V   Common and scientific names of Thallophytes   157
   VI   Groves of *Sequoiadendron giganteum* in California   158

REFERENCES   165

INDEX   171

Figures

Frontispiece: The General Grant Tree, Kings Canyon National Park.

1 Mother of the Forest, Calaveras Grove, showing scaffolding for the
   removal of the bark.   7
2 The felling of the Mark Twain Tree, Big Stump Grove.   8
3 The Boole Tree, Converse Basin.   11
4 Weeping sequoia, Roath Park, Cardiff, Wales.   20
5 The Wawona Tunnel Tree, Mariposa Grove.   21
6 Sequoyah, a Cherokee Indian for whom the giant sequoia may
   have been named.   26
7 A portion of the Lord's prayer printed in Sequoyah's Cherokee
   syllabary.   27
8 Two-week old sequoia seedling.   31
9 The awl-shaped leaves of mature sequoia foliage.   32
10 Shade-killed young sequoias, Mariposa Grove.   33
11 Young spire-top sequoia.   34
12 Sequoia bark pattern, showing parallel ridge form.   35
13 Sequoia bark pattern, showing spiral form.   36
14 Sequoia bark pattern, reticulate form.   37
15 Sequoia bark pattern, showing thin, smooth bark.   38
16 The Alabama Tree, Mariposa Grove, showing classical
   round-topped form.   39
17 The General Sherman Tree, Giant Forest, the world's largest tree.   45
18 Graphic comparison of the world's four largest trees.   46

19 Living remnant of severed sequoia trunk section   49
20 Sequoia with buttressed trunk, Giant Forest.   50
21 Giant sequoia cones.   51
22 Lichen-encrusted sequoia cone.   52
23 Sequoia cone illustrating the 3:5 Fibonacci ratio.   53
24 Giant sequoia seeds.   54
25 Basal area regression curve, the basis for estimating the age
    of living specimens.   60
26 A sequoia burl, Mariposa Grove.   61
27 Present distribution of the giant sequoia.   70-71
28 The Senate Group, Giant Forest.   72
29 The lowest naturally seeded giant sequoia known, on gravel bar,
    South Fork of the Kaweah.   76
30 Giant sequoias in the palace grounds, La Granja, Spain.   81
31 Cross section of sequoia cone peduncle showing annual rings. 89
32 Sequoia cone on 11-month-old potted specimen.   92
33 Cone-load distribution in mature sequoia.   93
34 Chickaree, or Douglas squirrel.   96
35 Adult of the long-horned, wood-boring beetle, *Phymatodes nitidus*. 98
36 Numerous seedlings of the giant sequoia are to be found in
    trough of burned logs.   109
37 Dense sequoia reproduction in area burned by fire of 1955,
    Cherry Gap, Sequoia National Forest.   110
38 Snag-top sequoia, typical of old age.   111
39 The Black Chamber, Giant Forest.   112
40 Lightning-topped sequoia, Giant Forest.   113
41 Remains of the Wawona Tunnel Tree following its collapse in 1969. 118
42 Hypothetical "rotation" of a chickaree territorial use of
    sequoia trees for cone harvest.   130
43 Galleries of carpenter ants in the barks of a giant sequoia tree,
    Giant Forest.   135

Tables

1 Comparison of Dawn Redwood, Coast Redwood, and Giant Sequoia. 17
2 Germination for sequoia seeds of various ages.   95
3 The more common birds within a typical giant sequoia grove.   125

Preface

It is our intent to present as accurate and up-to-date an account as possible of *Sequoiadendron giganteum* (Lindl.) Buchh., known popularly as the giant sequoia, big tree, or Sierra redwood, and to correct much of the error, distortion, and inconsistency which has, unfortunately, pervaded the literature since the discovery of this species in 1852. What follows is a synthesis of the writings of others together with the results obtained from our field studies, begun in 1956.

The factual errors and distortions about the sequoia may have arisen from that curious mixture of man's attitudes and the romance attending the exploration and settlement of the American West. In that mixture, it seems, humility was too often subservient to curiosity: as though the tree's dimensions were less than admirable, the sequoia became taller, greater in diameter, and older than it actually was. Certainly, not all this was intentional. It must be realized that in those early days most visitors to sequoia groves were untrained in the natural sciences and that their instruments for measurement were crude at best. Even more frustrating is the realization that many scientists of the time accepted and passed on these errors, apparently with little challenge. Curiously, a few of the distortions have survived the test of time and appear in some contemporary writings, occasionally by authors of considerable note.

It must be acknowledged that, more recently, some of the early observations have been verified as indeed accurate by modern and more sophisticated instruments. But, in those early days, it was difficult to separate fact from fancy, and fanciful exaggerations, apparently having the greater appeal, were more often passed on as facts.

The contradictions of "fact," so prevalent in sequoia literature, eventually evoked challenge and led, finally, to objective investigations. As a result, much of the fancy and certainly some of the romantic appeal of the sequoia story disappeared as the sequoia became less ancient, shorter, and smaller in girth. We feel, however, that the story is no less fascinating for these later discoveries.

Our account here is certainly incomplete. It brings together what we consider the best possible information on the giant sequoia to date. The case of the giant sequoia has confirmed the maxim that any research worth its salt poses more questions than it answers. In predicting, therefore, that the end to this story may never be told, we hope its pursuit may provide many others with such pleasures and gratifications as we have shared in a most pleasant research laboratory—the sequoia forest communities of the Sierra Nevada.

Our research program was both encouraged and supported[1] by the U.S. Department of the Interior, National Park Service, the chief custodian of these majestic trees. We are deeply indebted to the service, and especially acknowledge the personal interest and encouragement of park administrators, biologists, naturalists, rangers, and forestry personnel. Largely thanks to them, many of our early hypotheses and premonitions have borne fruit to become segments of the sequoia story. We are also indebted to the following persons for invaluable assistance in the production of this book: Glenn Harris for technical services, especially those relating to accuracy of reference citations and quotations; Bonnie Doran for secretarial services; Ivan Linderman and Loren Green for art and graphic work; Winthrop Stiles III for photographic services; Carl W. Sharsmith and James P. Heath for their meticulous review of the rough draft; and the many others whose suggestions have been incorporated in this text.

Richard J. Hartesveldt
H. Thomas Harvey
Howard S. Shellhammer
Ronald E. Stecker

June 1972

[1]Contract 14-10-9-900-254

1
Introduction

Our hope is to present the story of the giant sequoia and the ecological interrelationships with its associated biota, including man, and with its inseparable abiotic environment. The story which follows may, at times, prove provocative and disturbing, but hopefully challenging to the imagination. The ecological concepts discussed are basic and not peculiar to the giant sequoia communities.

The presence of Western man, however, created problems among the sequoias not anticipated in the earlier years, namely, that of the impact of visitors upon the once pristine sequoian forests. Investigations designed to determine the extent of the impact brought to light many aspects of the sequoia story that were not previously known or but poorly understood.

Because of its rather singular attributes of enormous size and longevity, its majesty, and its rugged mountain setting, the giant sequoia has, from the time of its discovery, drawn people into its native Sierra Nevada in ever-increasing numbers. Man has seemed compulsively inclined to visit the largest specimen, the oldest specimen, to drive through the tree with the tunnel in its trunk, or to see still other specimens with novel attributes—novelty itself being an attraction. As men came in unplanned-for numbers, mostly in the three summer months, they placed a great strain upon certain groves or on limited areas within groves, causing degradation of both the living communities and their physical environments. The more heavily visited specimens were literally in danger of being "loved to death" by the admiring public. Growing concern over the integrity of this national treasure moved us to write this book.

As studies of the human impact progressed, shedding considerable light on its various aspects, corrective measures were conceived and implemented. A most valuable by-product of these studies was the determination of many gaps in the written life history of the species, especially in its ecological relation to other plants and animals. To better insure programs of protective management, specific studies were directed at these gaps, and gradually, as in a puzzle of many parts, the picture took on form and clarity. The giant sequoia's life story now holds even greater potential interest for scientist and layman alike. The resulting appreciation is often reflected in the respect and careful protection given these trees by visitors to the sequoia groves. We hope our interpretation of the sequoia story will further that end.

A major goal of ours is to maintain the highest level of scientific integrity without sacrificing readability. While we intend this presentation to be more factual than impressionistic, it may be somewhat difficult at times, and perhaps undesirable, to eliminate completely the latter aspect.

Scientific words and concepts must be employed to convey the story in its fullest meaning. There is no pretext for avoiding such terminology when concepts must be expressed exactly. We believe most of these terms, where their meaning is not implicit, are adequately explained in the text where first used. The appendixes list the scientific names of plants and animals found as associates in the sequoian communities but not importantly connected with the sequoia story. For the reader who wishes to enrich his experience and knowledge, the appendixes also contain additional material too detailed for inclusion within the text.

Discovery

It is intriguing to wonder what thoughts may have run through the minds of those who first saw these colossal trees, so greatly exceeding in size any tree previously recorded. One may think of their reacting with a flurry of adjectives and grandiloquent phrases expressing awe and wonderment. But such was not the case. For the people moving westward in the early and mid-19th Century, a first-priority consideration was that of just remaining alive. Then, too, discoveries were rather commonplace during that period of America's history, so that immediate responses may have been somewhat subdued, or perhaps the uncommon was expected.

The news of the tree's discovery, announced in 1852, seems to have captured the attention of the civilized world. Any lack of grandiloquence on the pioneers' part has since been rectified many times over by people with far more leisure, and the flow of impressionistic rhetoric has not yet ceased.

The first authentic record of the giant sequoia was published at Clearfield, Pa., by Leonard (1839). Leonard was chronicler for the Joseph Reddeford Walker party, which crossed the Sierra Nevada in the autumn of 1833. In almost stoic tones, he relates that they ". . . found some trees of the redwood species, incredibly large—some of which would measure from 16 to 18 fathoms around the trunk at the height of a large man's head from the ground." We must remember that the time was late autumn, the weather was growing colder, and their shoes were badly worn. Undoubtedly, the pioneers feared being trapped in the winter snows of the Sierra and were bent on reaching the more amiable

climate of the San Joaquin Valley. There was no mention of their having collected either foliage or cones. Their reference to "redwood species" indicates at
least a familiarity with the coast redwood, discovered 64 years earlier, in 1769;
but possibly this reference to redwoods was interjected as an afterthought while
the journal was being prepared for publication.

The route the Walker party followed across the Sierra is not clearly documented. Leonard did, however, refer to a very deep valley to the south of their
route which could have been Yosemite. If so, then the sequoia trees he described
must have belonged to either the Tuolumne or the Merced grove, both of which
are now included in the western portion of Yosemite National Park. None of the
other northern groves of sequoias fits the relationship of a deep valley to the
south quite so well as these groves do.

Despite the Walker party discovery in 1833, the world was not to learn of the
sequoias' existence for another 19 years. It seems that the printing shop in
Clearfield burned to the ground and that only two copies of Leonard's narrative
were rescued. The disposition of these copies following the fire appears undocu-
mented at this time, but clearly the contents were either not made known to the
world or simply not accepted by the public at large. At least one copy turned up
some 65 years later, when the Burrows Brothers Co. of Cleveland, Ohio, reprinted its contents in 1904 and again in 1908. By that time, however, the tree's
existence was hardly news, although Leonard's version of the discovery did
increase the confusion as to who really had seen it first. Perhaps the most
incredible aspect of the Walker party's discovery is that there is still no record of
its members ever having mentioned the big trees to anyone else. Possibly their
stories were laughed off as the preposterous exaggerations with which mountain
folk of the early West were often credited.

The loss of the Leonard narrative insured the prevalence of another tale of
discovery in the literature. A. T. Dowd, an employee of the Union Water Co. at
the town of Murphy's in the Mother Lode Country, apparently discovered one
of the two Calaveras Groves while tracking a grizzly bear he had wounded. His
report of the unusually large trees he had stumbled upon was regarded as an
unfounded extension of the truth by the men in the camp and not one of them
would consent to make the hike to see for himself. Rather than defending his
story of the trees, therefore, Dowd resorted to a trumped-up story about a huge
grizzly bear he had shot, and thus lured several others into accompanying him to
the grove, where his earlier claim was, of course, quickly verified.

An article in the *Sonora Herald*, in June 1852, reported Dowd's discovery of
the Calaveras Grove. Other than the Leonard narrative, this is the first printed
record of the giant sequoia to appear in the public press, and its publication
remains the sole reason for using the term "effective discovery date" for the
species. Shortly thereafter, the article was carried in San Francisco's *Echo du
Pacific*, and within a year London's *Athenaeum* and the *Gardener's Chronicle*
had announced the giant sequoia to Europe.

With the news out, others began to claim discovery of the tree—at earlier
dates than Dowd's, of course. The Walker party's failure to speak up on behalf
of its valid claim is again perplexing. Shinn (1889) and others record the story of
John Bidwell, who claims that in 1841 as a boy, he passed through a grove of
exceptionally large trees while on a hunting trip. Why he also kept this tempting

secret is puzzling indeed, and it was only after Dowd's discovery that he volunteered the comment, "Those are my trees; I'm glad they have been found." Bidwell, who later ran for President of the United States, reportedly conveyed this information to Col. John C. Fremont, although no written record apparently exists. This, and his failure to speak up on his own behalf until after the Dowd discovery, renders his story suspect.

Other contenders for the honor of discovery—J. Marshall Wooster, William Quirk, and a Mr. Sanborn—were collectively given credit for discovering the Calaveras Grove in May 1850 (Todd 1870). In a letter to the editor of the *San Andreas Independent*, dated 26 September 1857, Wooster relates carving their initials in the burnt part of one of the trees. He also claims, however, that a Mr. Whitehead, a prospector, had visited the same grove in April of that year. The carved initials of Wooster, Quirk, and Sanborn were verbally verified by "someone" at a later date.

Joly (1883) reported discovery of the sequoia in 1850 by a Capt. Boling; Krussman (1966) credits the Prince of Wied (Germany) with the honor between 1832 and 1834; John Barrington, in a personal communication, mentions the sending of a packet of seed to his father in Ireland in 1844; and Prince (1854) claims that he and 12 others were in the Calaveras Grove in 1849. Still others refer to the arrival of sequoia seeds in Europe before 1853. The most vulnerable point in these last-mentioned stories is that they were all written following Dowd's discovery in 1852, and therefore still remain suspect.

Once the sequoia was "discovered," its fame spread rapidly around the civilized world and brought visitors from near and far. Some came out of curiosity to verify the great tree as fact or to disprove it as fancy; a few came in awe, and some out of piety; others came to transport the tree's progeny to the far reaches of the earth; and a goodly number came to cut it down.

Human interest

Once the sequoias' existence and its novel attributes became known, publicity was quick to follow. The vital statistics of girth, height, and age were in great demand but in short supply. Anyone who had visited a sequoia grove was considered an authority, and his reports of the trees' dimensions were both indisputable and highly publishable. However, the circumferences were measured by methods that seem wanting in the light of today's demands for precision. Pacing, outstretched arms, and lariat lengths were all in common employ. Undoubtedly, the lariats' elasticity was greatest when stretched out for measurement. Some measurements were admittedly "by eye." Only the relatively recent literature mentions steel tapes of known accuracy. Yet some of the older figures have been repeated over and over as gospel.

Whereas the more conscientious measured the circumference in a horizontal plane above the trees' butt swell, others made ground-level measurements, which were then converted directly into diameters without the slightest compensation either for butt swell or for the measurement possibly being made on a steep slope. Others reported unabashedly the circumference of fused doubles and triples. The trees' attraction assuredly grew when diameters of 45-50 ft were recorded in several publications, all using the same source of information. But not everyone accepted the figures as true, and challenge was inevitable. Starker (1935) said of the studies that followed, "Many claims have shrunk under the glare of investigation, some dissolved into the atmosphere."

The trees' heights were understandably more difficult to measure than their diameters. Triangulation was crude at best and might better be called guesswork. Fallen trees *should* have been another story, but were not. It is beyond comprehension that fallen specimens could be so inaccurately measured; many works reported the "Father of the Forest" in the Calaveras Grove to be 450 ft long as it lay on the ground—140 ft longer than the tallest specimens measured by modern surveying instruments. There are several early reports that the tallest sequoias approached 600 ft, and one Londoner even predicted that specimen trees, if undisturbed, would eventually reach 50 ft in diameter and 1000 ft in height (Anon. 1876).

With the credibility gap between early Westerners and the rest of the world, it occurred to American showmen that they could prepare and ship sections of the big trees to almost any place on earth for exhibition purposes, thus silencing the doubting Thomases. Exhibit sections were prepared for this purpose with great labor and expense. But the American fancy for size so exceeded the availability of downed specimens that, to satisfy the curious, some of the larger living trees were selected for sacrifice, apparently without qualms or regrets.

The carnage began in the same year as Dowd's discovery, 1852. Saws of such gigantic proportions being understandably not available, pump augers were used to weaken the first of the many trees cut. According to Remy (1857), 25 men worked 10 days drilling the holes that finally set it off balance until it toppled. The tree dropped with a thundering crash, its reverberations exceeded only by the furor of a private citizenry incensed over its destruction. The trunk reportedly hit the ground with such force that "mud and stones were driven near 100 feet high where they have left their mark on the neighboring trees" (Anon. 1855a). If some Americans seemed callous over the felling, others were certainly greatly troubled. Several articles, singularly alike in tone, expressed unbelieving revulsion: this was, in time, to forge a movement which later resulted in the public reservation of nearly all sequoia lands.

An example of the more classic rhetoric in this vein comes from the editor of *Gleason's Pictorial Drawing Room Companion* (Anon. 1853):

To our mind it seems a cruel idea, a perfect desecration, to cut down such a splendid tree. But this has not been done, however, without a vast deal of labor. It was accomplished by first boring holes through the body with long augers, worked by machinery, and afterward sawing from one to the other. Of course, as the sawing drew to a close, the workmen were on the alert to notice the first sign of toppling, but none came; the tree was so straight and evenly balanced on all sides that it retained its upright position after it had been sawed through. Wedges were then forced in, and a breeze happening to spring up, over went the monster with a crash that was heard for miles around. The bark was stripped from it for fifty feet from the base, and is from one to two feet in thickness. It was taken off in sections, so that it can be placed, relatively, in its original position, and thus give the beholder a just idea of the gigantic dimensions of the tree. So placed it will occupy a space of about thirty feet in diameter, or ninety feet in circumference, and fifty feet in height. A piece of the wood will be shown, which has been cut out from the tree across the whole diameter. We are told that this piece of wood shows a vestige of bark near the middle, and that this bark was evidently charred many centuries ago, when the tree was comparatively a sapling. At last accounts, the tree was in Stockton, on the way to San Francisco, where it was to be exhibited previous to its shipment to the Atlantic states. Probably it will not be very long, therefore, before our readers will be able to get a view of this monster of the California woods for a trifling admission fee. In Europe, such a natural production would have been cherished and protected, if necessary, by law; but in this money-making, go-ahead community, thirty or forty thousand dollars are paid for it, and the purchaser chops it down, and ships it off for a shilling show! We hope that no one will conceive the idea of purchasing Niagara Falls with the same purpose! The Mammoth Cave of Kentucky, is comparatively safe, being *underground*; and then it would be impossible to get it all the way through the limited size of the entrance! So, for the present, at least, we need not except the cave this way. But, seriously, what in the world could have possessed any mortal to embark in such a speculation with this mountain of wood? In its natural condition, rearing its majestic head towards heaven, and waving in all its native vigor, strength and verdure, it was a sight worth a pilgrimage to see; but now, alas! it is only a monument of the cupidity of those who have destroyed all there was of interest connected with it.

However well taken, the points made above did little to slow the destruction. A second specimen was to be exhibited in the Crystal Palace at Sydenham, England.

Because means of transportation were primitive, the weight of large specimens created difficulties. The tree chosen for the Crystal Palace display was the "Mother of the Forest," another resident of the Calaveras Grove. Its bark was stripped to a height of 120 ft above the ground from scaffolding erected for that purpose (Fig. 1). Because the weight of the trunk's whole section would have been tremendous, only the bark was shipped. Even this posed engineering problems, for the "Mother" had a basal diameter of 31 ft. The remaining portion of the tree (most of it) was left in place, where it fared rather poorly. It reportedly remained "alive" for a few years; but, divested of its bark, it was assured of premature death. Even so, its remains stood intact until partially destroyed by fire in 1908, and the remaining snag is a prominent landmark of the North Grove today.

The skinning of the tree was utterly deplored by John Muir, who often set the tenor of feeling about such matters. In Muir's words, this was ". . . as sensible a scheme as skinning our great men would be to prove their greatness" (Wolfe 1938). The display at Sydenham was immensely popular, however, and remained so until fire consumed both the Palace and the "Mother's" vestments in 1866. With the tree's removal from its ancient mountain home, hastened by many centuries, its value to mankind came to an untimely end.

In 1876, another tree was cut from the Grant Grove for Philadelphia's Centennial exhibition. The uneven surface of its stump bears testimony to man's struggle in bringing it down. Except for the portion removed for exhibit, the trunk still lies in front of its more fortunate neighbor, the famed General Grant Tree.

One of the better-known sequoias felled for exhibition in 1891 was the Mark Twain Tree in what is now called Big Stump Grove, Kings Canyon National Park

Fig. 1. Mother of the Forest, Calaveras Grove. In order to prove the great size of the newly discovered mammoth trees of California, the bark of this 31-ft sequoia trunk was carefully removed by means of scaffolding erected to a height of 120 ft. The sections of bark were reassembled for a display at the Crystal Palace, Sydenham, England. The dead snag of this once great tree remains as a monument to man's mood during the 1850s. *Photo by permission of Harpers Magazine.*

(Fig. 2). Early photographs show a near-perfect specimen without serious fire scars. Because of its excessive size and weight, an extensive feather-bedding trench was dug to prevent its breakage in felling. Some 8 days of labor were required for the felling, a monument to the engineering skill of the loggers, whose pride undoubtedly exceeded their monetary recompense. Collis P. Huntington gave the basal section of the tree to the American Museum of Natural History in New York City, where it remains today. The next higher section, presented to the British Museum in London, has remained there since. The remainder of the tree was cut up for grape stakes and fence posts, so that only the stump remains. Surely, these cross sections of the tree have been of great interest to viewers, but can it possibly be as great as if it were today a living museum piece in its native Big Stump Grove?

Though much to be regretted, the cutting of exhibit sections was only a fraction of the tragedy that was to befall the giant sequoia.

Fig. 2. The Felling of Mark Twain Tree, Big Stump Grove. In what is now a part of Kings Canyon National Park, this excellent specimen was cut in 1891 for museum display sections. A great loss to the lovers of nature, its felling was regarded as a great feat of logging engineering. *Photo by* National Park Service.

Sequoia lumbering operations

Logging entrepreneurs were interested in far more than a few verifiable measurements to satisfy the curious. The thought that a single sequoia log contained more board footage than a whole acre of northern pine held, for a Lake States logger, a pocket-jingling interest. Imagine the thrill of cutting 3000 fence posts from one tree, enough to fence in an 8000-acre ranch, plus some 650,000 shingles that would cover between 70 and 80 roofs (Andrews 1958); or imagine one tree providing enough wood for a telephone pole 40 miles high! These are but a few of the size criteria the lumbermen used. The literature, filled as it is with just such materialistic comparisons, bears out their eminent success in this field.

Several groves in the southern Sierra were logged of virtually all marketable species, including the giant sequoia. No matter how questionable the cutting, a market for it existed, and so the sequoia was cut. Its wood, resembling that of its coastal cousin, although more even-grained and much more brittle, was marketed under the same name, which probably adds to confusion between the two trees in the public mind today.

Although the wood's great resistance to decay was a distinct advantage, its low tensile strength and brittleness made it unsuitable for most structural purposes. When felled, the dry, fine-grained sequoia often broke across the grain, or in almost any direction. Steele (1914) described it picturesquely as breaking into "more wasteful shapes than so much frozen water." Consequently, as the cedar gave out, the king of trees was converted into such plebeian items as fence posts, grape stakes, shingles, novelties, patio furniture, and pencils for Europe—ignoble uses for a most noble tree. While the storm of resentment gathered, whole groves were cut down for these purposes beginning in 1856 and continuing intermittently until the mid-1950s.

The giant sequoias' size, which was, in essence, the trees' undoing, posed various problems for the most experienced logging engineers of the time. But the problems of logging were a challenge, and challenge in the old West daunted few and encouraged many. Always, Yankee ingenuity rose to the occasion, as manifest in the felling, skidding, and milling. The task of getting the trees down was of Herculean proportions and the slightest miscalculation could result in great losses of wood and, of course, danger for man. To log a tree of sideshow proportions took men with sideshow imaginations. Undercuts on the larger specimens were enough for a man to stand in upright, or pose upon a horse or mule. Saws had to be welded together to span the breadth of the larger trees.

Felling often caused the wood to shatter, wasting as much as 75% or more of individual trees. Challacombe (1954) reflects the feeling of many; it was a "real national tragedy," and the term "arboricides" was coined specifically in reference to the sequoia loggers.

With increasing lumber prices, more and more sequoias were cut. Some were left shattered on the ground and, although a few of the remnants were salvaged when intact, this was small consolation to those vigorously opposing their cutting. The shattering of the big logs had a double minus value: not only was the splintered wood useless for harvest, but the debris, according to Muir (1894), was "a certain source of future fires," a prediction which frequently has proven true. Despite the general belief that sequoia wood is not especially flammable, it burns hotly when splintered and dry.

The sections of sequoia logs that did not shatter with felling still presented problems of handling and transportation. Logs 20 ft and more in diameter could not be handled in the same way as the "diminutive" species of sugar pine and ponderosa pine. Where splitting by wedges was not feasible because of size, auger holes drilled into the ends of the logs were filled with explosives to blast the huge trunks apart. This method was a gamble, often producing nothing but a great quantity of unusable splinters.

Reduced to a workable size, the sequoia logs were milled in the normal manner, although some new methods of transportation were introduced. In the Converse Basin operations, the wood was first milled in the area of cutting and then sent 54 miles by flume to Sanger, where it was further milled to finer requirements. The flume's water capacity and its gradient controlled the rate of water flow. Andrews (1958) vividly reports this portion of the sequoia tragedy. Despite its depressing overtones, it is well worth reading. The author records flume velocities of up to 50 mph, a speed of commercial log transport unmatched in that period. The flume was also used to transport supplies, mail, and occasionally human beings, whose safety was understandably in jeopardy.

After several years, a large portion of the flume burned in a forest fire and the rest was finally dismantled, a fitting finale to an era of wanton forest destruction. The devastation and wastage in sequoia logging are almost beyond belief. Healing will take centuries; the shambles remaining are perhaps the greatest monument ever to man's destructive lumbering enterprises in this country. Of the many thousand sequoias in the Converse Basin, only one escaped the ax. Curiously, it was the largest.

In a spectacular setting overlooking the Canyon of the Kings River is a tree with the largest diameter of all sequoias—35 ft. Its size was undoubtedly its salvation. Because of the tree's great bulk and rocky habitat, it is unlikely that enough wood could be salvaged to make it worth the felling. The logging company was thus persuaded to spare the great tree, which was then named for Frank A. Boole, the Superintendent of the Converse Basin Mill, who had overseen the cutting of the Basin's 2600-acre sequoia forest. Today, the Boole Tree (Fig. 3) seems a monster out of place among the diminutive but thick stands of Scouler willows which encroached after the logging. Its 268 ft stands out starkly against the distant skyline of Spanish Mountain north of the Kings River. In its greatly modified environment, with few serious competitors, the Boole Tree is probably growing faster than before the logging. Ironically, it may well escape future serious fires because of the greatly reduced fuel in its vicinity, and it will perhaps continue to grow uninterruptedly for many centuries. Still, this preservation of one tree hardly compensates for the destruction of its more easily merchantable compatriots.

By the time of their final inroads, the loggers had cut some 34% of the original sequoia acreage. Fortunately, not all the groves they cut were ruined as the Converse Basin was. An informative and interesting record of the logging era, with good detail, is "The Status of *Sequoia gigantea* in the Sierra Nevada," a report to the California State Legislature (1952) compiled and written largely by Frederick A. Meyer, then chief state park forester, from data gathered by him

Fig. 3. The Boole Tree, Converse Basin Grove, Sequoia National Forest. The world's third largest tree stands alone among the diminutive Scouler willows. Named after Frank Boole, it commemorates the man who supervised the cutting of virtually all of the other sequoias in this large grove. Its basal diameter exceeds that of any other living sequoia tree. *Photo by* H. Stagner, courtesy National Park Service.

and by Dean F. Schlobohm of the California Division of Forestry. We share the thought Meyer offers in his summary that, in spite of the logging desecration, the resulting forest and landscape teach us lessons of academic worth. The young sequoias that had seeded so thickly into the much disturbed soils grew with great rapidity and vigor, and definitely disproved the long-standing hypothesis that the sequoia was a decadent, slow-growing tree well on its way to extinction. Furthermore, the sequoia was revealed as one of the earliest trees in the stages of plant succession, a fact poorly understood until relatively recent time.

That some people, at least, did care about such things was another valuable lesson; but it took the destruction of a great many sequoias to weld public sentiment into a momentous, though somewhat sporadic, movement that eventually reserved for aesthetic and scientific purposes most of the original sequoia lands. The reservation began during the Lincoln administration in the heat of the Civil War. Americans must be forever grateful for the efforts of the few dedicated people and citizen groups who led that crusade.

Public reservation of sequoia lands

In a piece of landmark legislation, the Federal government in 1864 deeded the Mariposa Grove and the Yosemite Valley to the state of California, to be administered as part of the Yosemite Grant. The bill, introduced by California Senator John Conness, a native of Ireland, set the tone for the preservation gradually extended to most sequoias. The lands given over to California were meant ". . . for public use, resort, and recreation and shall be inalienable for all time." Although the bill did not define the word "inalienable," no one challenged it or asked its intent. This grove, then, received public protection before the lumber industry had a chance to develop an interest in it.

Despite Yosemite Valley's protected park status, John Muir was apprehensive about both logging and grazing of sheep in the highlands above. He foresaw accelerated erosion and impairment of Yosemite Valley. With written attacks on the practices of the "muttoneers," Muir urged establishment of a Yosemite National Park which would include all the lands draining into the valley. He further voiced fears that the destructive logging of his beloved sequoias would result "in a few decades . . . in a few hacked and scarred monuments" (Muir 1894).

His efforts, assisted by the deep interest of editor Robert Underwood Johnson, strongly contributed to passage of further remarkable Federal legislation in the autumn of 1890. This was preceded by several unsuccessful attempts to create reservations above Yosemite Valley, and farther south in today's Sequoia and Kings Canyon National Parks. Congressmen Lewis E. Payson of Illinois and William Vandever of California were instrumental in the passage of legislation which created Sequoia and General Grant National Parks on 25 September 1890, and Yosemite National Park on 1 October 1890. There were notable similarities in the two bills, but some unusual and unexplained differences between them suggest that the whirlwind of congressional activities leading to their passage may have been opportunistic. Whatever the reason, much of the sequoia land was reserved before the lumber industry became seriously interested in obtaining the rights to log it off.

Berland (1962) thought that including the Giant Forest in Sequoia National Park was somewhat erratic. Yet the preamble of the 1 October act explicitly stated that:

> ... rapid destruction of timber and ornamental trees in various parts of the United States, some of which are the wonders of the earth on account of their size and the limited number growing, makes it a matter of importance that at least some of said forest should be preserved.

Apparently, sequoias were not mentioned by name, but the reservations were clearly intended as parks for public enjoyment.

Representative Payson's bill for the reservation of land above Yosemite Valley and the Mariposa Grove contained slightly different wording, although both bills apparently were patterned rather closely after the Yellowstone act of 1872. The bill, an alternate for one introduced the previous March by Representative William Vandever of California, declared the purpose was "to set apart a certain tract of land in the State of California as a forest reservation." Neither the word "park" nor the word "sequoia" appears in the text (Ise 1961); but the bill stated explicitly that "regulations shall provide for the preservation from injury of all timber, mineral deposits, natural curiosities or wonders" (26 Stat. 650).

Payson's bill found strong favor with California Congressmen, the Governor of California, and the Secretary of the Interior. Once again, opportunism probably moved Congress to act quickly, so that the bill was passed by both Houses in a single day and signed into law by President Benjamin Harrison on 1 October 1890. Land, which included both the Tuolumne and Merced groves, was soon withdrawn from the public domain. The land was soon given the title "park" by the Secretary of the Interior.

As provided by these two bills, a considerable percentage of all sequoia land was now in public reservations, although logging of sequoias continued or was threatened on lands adjacent to Sequoia and General Grant National parks. The famous Calaveras Groves far to the north were excluded from these preservation efforts.

There was, however, much concern over the future of the Calaveras Grove. This unit of sequoias had the sentimental distinction of being the first to have drawn the world's attention to these trees and, at the turn of the century, may still have been the most visited grove. The land had been sold into private ownership for $100,000, and the owner, because of an initially low return on his investment, thought of logging the big trees. The furor that arose over this prospect had substantial backing, with people turning to both state and Federal governments to intervene in the threatened destruction through purchase of the Grove. The state of California showed no serious interest in its acquisition at the time, perhaps because it hoped that the Federal government would purchase it as a national park unit (Anon. 1903). There was widespread interest in its preservation, and Theodore Roosevelt, then Governor of the state of New York, strongly encouraged Secretary of the Interior Ethan Hitchcock to do all in his power to save the grove. Such help, however, was not forthcoming, and, when Roosevelt became President, a petition was sent to him bearing 1,437,260 signatures and asking for federal purchase of the land. Although Roosevelt generally fought for conservation issues, he failed to persuade Congress to appropriate the money. After several more attempts at such legislation, the North Grove was finally included in a bill signed by Roosevelt in 1909 creating the Calaveras Bigtree National Forest.

It was not until 1931, however, that the grove acquired park status. Through matching funds raised by the Save-the-Redwoods League and the Calaveras Grove Association, the North Grove was finally added to the growing state park system. Public ownership of the much larger South Grove, because of its much higher price-tag, was not due for another 23 years.

After these many years of planning and fund-raising, the Save-the-Redwoods League acted as intermediary for a gift of $1 million from the Rockefeller Foundation, and another $65,000 from the Calaveras Grove Association. The state provided $1.07 million from state park matching funds, and from the U.S. Forest Service came land valued at $350,000. While the purchase was consummated on 29 April 1954, the land, being inaccessible to the public, was not formally dedicated as a part of the state park until 9 September 1967, when the long struggle to preserve the Calaveras Groves finally reached fruition.

In the southern Sierra, the unappropriated sequoia lands remained a thorn in the sides of many. Money was again the problem, and the Federal government lacked what was needed for purchase. Here, the benefactor was the National Geographic Society. In 1916, it began a fund-raising campaign to purchase lands within and adjacent to Sequoia National Park. By 1921, the society succeeded in adding nearly 2000 additional acres of sequoia forest to the park, at a cost of $96,330 (White 1934). The last remaining large piece of sequoia land, the Redwood Mountain Grove of 3720 acres, was added to the park system when Kings Canyon National Park was created in 1940. While minor adjustments and additions to the public ownership followed, the bulk of the trees was safely reserved by that time.

The present distribution of total sequoia acreage by ownership is approximately as follows:

National Parks	68%
National Forests	21%
Bureau of Indian Affairs	1%
State and County	2%
Private owners	8%

The current policies of all public ownership agencies preclude lumbering of the giant sequoias. Even on private lands, there is little apparent threat of further cutting. For all practical purposes, the era of sequoia logging is over and, except for the threat of fire and ecological damage by man, the remaining specimens appear safe for future generations' spiritual and scientific benefit.

Significance of the giant sequoia

Man has invested the giant sequoia with a significance that probably has no counterpart among other trees. The reasons, of course, vary, whether deriving from the scientific or the lay community. Undoubtedly, its great size, longevity, and comparative rarity have prompted the ardor and respect expressed for the tree ever since its discovery, as evidenced in the abundant writings about the sequoia over the past 120 years. Approximately 3000 literature citations are now catalogued for this species in about a dozen languages, with English leading the field.

Curiosity about a tree of such novel dimensions was understandable in the years immediately following its discovery. An even greater significance was attached to it because of its assumed rarity. Although the novelty wore off somewhat with the discoveries of new groves, man's regard for the sequoia was enhanced only by increasing knowledge of its seemingly unique attributes.

Obviously, the lumberman and the sideshow opportunist regarded the giant tree as a source of board footage and personal profit. But the giant sequoia, unlike other species in the Sierran forests, proved to be of small importance as a timber, and perhaps the great brittleness of its wood was its eventual salvation. Certainly the carnage wrought by the lumbermen aroused the feelings and brought forth public efforts that succeeded in reserving nearly 90% of all sequoia acreage. Truly, the reservation of no other species of tree rests upon so dedicated a foundation.

The many superlative attributes of the giant sequoia are often still confused in the public mind with those of its relative, the coast redwood, which is also a tree of admirable proportions, but whose range nowhere overlaps or even closely approaches that of the giant sequoia.

If measured by volume of wood in the outstanding specimens, the giant sequoia is undisputedly the world's largest tree. Even so, exaggerations were commonplace in earlier years. It is now known that one species of tree has a greater diameter than the giant sequoia (see "Other Large Trees"), that three grow to a greater height, and one, the bristlecone pine, lives to a greater age. While such attributes have been of largely popular appeal, efforts were made to explain their scientific importance as well. Today, many other biologically and ecologically interesting qualities of this tree further insure man's high regard for it. Consider, for instance, that it carries a remnant gene pool which bridges the eons back to the Cretaceous, some 125 million years in the past. Here is a world of scientific interest perhaps never to be fully explained.

Long before man discovered the existing sequoian species, fossil remains of several related forms had been found and named. The records of these ancestral forms are known from much of the Northern Hemisphere, and those which seem directly ancestral to the giant sequoia are known from northern Europe, Greenland, and North America. Evidence suggests that these forests at times were enormous in extent. It is possible that pterodactyls, the large flying reptiles, inhabited these ancient sequoia forest communities (Ellsworth 1924).

The closest direct ancestral relative of the giant sequoia, according to fossil evidence, lived in what is now southern Idaho and western Nevada. Forests of these trees existed there as much as 10-20 million years ago, before the last great rise of the Sierra Nevada. As conditions became cooler and drier with the Sierra's rise, the survivors of this change still managed to prosper along the southwestern edge of their range, not far from the present eastern boundary of California. While the Sierra's elevation was still only a few thousand feet, this species migrated westward through the lower mountain passes and on to its western slope. As the Sierra continued to rise to its present imposing height, a gradual but vast climatic change took place: the land to the east became too dry for the sequoias, leading to their extinction there, and finally the sole survivors of a once widespread race were the relict groves left in a string along the western slope of the Sierra Nevada.

The present distributional range of the sequoia and its closest living relatives invites us to speculate on past genealogical changes and to ask just where the species is headed now. For that matter, similar questions arise over the entire redwood family, whose past distributional area, compared with the small remaining one, is impressive to say the least. Today, the family Taxodiaceae is represented by only 10 genera and 15 species in the entire world (see Appendix 1). Each species has a limited areal range. Only *Taxodium* (southern and pond cypresses) and *Sequoia* (coast redwood) have fairly extensive ranges, while that of *Metasequoia* (dawn redwood) is so small and its location so remote that it was unknown to science until 1944. Of the 15 species constituting the redwood family, only five are native to the New World. The other 10 are found in the Asiatic-Pacific portion of the world. The family's two sequoian forms in America are confined to the Pacific coastal area, and the range of the giant sequoia is much smaller than that of the coast redwood.

In the redwood family, the two genera apparently most closely related to the giant sequoia are the coast redwood and the dawn redwood. These three genera, or any two of the three possible pairs, share many characteristics, of which we will highlight only a few. An expanded comparison is shown in Table 1.

While many differences are visible among these trees, perhaps the most evident ones are in the foliage. In striking contrast to the dawn redwood, with its deciduous leaves, the giant sequoia and coast redwood are evergreen. Each fall, the dawn redwood sheds its short branchlets of leaves and the tree remains barren until spring, unlike many other coniferous trees. The giant sequoia's leaves are all scale-like, while those of the dawn redwood are flattened and needle-like. Most of the leaves of the coast redwood are also flattish and needle-like, but some resemble the overlapping, scale-like leaves of the giant sequoia. The leaves of the dawn redwood are arranged opposite to each other, while in both other genera they are placed spirally on the stems. The distinctive arrangement in the dawn redwood leaf is repeated in the cone scales, which are actually modified leaves. Its seed cones are shed yearly; those of the coast redwood may persist on the trees for perhaps a year or two after the seeds have been shed. In the giant sequoia, however, the seed cones remain green after they mature at the end of the second year, and may continue alive and closed for as much as two decades.

The coast redwood is well known for its ability to sprout from its base or from its stumps and roots following destruction by fire or logging. This vegetative reproduction is undoubtedly an adaptation to fire, assuring more rapid recovery for the species. Although the giant sequoia has other adaptive

TABLE 1. Comparison of Dawn Redwood, Coast Redwood, and Giant Sequoia. From Chaney 1950; Munz 1959; Stebbins 1948.

	Dawn Redwood (*Metasequoia glyptostroboides*)	Coast Redwood (*Sequoia sempervirens*)	Giant Sequoia (*Sequoiadendron giganteum*)
Size	Height—to 140 ft	to about 370 ft	to about 310 ft
	Diameter—to 6 ft	to 16 ft	to 35 ft
Leaves	Needle-like	two types; needle-like and awl-shaped	awl-shaped
	with small stalk	sessile	sessile
	deciduous	persistent	persistent
Long branchlets	Bear short shoots in opposite pairs	bear short shoots in alternate array	bear short shoots in alternate array
Short branchlets	Leaves opposite	leaves in spirals	leaves in spirals
	leaves in two rows	leaves in two rows except at tips	
	deciduous	deciduous	deciduous
Seed Cones	About 1 inch long	0.75-1.50 inches long	2-3 inches long
	deciduous		
		some persistent but open after first season	persistent and may remain green 20 years
	scales opposite	scales in spirals	scales in spirals
	seeds in one row on each scale	seeds in one row on each scale	seeds in two rows on each scale
	mature in one season	mature in one season	mature in two seasons
Pollen Cones (staminate)	scales opposite	scales spiral	scales spiral
Buds	scaly	scaly	naked
Chromosomes	22 per diploid cell	66 per diploid cell	22 per diploid cell

relationships with fire which will be explained in some detail later, it has never been known to sprout from its base. The small sequoias occasionally growing from the trunks of larger specimens are, in reality, separate trees.

One important difference, not readily seen, among the three sequoia forms is the number of chromosomes in their reproductive cells. Both the giant sequoia and dawn redwood contain 11 chromosomes per reproductive cell, while the coast redwood has 33 per reproductive cell. On the basis of similar chromosome numbers, Stebbins (1948) suggests that "the dawn redwood may actually be a direct descendant of the present coast redwood." It is generally held that the closest relative of the giant sequoia is the coast redwood, but that the dawn redwood and the coast redwood are more closely related. Because of the similarities in these trees, the term redwood has been applied to all three.

Although the extent of the distributional range of the giant sequoia during the geological past and its immediate predecessor is but poorly known, its current restriction in the form of 73 groves, the total area of which is estimated at 35,607 acres, has been seen by some as heralding the final chapter of a long and successful genealogy. While the assumption appears logical, its validity will, of course, remain for a future generation to record. The species does appear trapped in its remnant "cells," but there is no evidence that its groves are now shrinking in size. Most of the grove perimeters seem relatively stable, and some groves show good evidence of expansion during the past few centuries.

The collective attributes of this species have, from the very beginning, whetted the appetites of both scientific question and inquiry. The admirable longevity of individual specimens and the ancient lineage of their predecessors have lent to it a significance for mankind that is well beyond the realm of botanical sciences. Geology, climatology, entomology, genetics, phytogeography, and other fields have all gained from knowledge of the sequoia. With the many recent additions to such knowledge, its significance for man has only increased, and is not likely to lessen with time.

Sequoia varietal forms

After the sequoia was introduced in Europe in 1853, several forms or sports appeared in nursery stock and were assigned horticultural names. Man's careful selection has resulted in several such forms, assumed to represent mutant strains; in the wild, however, where similar mutations doubtless occur, the seedlings are eliminated by the environment as rapidly as they appear, and therefore, not surprisingly, none has ever been noticed or recorded. In Europe, a much greater effort to grow sequoias in nurseries gave these forms, once noticed, correspondingly better care than in the United States. Den Ouden and Boom (1965) list some 14 horticultural forms, of which only 2 may be considered common.

The weeping sequoia (*Sequoiadendron giganteum* 'Pendulum') probably originated in Nantes, France, in 1863, while another specimen of the same form was grown from seed at a nursery in Carlisle, England, and still another at Versailles, France. This form is the commonest of the species' horticultural varieties, with specimens found in the British Isles, France, Switzerland, and perhaps elsewhere in Europe.

The growth form of the weeping sequoia is one of shortened, drooping branches, in striking contrast to the sequoia's normal form. Some of the trees are straight of habit, but commonly they bend over in grotesque forms, more interesting than beautiful. A specimen in Cambridgeshire, England, takes the form of a large hoop, 40 ft long. One, at Somerset, forms a 42-ft arch, while one in Sussex turns horizontal at 40 ft. Nelmes (1964) refers to the specimen in Roath Park in Cardiff, Wales, as the "ugliest tree in Britain" (Fig. 4). This form is not common in the United States, where the only living specimens known at present are on the Stanford University campus in Palo Alto, and the San Jose State University in San Jose.

The only other horticultural form fairly common in Europe is the golden sequoia, *S. giganteum* 'Aureum,' which is possibly identical with one known as *S. giganteum* 'Aureovariegatum.' This form was developed at the Lough Nurseries in Ireland in 1856. Its foliage is a variegated golden yellow. The largest specimen recorded is 66 ft tall and grows in Gloucestershire, England.

Other horticultural forms are, in their appearance, dwarfed, columnar, white-variegated, pyramidal, glaucous, and silvery. Four of them are no longer in cultivation, the stock having died. All these forms are generally propagated by cuttings in hot frames rather than by seeds.

Nomenclature

Naming the giant sequoia, we believe, has been a process beset with such difficulties as few other well-known species of plants have suffered. Controversies over the various names began early and, from time to time, rose to clamorous proportions. No less than 13 scientific names have been proffered for this species. Although this number is not excessive for plant species, considerable disagreement accompanied the naming and, occasionally, certain accepted rules of botanical nomenclature were abandoned. Botanists of considerable note were involved. Furthermore, the tree has had five English common names, and the result has been confusion for the general public. While a full account of the contentious intrigue and chauvinism over the naming is beyond the scope of this book, some aspects of the story are worth reporting.

It seems logical to assume that, over the centuries, several tribes of California Indians were familiar with sequoias and had words or names for them. Powers (1877) lists only one such name, used by the Mokelumne Tribe in the Miwok tongue: "woh-woh'nau," or "wawona," which is more common today. He records that the word was formed in imitation of the hoot of an owl, the guardian spirit and deity of the sequoia trees. It was thought bad luck for any person to cut or otherwise damage them. The literal translation apparently means "big tree," but the word "wawona" is best known to the world as the name for the famed Tunnel Tree of Yosemite's Mariposa Grove (Fig. 5).

The Walker discovery party offered no common name for the giant trees they had found other than "trees of the redwood species . . .," indicating that they knew of the coast redwoods at least at the time of their writing. But this could hardly be called a christening. Dowd apparently made no suggestions after his 1852 rediscovery, but the term "mammoth tree" was rather common in writings immediately following his find. This designation was soon largely discarded in its English usage in favor of the simpler term "big tree," although "mammoth tree" is still preserved as "Mammutbaum" with German-speaking Europeans. "Big tree" is still common today, but in disfavor because the name describes several other trees as well. The terms "giant sequoia" and "Sierra Redwood" are probably in much greater use today. Even the specific epithet *gigantea* is used as a common name, as is *sempervirens* for the coast redwood. Unlike scientific

Fig. 4. Weeping sequoia, Roath Park, Cardiff, Wales. One of 14 known horticultural forms, the weeping sequoia has no one typical form; most are bent and grotesque. This one was labeled, "The Ugliest Tree in Britain." *Photo by* W. Nelmes, Roath Park.

Fig. 5. The Wawona Tunnel Tree, Mariposa Grove. This tree, tunneled in 1881, has long been a favorite with park visitors and is perhaps the world's best known tree. Pictured here is President William Howard Taft (hat off in carriage), John Muir, Major Forsythe, Congressmen McKinley and Englebright, Governor Gillett, Charles Forbes, and Captain Butts. 8 October 1909. Boysen *photo, courtesy* National Park Service.

names, common names are often provincial and thus subject to personal preference and emotion. However, with no ground rules by which to "legislate" in favor of one acceptable common name, the variety now in use is probably here to stay. As we noted, even scientists have met with difficulties in giving this species a scientific name, which itself has quite a history.

Fossil sequoian ancestors were known for many years before discovery of the two living species, and the generic term first given them was *Steinhauera* by Presl (1838) of Czechoslovakia. His description of the genus being rather poor, it is difficult to know whether the two living species are closely enough related to *Steinhauera* to warrant their assignment to that genus. While the rules of botanical nomenclature forbid assigning the name of a fossil genus to a living one, this was done in 1904 by German botanist Karl Kuntze (Post and Kuntze 1904), who attempted to revise some 30,000 plant names. His *Steinhauera gigantea* was not at all well received and is usually cited in the literature only as a curiosity.

In 1828 Lambert named the coast redwood *Taxodium sempervirens*, which troubled an Austrian botanist, Stephen Endlicher, a specialist in coniferous trees. He found good reason to segregate it from the genus *Taxodium*, assigning the name *Sequoia sempervirens* to the coast redwood, and *Sequoia gigantea* to a horticultural form of the tree, possibly his *Sequoia sempervirens* 'Glauca' (Endlicher 1847).

The giant sequoia, first seen in 1833, remained unknown to the scientific world—and to the world in general—until 1852, 5 years after Endlicher's use of the name *Sequoia*, and it remained unnamed until 1853. Endlicher died in March 1849, and could play no role in the ensuing problems over the tree's naming. In June 1852, Dowd sent branches bearing both foliage and cones to Albert Kellogg, one of the founders of the California Academy of Sciences and a scientist of considerable note. Kellogg did not immediately proffer a scientific name and description for the new species, but in May 1855, he and Dr. Behr of the Academy finally named it *Taxodium giganteum*, thus adhering to the genus which Lambert had assigned to the coast redwood. By then, however, the species had acquired five other names, which invalidated their proposal. Furthermore, the tree is not as closely related to *Taxodium* as Kellogg and Behr had presumed, although it is classified in the same family. The literature does not explain why Kellogg and Behr delayed 3 years in offering a name. Whatever the reason—and lack of interest was not a likely one—the price was the naming of the tree by a European.

Apparently, some question also exists about the role another American botanist, John Torrey, played in naming the sequoia. One parcel of specimen materials sent to him was purportedly lost in transit across the Isthmus of Panama. According to Bloomer (1868), specimens did perhaps reach Torrey, whom he quotes as naming the tree *Sequoia gigantea* in August 1855. Since no formal publication by Torrey confirms this, any claim he may have otherwise made to its naming is invalid. Whether he knew that Joseph Decaisne of France had earlier assigned it the same name, or that Kellogg and Behr had assigned a name 3 months before, cannot be determined.

The species was given its first scientific name after the visit of a William Lobb, who in the summer of 1853 was collecting plants for the nursery of James

Veitch of Exeter, England. In San Francisco, Kellogg showed the visitor the cones and foliage brought in by Dowd and gave him a description of the tree. Lobb, who must have recognized it as a member of the family Taxodiaceae, may have also realized the potential interest of the nameless tree to his employer's customers. After hastening to the Calaveras Grove where he collected cones, seeds, foliage, and seedlings, he sailed immediately for England, arriving there by 15 December 1853. While his hasty departure for home was probably in his employer's interest, possibly another motive prompted him—the prospect of presenting his specimens to John Lindley, an English botanist. Lindley lost little time in capitalizing on the tree's lack of a name. He wrote a description of the tree and published it 2 weeks later in the *Gardener's Chronicle* (Lindley 1853), including the tree's first scientific name—in honor of Arthur Wellesley, Duke of Wellington. "As high as Wellington towers above his contemporaries," said Lindley, "as high towers this California tree above the forest surrounding it. Therefore, it shall bear for all time to come the name *Wellingtonia gigantea*." Neither Lindley nor the beloved Wellington had ever seen this tree. Both were English, neither had ever been to California, and Wellington, it was reported, had no particular interest in plants. So the battle began.

Americans were understandably incensed over the name, despite their own curious foot-dragging. A strictly American species honoring a British war hero, and named by a Briton in Britain! Lindley was soon judged *non compos mentis* by most American botanists for his "scientific indelicacy," and many abandoned academic dignity to qualify Lindley's name with various uncomplimentary adjectives.

Though quick to respond with names of their own to counter the unpopular *Wellingtonia*, Americans had rather poor success. Kellogg and Behr had finally assigned the name *Taxodium* to the tree. American botanist C. F. Winslow stated that, if it were indeed a *Taxodium*, it should be called *T. washingtonianum*; if it were a new genus, he suggested that it be named *Washingtonia californica*, with the obvious intent of honoring an American military hero who actually liked plants. The tree proved not to be a *Taxodium*; *Washingtonia* is and was then the name of a genus of palms and therefore illegitimate, and the International Code of Botanical Nomenclature prohibits the assignment of provisional and alternative names, so both American attempts at rescue proved abortive (Rickett 1950).

Botanists of other nations must have been more than mildly amused over the struggle. One of them came to the aid of the desperate Americans, and successfully so. In 1854, French botanist Joseph Decaisne asserted in a detailed lecture that the coast redwood and the big tree surely belonged to the same genus, and he therefore reassigned Endlicher's *Sequoia* to replace *Wellingtonia*, while maintaining Lindley's specific epithet, *gigantea*. Whether Decaisne was inflicting mild revenge on the British for Wellington's defeat of the French at Waterloo, or whether Americans had prodded him to make the change remains a moot point (Anon. 1855b). Neither is it certain whether Decaisne knew that Endlicher had already used the name *Sequoia gigantea*, and that homonyms are also untenable under the accepted code of nomenclature. The name *Wellingtonia* soon began to disappear from British literature as botanists like Joseph Hooker agreed to the new generic name. As a common name for this tree, however,

Wellingtonia is still generally used in the British Isles today.

Not all botanists agreed with Decaisne concerning his new generic name. In 1855, Berthold Seeman, a German naturalist living in England, eliminated the error of using the earlier homonym *Sequoia gigantea* by proposing the compromise, *Sequoia wellingtonia*. Despite the validity of this name, the plight of the tree's nomenclature seemed only to grow. Botanists, while aware of the earlier homonym, accepted and used *Sequoia gigantea*, although by no means exclusively, until American botanist John T. Buchholz (1938) gave the tree its present name, *Sequoiadendron giganteum*. Buchholz, following a series of scholarly investigations, pointed out that the two California sequoias were strikingly different in their embryogeny, and not as closely related as previously believed. He further adduced more than 50 known botanical differences between *Sequoia* and *Sequoiadendron*. This, and the two trees' lack of a common fossil ancestor in their immediate past, justified his generic segregation. Buchholz's was the 13th scientific name assigned to this species over the years, as the following list shows:

Synonymy of *Sequoiadendron*
(St. John and Krauss 1954)

Sequoiadendron giganteum (Lindl.) (Buchholz 1939).

    Wellingtonia gigantea Lindl. (Lindley 1855).

    Americus gigantea (Lindl.) Anon. 1854.

    Sequoia wellingtonia Seem. (1855).

    Sequoia gigantea (Lindl.) Decaisne 1854.

    Taxodium Washingtonianum Winslow. (Winslow 1854).

    Washingtonia Californica Winslow. (Winslow 1854).

    Washingtonia Americana Hort. Am. ex Gordon. (Anon. 1862).

    Gigantabies Wellingtoniana J. Nelson, under pseudonym Senilis. (Nelson 1866).

    Taxodium giganteum (Lindl.) Kellogg and Behr. (Kellogg and Behr 1855:53).

    Americanus giganteus (Lindl.) Anon. emend. Gordon, *Pinetum* 330, 1858. Published in synonymy.

    Sequoia washingtoniana (Winslow emend. Sudw.) Sudw., *U.S. Dep. Agric. Div. Forestry Bull.* **14**:61. (Sudworth 1897).

    Steinhauera gigantea (Lindl.) Ktze. in Voss, *Deut. Dendrol. Gesell.*, Mitt. 16 (1907):90. (Voss 1908).

Perhaps under suspicion as the unlucky 13th, the Buchholz name was slow to gain acceptance. Dayton (1943), in an opinion survey of some American botanists, records amazing resistance against using the new name, with much expression of strongly emotional rather than academic opinions. And there was the problem of a national park bearing the name of the former genus. However, Sequoiadendron National Park has never been seriously suggested.

Perhaps more justifiable was the fear that, if Buchholz had correctly interpreted the relationship, the rules of nomenclature would force a return to the use of *Wellingtonia*. The latter, however, had already been assigned in 1840 to a plant in the family Sabiaceae, and thus became illegitimate as a name for the giant sequoia. Present well-substantiated evidence supports the generic segregation of the giant sequoia to *Sequoiadendron giganteum* and should close the matter. The common name is less well established, however; the National Park Service uses "giant sequoia," while the U.S. Forest Service and the California Division of Beaches and Parks prefer "Sierra redwood." Still others use the older name "big tree." Perhaps the confusion of names is not yet resolved.

Origin of the name sequoia

The name *Sequoia* has been most popularly represented as the Latinized version of "Sequoyah," the name of a remarkable Cherokee Indian (Fig. 6) from the southern Appalachian Mountains. He was the son of a Cherokee mother and a German immigrant father, and his Christian name was George Guess, or Gist. Being highly gifted, Sequoyah became a talented silversmith. His keen intellect led him to realize that the Indians' plight was partly due to their having no written language. Apparently troubled by this, Sequoyah began to experiment with symbols which he made to represent the various syllables of the Cherokee language, a language with many guttural sounds not easily adaptable to written English. He reportedly worked for 12 years, finally narrowing his syllabary to 85 symbols in 1821. His system proved easy to use and it is said that most of his tribe learned to use it. The *Cherokee Phoenix*, a newspaper begun in 1828, was printed in these syllabic characters, as were the Bible (Fig. 7) and a few other works (Martin 1957-58). Although popular writings often recorded Sequoyah as a chieftain, he held no such position in the Cherokee Tribe.

When gold was discovered in Cherokee country, the Indians were forced off their lands and those that were not killed, including Sequoyah, were "beneficently" placed on reservations in Oklahoma. Completely out of their element in a strange and hostile land, the Cherokees fared badly and began to wander. Sequoyah reportedly died during a trip to Mexico, possibly attempting to restore some meaning to the Cherokees' shattered lives (Mooney 1900).

Despite Sequoyah's short and unfortunate stay in his adopted state, and his burial as an outcast at an unknown spot in Mexico, Oklahoma claimed him as a citizen. In tardy recognition, he is one of two outstanding Oklahomans in Statuary Hall in Washington, D.C.

Certainly this compassionate and talented man, on whom such indignities were imposed, deserved the honor, and should have his place in the sun. Unforgivably, however, Endlicher omitted the etymology of his new genus in his *Synopsis Coniferae*, contravening another recommended procedure of botanical nomenclature. No one has ever found mention in his writings of Sequoyah's name or of his unique Cherokee syllabary. It was apparently assumed that Endlicher, a known philologist, admired the Indian for his linguistic accomplishments. The assumption became widespread, and some botanists, such as Asa Gray, searched the Endlicher papers for confirmation, but in vain. French

Fig. 6. Sequoyah, Cherokee Indian. A man of many talents, Sequoyah devised a syllabary that permitted his people to read and write in their own language. It is believed by many persons that the genus *Sequoia* is the latinized version of Sequoyah who lived 3000 miles to the east of this species. *Photo courtesy of* Library of Congress.

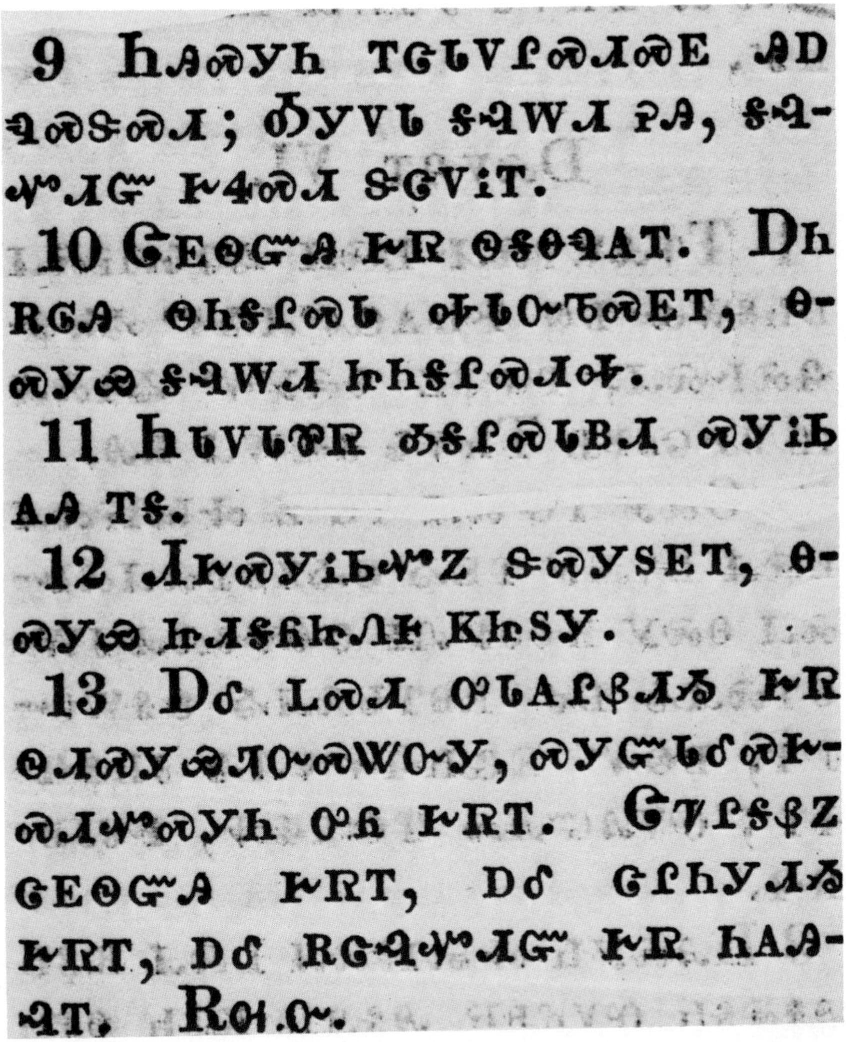

9 ᏂᎯᏍᎩᏂ ᎢᏣᏓᏙᎵᏍᏗᏍᎬ ᎯᎠ
ᏄᏍᏕᏍᏗ; ᎣᎩᏙᏓ ᎦᎸᎳᏗ ᎮᎯ, ᎦᎸ-
ᏉᏗᏳ ᎨᏎᏍᏗ ᏕᏣᏙᎥᎢ.
10 ᏣᎬᏫᏳᎯ ᎨᏒ ᏫᎦᎾᏄᎪᎢ. ᎠᏂ
ᎡᎶᎯ ᏫᏂᎦᎵᏍᏓ ᏧᏓᏅᏖᏍᎬᎢ, Ꮎ-
ᏍᎩᏯ ᎦᎸᎳᏗ ᏥᏂᎦᎵᏍᏗᎭ.
11 ᏂᏚᏙᏓᏆᏒ ᏧᎦᎵᏍᏓᏴᏗ ᏍᎩᎥᏏ
ᎪᎯ ᎢᎦ.
12 ᏗᎨᏍᎩᎥᏏᏉᏃ ᏕᏍᎩᏚᎬᎢ, Ꮎ-
ᏍᎩᏯ ᏥᏗᎦᏲᏥᏁᎨ ᏦᏥᏚᎩ.
13 ᎠᎴ ᏞᏍᏗ ᎤᏓᎪᎵᏰᏗᏱ ᎨᏒ
ᏫᏗᏍᎩᏯᏘᏅᏍᏔᏅᎩ, ᏍᎩᏳᏓᎴᏍᎨ-
ᏍᏗᏉᏍᎩᏂ ᎤᏲ ᎨᏒᎢ. ᏣᏤᎵᎦᏰᏃ
ᏣᎬᏫᏳᎯ ᎨᏒᎢ, ᎠᎴ ᏣᎵᏂᎩᏗᏱ
ᎨᏒᎢ, ᎠᎴ ᎡᏣᎸᏉᏗᏳ ᎨᏒ ᏂᎪᎯ-
ᎸᎢ. ᎡᎺᏅ.

Fig. 7. The Lord's Prayer, from the Cherokee Bible, using Sequoyah's syllabary. *Photocopy by* University of Michigan Library, *by permission of* the American Bible Society.

botanist de Candolle agreed with Gray that "the supposed origin of *Sequoia* from Sequoyah or Sequamal is entirely fanciful." Although Koch (1873) believed its origin to lie in one of the California Indian languages, his contention lacks support.

Gray thought that the stem of the word had derived from the Latin *sequi* or *sequor*, which means "following," and was an allusion to the two extant species as followers or remnants of many related forms now extinct (Bellue 1930). If there was an association with Sequoyah in Endlicher's mind, Gray felt, surely it was an afterthought (Anon. 1891). De Candolle dismissed the word's origin as unimportant, but others did not, hoping perhaps to rescue a name of American origin for an American tree. Whatever the origin, the name of this remarkable tree has remained generally associated for more than a century with that remarkable Indian, Sequoyah. Perplexity and doubt notwithstanding, let it so remain.

2
The Tree as an Individual

Description

Human propensity for superlatives has led to a rather one-sided view, as the giant sequoias described were mainly the larger specimens. Perusing the literature might lead us to suspect that young trees were scarce indeed, and seedlings nonexistent.

Seeing the trees themselves, we realize that descriptions are inadequate to do them justice. Records of the various measurements fail to convey the trees' massive beauty, and even pictures cannot reproduce their awesomeness.

Writers have long been inclined to compare the tree with other objects of known dimensions. The number of horses and riders that could stand in the hollowed cavern of the trunk, the arm lengths required to span its width, or the number of houses that one could build with its wood are familiar examples of such comparisons. Hinds (1893) declared that a mature sequoia tree is 3,125,000,000,000,000,000,000 times larger than a single bacterium—a comparison of questionable value, the author neglecting to say which sequoia was meant, and which species of bacterium.

As stated earlier, the erroneous and exaggerated sizes and ages of these trees have been refuted in recent years through the use of standardized measurement procedures and more sophisticated instruments. Despite this, standard procedures are not necessarily followed and reference points from which measurements were made are not necessarily given. The dimensions used in this account are official figures obtained from the National Park Service and the U.S. Forest Service.

Because the tree's appearance varies greatly with age, we will discuss each major stage of its life cycle.

Seedling stage

As germination progresses, the emerging sequoia seedling stands from three-quarters of an inch to an inch high by the time the seed coat is shed from its spreading cotyledons (Fig. 8). The number of cotyledons or seed leaves, varying from three to six, is usually four. They are bright green on the upper surface, reddish on the underside, and rather sharp-pointed. To the novice observer, they may closely resemble the seedlings of the white fir. The latter's seed leaves, however, are bluer in color, have blunter tips, and green undersides, all of which clearly distinguish them from the neighboring young sequoias.

Where site conditions approximate the optimum and the seedlings survive, the linear secondary leaves normally begin to appear within a matter of weeks as a rosette in the center of the developing crown. Depending upon soil moisture conditions, the cotyledons wither and fall away within a few to several weeks. Branching begins by late summer and the more vigorous specimens may have as many as six branches by autumn when the plant is perhaps 3 or 4 inches tall. By this time, the leaves of the newer foliage begin to resemble the awl-shape of those on the adult trees (Fig. 9), but spread much more from the stem and have longer tips than the leaves of the mature foliage. The root system is well branched and may be said to have a taproot often 4-5 inches long at this stage. Older trees lack taproots completely.

If the readily available soil moisture is plentiful during the second year of growth, the seedling may attain a stature of 8-12 inches and begin to acquire a somewhat roundish or oval crown of many branches. The foliage is now clearly recognizable as the giant sequoia's, being distinct from that of any other North American tree. The roots, still maintaining the juvenile taproot pattern, may now penetrate the soil to a depth of 10-15 inches.

Mature foliage of sequoias consists of awl-shaped leaves, 1/8 to 1/4 inch in length on the new shoots. The leaves are closely attached and persistent on the twigs in their basal portions only; the slightly spreading tips are free from the stem and bear sharp prickle points. Their overlapping, shingle-like arrangement gives the stems a rope-like appearance, with the stem completely concealed. The leaves are so persistent that they never fall singly, but are shed intact with the entire twigs to which they are attached after several years of photosynthetic service to the tree. Even as the stem sizes increase in radial growth, the original leaves persist, becoming more widely spaced; eventually the developing bark seems to engulf them, or they are sloughed off with the deciduous bark scales. Both time and shading vitally affect the shedding of the twigs, especially of those in the crown's interior where light is reduced.

In the better sites, upward growth of the leader shoot of seedlings will usually greatly exceed the rate of lateral growth, so that the developing crown becomes narrowly conical and sharply pointed at its tip. The seedlings in poorer sites grow slowly at best and may not outwardly show any growth increment at all. With greater shading, the struggling plant may lose parts of its foliage and thus shrink in overall size, but may maintain a somewhat globular crown for many years. When heavily shaded, the trunks are twisted and contorted into many forms, evidently lacking sufficient light for normal development. Persistent shade brings death to these shade-intolerant trees (Fig. 10).

Fig. 8. Two-week-old sequoia seedling. At this age, the typical seedling is about 0.75 inch tall, and bears four cotyledons of seed leaves. Depending upon soil moisture conditions, secondary leaves will make their appearance within 2-5 weeks.

Fig. 9. Mature sequoia foilage is unique in appearance among trees. Its spreading, awl-shaped leaves overlap each other in a spiral form that gives the branchlets its typical rope-like form. The leaves, which are sharply prickle-pointed, are persistent and shed mostly with the entire branchlet.

Fig. 10. Shade-killed young sequoias, Mariposa Grove, Yosemite National Park. Seeded in about 1912, these trees died in the dense shade of white firs which are more shade-tolerant than the sequoias. In the absence of canopy-opening fires, shading is a major death factor to young sequoias. *Photo by* R. J. Hartesveldt.

Fig. 11. "Spire-top" sequoia. Young sequoias in the better sites grow upward rapidly and maintain this narrowly conical crown form up to 100 years and more. The larger spire-tops are usually found in locations where sunlight and soil moisture are optimal. *Photo by* R. J. Hartesveldt.

Fig. 12. Sequoia bark pattern showing parallel ridges. Although a common pattern, most common is this pattern blended slightly with the reticulate pattern. The Mariposa Tree, Mariposa Grove, Yosemite National Park. *Photo by* R. J. Hartesveldt.

Fig. 13. Spiral bark pattern. Perhaps the least common of the major bark patterns, the spiraled form seems to be more common in the Mountain Home Grove than elsewhere. This genetic population suggested that this grove has been separated from other groves for a long period of time. Most spiraled specimens show a right-hand twist; a few of them twist to the left. *Photo by* R. J. Hartesveldt.

Fig. 14. Sequoia displaying strongly reticulated bark pattern, Redwood Mountain Grove, Kings Canyon National Park. *Photo by* R. J. Hartesveldt.

Fig. 15. Sequoia displaying thin bark, Grant Grove, Kings Canyon National Park. Some sequoias lose their bark scales readily and present a smooth, thin bark. The protective value of the fire-resistant bark is thus much reduced, a factor which may well explain the scarcity of such trees. *Photo by* R. J. Hartesveldt.

Fig. 16. The Alabama Tree, Mariposa Grove, a classical example of the round-top crown form of older sequoias. This crown form indicates a relative lack of fire damage to the base of the trunk. Fire has been a ubiquitous factor in the Sierra Nevada over many years so that this crown form is relatively rare. *Photo by* R. J. Hartesveldt.

Sapling stage

For several years, the young striplings in the better sites continue to grow rapidly in height and to maintain their narrow, conical crown form, which is now called a "spire-top" (Fig. 11). This sharp-pointed crown may persist for 100 years or more where the light is good, and the growing tip may be as much as 150 ft or more above the ground. The slightly ascending limbs are often dense with foliage, giving the crown a compact form which readily separates it from its associated firs and pines. Seed-bearing cones may also be common at this time, an added means of identifying the sequoia among its associates.

At this stage of development, the root system has spread out laterally and the taproot is gone. The depth to which the main root system grows is seldom more than 2 or 3 ft, and ranges outward to 100 ft or more, depending upon soil moisture conditions.

The trunk's diameter may be as much as 4 ft at breast height (4.5 ft above the ground), and the brownish bark may attain a thickness of 1-2.5 inches. If, as rarely happens, a sequoia survives to this stage in the open, its branches may persist nearly to the ground level. Where shaded, the lower branches die and begin to fall away, so that the crown becomes confined to the upper third or upper half of the tree.

The rapid upward growth favors the tree's survival but also invites possible damage to it. Where the tree survives a severe struggle for light by over-topping its competitors, wind and snow may damage its tall, slender stem, either or both breaking off the top or bending it beyond recovery. As it protrudes above the general crown level, it also becomes subject to lightning strikes.

The bark

As the sequoia ages, the grayish scales of the bark begin to slough away and expose the predominantly cinnamon-red bark which gives this tree its characteristically striking appearance on a sunny day. Although its synonym, redwood, may have been derived from the bark color, the more likely origin is the reddish color of the heartwood.

The eventual thickness of the bark is apparently a genetically controlled trait; some specimens seem to have less tightly bound bark scales than others, which results in a sloughing off and, eventually, thinner bark. The species is well-known, however, for the bark's massive thickness, perhaps greater than that of any tree on earth, and certainly a major attribute leading to the tree's longevity. The bark, being soft and fibrous, is a poor conductor of heat, and it contains but little pitch: all these features are important in its renowned resistance to fire damage. As the trunk grows outward, the bark must split longitudinally to accommodate this growth, and over several hundred years the bark ridges' average thickness is about 10 inches. Occasionally, individual sections of bark will exceed 24 inches, and we measured one very limited portion on a tree in Redwood Canyon, Kings Canyon National Park, that was 31 inches thick. The popular literature mentions thickness of 3 ft and more, figures which have never been verified. These represent careless estimates, or perhaps the total thickness of bark on both sides of the tree trunk. Age seems to increase the sloughing off of bark scales, the specimens with the thickest-bark being generally intermediate in age with 8-12 ft trunk diameters.

Another probable genetic trait is the pattern of the bark formed by the flutings and ridges. Perhaps the most basic pattern is a combination of the long parallel ridges and flutings and the reticulate pattern. In this pattern (Fig. 14), bark ridges coalesce or grow together at irregular and often distant points. Less common is the long parallel pattern in which the bark ridges are roughly parallel to each other and the trunk and seldom join each other (Fig. 12). The basic reticulate pattern (Fig. 14) is relatively uncommon, but outstanding in its appearance, and often bears very deeply fluted recesses.

In some localities, bark with spiralled flutings is common (Fig. 13). In the Mountain Home State Forest, a significant proportion of the total sequoia population has bark of the spiralled variety, most of which spirals to the right. Still other trees drop most of their outer bark scales, subduing the ridges to the extent that the older trees present a smooth-bark surface (Fig. 15). The bark of these trees is relatively thin, and often large segments of the trunk are riddled with sapsuckers' holes.

Much has been said about the fire-resistance of the sequoia's bark. Very definitely, it is a major factor contributing to this species' longevity. In normal circumstances, there is little or no pitch associated with the bark, which has a fire-resistant property often described as asbestos-like, especially where it is thick. "Asbestos-like" is perhaps a far-fetched analogy, because bark is organic and chars readily with continuous fire from an external source. The loose outer scales will burn with ease, as eloquently described by Muir (1878). The thicker parts of the bark do not hold a flame well, and are seared through only when accumulations of fuel beneath it burn for a long time, or when fire is repeated several times over, as it is especially on the up-slope sides of the trees where fuel accumulates as it moves slowly down-slope by gravity. The very long fire scars that run up trunks are probably largely due to heat from the burning of less fire-resistant adjacent trees such as firs and pines. Fire-scarring often begins in the tree's youthful stages and is repeated over and over again in the event that the tree survives. Cross sections of logged sequoias sometimes disclose fire scars that have completely healed since the damage was incurred. Even remnants of the bark are often embedded in the wood.

Maturity

The value of assigning the term "maturity" to a life stage of this species is questionable. Some trees first produce cones and seeds at the early age of 15-20 years, when they are still slender spires. Where individuals have managed to escape the damaging effects of fires, the rate of vertical growth finally slows in comparision to that of the lateral limbs. Thus the crown, previously pointed at the tip, gradually assumes a broadly rounded form, which many writers have assigned as the mark of maturity. The ubiquity of fire has reduced the perfect round-top, classical in its grace and beauty, to a relative rarity. The Alabama Tree and Galen Clark Tree in Yosemite's Mariposa Grove (Fig. 16), and the

Roosevelt Tree in the Giant Forest are excellent examples of this crown form. Where fires intrude through the bark and sapwood, the resulting disruption in the flow of water and minerals to the crown causes a part of the crown, usually the uppermost portions, to die back, which further results in an irregular crown and most often a dead, snag-top (Rundel 1973). Snag-tops are far more common in this stage of the sequoia's life cycle than is the rounded crown form.

The trunks of well-formed trees at this stage may be 10-20 ft or more in diameter above the butt swell. Perhaps the most salient feature of these grand specimens is the trunk's very slight upward taper. This attribute continues into old age, at least in the larger specimens such as the General Grant Tree (see Frontispiece). This characteristic is more prominent in sequoias than in any other Sierran tree. The height of mature specimens varies with both site quality and the degree of fire damage to the trunk's base. Bottomland trees seem generally to be the tallest ones, and specimens of more than 300 ft are certainly not rarities. Despite the rather commonly cited heights of 350-400 ft, there is little to substantiate such claims. One specimen recorded as being 320 ft has been remeasured at 220 ft, and the earlier figure is now regarded as a typographical error. The tallest known specimens recorded by instrument are 310 ft tall, one in the South Grove Calaveras Big Tree State Park (State of California 1924) and the other in the Redwood Mountain Grove, Kings Canyon National Park.

A better figure for the average height of mature specimens is 250-275 ft. Most of these trees bear dead tops, which proclaim a reduction from a former taller stature during a rather indefinite period of years. There is small chance, therefore, that they will exceed their present heights. Occasionally, lateral limbs take over the role of leader shoot and extend upward to greater heights than the original central stem.

The distance up to the first limbs is often impressive too. With the falling away of the lower limbs, the trunks are often bare for 100-150 ft and occasionally more. On the General Sherman Tree, for instance, the largest limb, with a basal diameter of nearly 7 ft, starts at the 130-ft level, and continues in a broad curve for an estimated 125 ft, thus constituting a sizable "tree" in itself.

Apparently, the areal dimension of a sequoia's rooting zone, based upon limited examination, is very nearly an inverse measure of the availability of soil moisture. Along the drainage bottoms where subsurface moisture flow may continue through most of the growing season, lengthy roots are not necessary and may not extend more than 40 or 50 ft away from the trunk. Where the soil is well drained, however, roots grow outward, commonly to a distance of 100 ft and more. Although Muir (1901) reports roots 200 ft long, there is only one other record of sequoia roots growing to that length.

In one study, trenches were dug outward from the base of an almost unburned 12-ft specimen in a well-drained site in the Giant Forest. Roots were followed until they disappeared at a distance of 125 ft from the tree. Assuming a roughly circular pattern of root growth around the tree, the rooting area was calculated at roughly 49,000 ft^2, or 1.13 acres. Rooting depths were also measured to calculate the volume of soil occupied by the tree's roots. At the base of the tree, main lateral roots went down nearly 4 ft, but almost immediately proceeded upward until all the feeder roots at the extremities were within a foot of the soil surface. Length and depth measurements established that the volume of soil occupied by roots was about 91,500 ft^3.

Within the volume of soil mentioned above, as much as 137,000 gallons of soil moisture could be stored at tensions between field capacity and the wilting point. Although not all of the water within this range is available for plant use, the amount of storage remains impressive. This water is shared, of course, with other plants having their roots in the same volume of soil. Occasionally, during the summertime, soil moisture is replenished to a small degree by thunder-showers. But winter snow melt and spring rainfall are the basic sources of supply of soil moisture for giant sequoia growth (Hartesveldt 1965).

The shallow depth of the roots of so large a tree surprises nearly all park visitors. How do such trees remain standing without a deeper anchoring system? Of course, they don't always. The shallow root system is often the tree's undoing and fallen trees expose roots that seldom appear to have gone deeper than about 3 ft. The largest lateral roots are usually a foot or less in diameter although they occasionally exceed 2 ft for a short distance. The trees, it seems, would need to be well balanced to maintain their equilibrium with such a shallow disc of radiating roots to hold them in the soil. Many of them seem perfectly perpendicular, the epitome of a long-enduring record of life. But the number of leaners is surprisingly large, and it remains a mystery what keeps some, such as the huge Grizzly Giant with its 17° lean, from toppling to their death.

Very significant is the number of small feeder roots that branch and rebranch in every direction: they present an enormous surface area for the intake of enough moisture to maintain a crown whose foliage may weigh more than a ton. No one has yet made a surface area calculation, perhaps because of the obvious technical difficulties and labor involved. In the upper 2 ft, the soil contains a striking number of these feeder roots, and they are also abundant at the mineral soil surface, where they catch even the slightest precipitation from short summer thundershowers. Below 2 ft, their numbers dwindle rapidly, although individual roots occasionally penetrate to a depth of 5 ft or more in the drier, better-drained soils. Undoubtedly, the complex intertwining of roots also helps support these huge trees.

Where the zone of soil moisture saturation is near the surface, the roots of bottomland and meadow-edge specimens are considerably shallower. Here, poor oxygenation of the roots prevents or sharply reduces the rate of water passage into the root xylem tissues, and often the roots die.

We will say more about maturity in the chapter on "Life History of the Giant Sequoia."

Maximum size at maturity

Man's insatiable curiosity to determine which is the very largest giant sequoia culminated in a flood of correspondence in the 1920s and 1930s which still bulges the old files of both the National Park Service and the Forest Service. The crescendo of demand for such information led finally to a formal study of contenders for the title. Diameter and height had long been the measurements most commonly cited; but in trees so massive, total volume of the trunk portrays the true size best although other parameters are also useful. Volume, as an expression of size, is a bit more difficult to visualize; it is certainly the most difficult figure to obtain, requiring sophisticated instrumentation and calculation techniques. Accurate measurements were generally lacking during this period of increasing interest in the greatest size.

Such was the controversy over which park or which county had the world's largest tree that a group of surveyors, in the summer of 1931, undertook to measure accurately several of the top contenders by means of transits and other surveying instruments. The world's four largest trees were identified in this study and reported by Jourdan (1932) as follows:

	General Sherman	General Grant	Boole	Hart
Height to top of trunk in ft	272.4	267.4	268.8	277.9
Volume, excluding limbs in ft^3	49,660.0	43,038.0	39,974.0	32,607.0
Volume of burns in ft^3	350.0	2,194.0	1,420.0	1,639.0
Restored volume in ft^3	50,010.0	45,232.0	41,394.0	34,246.0
Mean diameter of restored base in ft	30.7	33.3	33.2	26.5
Mean diameter in ft at 60 ft	17.5	16.3	15.3	14.5
Mean diameter in ft at 120 ft	17.0	15.0	13.9	12.9

Of the four above, the General Sherman Tree (Fig. 17) is clearly the largest in volume, mainly because it tapers only slightly. Figure 18, taken from the Jourdan report, compares graphically the taper of the four trees, showing why the General Sherman Tree is the largest even though it has a diameter at breast height (dbh) nearly 3 ft less than the Grant and Boole trees. Another tree not measured in this survey, the Grizzly Giant in Yosemite's Mariposa Grove, is generally considered the world's fifth largest tree, according to transit measurements by park engineers.

No one has remeasured the above trees since 1931, so there is a 40-year lag in the statistics. According to our increment borings, taken in 1965, the General Sherman Tree had an annual growth rate of almost a millimeter (1/25th inch), or a radial growth of about 1.5 inches during the 40-year growth period since the study. If added evenly to the entire tree trunk, the net accumulation of wood for that period would be about 1500 ft^3, or the amount of wood used in the construction of an average-sized house. This puts the yearly average of new wood production at about 40 ft^3, or approximately the volume contained in a tree 1 ft in diameter and 50 ft tall. Such a yearly increment of almost 500 board feet of wood helps substantiate the surprising claim that the world's largest tree may also be the world's fastest-growing tree.

Fig. 17. The General Sherman Tree, Giant Forest, Sequoia National Park. Although this is the largest of all trees on earth on a volume basis, it is probably far from the oldest. Situated in a drainageway with a good soil moisture supply, the Sherman's annual growth rings are wider than those of much smaller specimens on drier sites. Estimates place this tree at 2200 years. *Photo by* National Park Service.

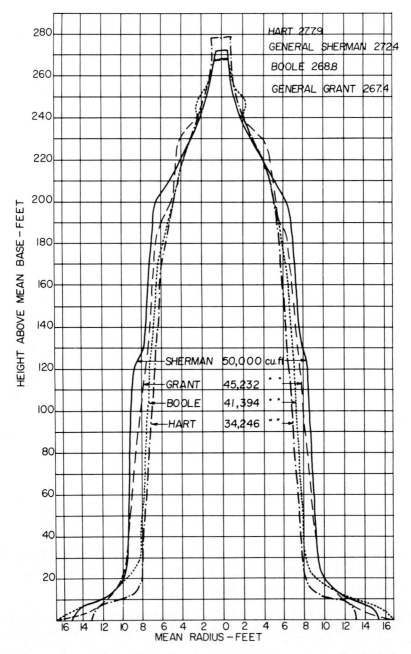

Fig. 18. Graphic comparison of the dimensions of the world's four largest trees. Despite the fact that the General Sherman Tree is smaller in diameter than the Grant and Boole trees, the slight taper to its trunk provides the added volume that gives it the top honor. *Line drawing by* Ivan Linderman, *permission of* Engineering News-Record.

Fused trees and grafted roots

Because of the high density of seedlings in some areas, two or more adult trees growing in close proximity often compete for the same trunk space. When the bark of such trees begin to touch, the pressures created must, in time, destroy the soft, fibrous bark so that phloem, cambium and eventually sapwood (xylem) tissues become fused and continuous around the trees' entire perimeters. The fusion is evident in several specimens where subsequent fires have carved deep caverns and exposed the fused tissues. Here it is not easy to determine just where the wood of one tree ends and that of the other begins. Fusion is basal only, of course, but the fused trunks sometimes continue upward for 20 or 30 ft. In large specimens, the combined circumference may considerably exceed the circumference of the larger single-stemmed trees; some early records of excessively large trees were probably measurements of such dual specimens.

Still another form of tissue fusion evident in the sequoia, but not studied much, is root-grafting. There are several examples of sequoia trunks without crowns that are still "alive." This happens most commonly when a smaller specimen in close proximity to a large sequoia has succumbed to shading, but still continues to "grow" by adding radial wood tissue. One large specimen exists in the Redwood Mountain Grove next to a dense cluster of large, vigorous sequoias. Increment borings indicate that, despite its loss of foliage, the "snag" is still growing at roughly one-third the rate of its nourishing benefactors some 12 ft away.

In other circumstances, where stumps or separated "flying buttresses" of roots are so attached, but with the bark removed to the ground level, the bark has regrown until it covers the entire remnant, giving it an appearance not unlike that of a cypress knee (Fig. 19). Walter Fry in 1903 noted one such specimen in the Giant Forest Lodge area regrowing its bark very near the ground level. The remnant, about 2.5 ft tall, is now completely overgrown with new bark.

Old age

A great majority of sequoia specimens 15 ft and greater in diameter display fire scars that encompass large segments of the trunk's original circumference. Coupled with their great size, this is certainly what gives the older and larger sequoias their uniquely massive appearance and irregular, craggy crowns. Few, indeed, are without a snagged top; the fire scars that caused them to die back are often large and greatly varied in form. These scars undoubtedly give the sequoias the craggy character for which they are best known.

Cavernous fire scars at the bases of sequoia trees have been used for both human living quarters and for stables. Perhaps the one best-known is the Stable Tree in the Mariposa Grove which the U.S. Cavalry used during its administration of Yosemite National Park. The tree fell to its death in 1935. Some specimens have tunnels all the way through the trunk; others are completely hollowed out like a chimney, so that a person standing in the hollowed base can see blue sky through the burned-out upper trunk. A specimen in the Mariposa Grove, the Corridor Tree, has resulted from several fire scars coalescing and forming a corridor between the remnant "flying buttresses" of the swollen base. The intact central section of the heartwood still supports the bulk of the tree's weight.

Perhaps the most remarkably scarred of all sequoias is the Black Chamber in Giant Forest (Fig. 41), which had once a diameter of about 18 ft at ground level. Fires have destroyed 96% of its circumference and most of the trunk's wood tissue. Yet the tree, very much alive, is growing radially at the normal rate of about one millimeter per year. It has a crown of vigorous foliage and is loaded with cones.

No one has ever satisfactorily explained the swollen or buttressed bases of the sequoias. While leaning specimens are known to add compression wood on the down-lean side, perfectly straight specimens often have the largest and most spreading bases (Fig. 20). Furthermore, the suggestion that trees in wet soil and on slopes grow such bases for additional support does not withstand field inspection. Some do and some do not. Many specimens on steep slopes have virtually no swelling in the trunk's basal region, so that the function of the swollen base remains doubtful.

The great outward growth of the trunk over the centuries creates another pronounced, though not completely peculiar, feature in this species. Soil, which must be displaced to accomodate the tree's radial growth, is forced outward as the tree expands (Zinke and Crocker 1962), and piles up around the trunk until the tree appears to stand upon a slightly raised pedestal. Such soil becomes somewhat compressed and is referred to as a peripheral pressure ridge. It is most noticeable on the more level sites, where erosional soil movements are minimal. In the absence of fires, the accumulating duff, leaf litter, cones, and bark scales further accentuate these ridges.

Cones and seeds

The seed-bearing cones of sequoias mature at the end of the second year: they are now ovoid, and average between 2 and 3.5 inches in length, and 1.5-2.25 inches in diameter. The cone scales, whose average number is 34, become thickened at the apices and are flattish to slightly recessed, giving the whole cone a solid, compact appearance (Fig. 21). Cone scale variation seems to be genetic: certain trees produce predominantly small cones, while the cones of others are all abnormally large; some have as many as 56 cone scales (Beidleman 1950). One exceptional cone has been found which possesses extra spirals of cone scales for a total of 62 scales.

At maturity, the cone scales are forest- to olive-green, and each scale contains a double row of vascular tissue which supports the growth of the expanded fleshy tips. The cones remain green and growing after maturity and continue to grow in size until the lower lips of the scales have become rounded and bulbous. Now they become darker and, after a few years, begin to support a growth of lichens that may in time literally cover the entire cone (Fig. 22).

Cone scales are arranged in ascending spiral rows so that, for each species of conifer, there is a definite number of rows around a cone. However, counting to the right and to the left produces different numbers, the ratio thus becoming a diagnostic characteristic. For the giant sequoia, we find three whorls to the left and five to the right when counting from its stem. For the ponderosa pine, the respective numbers are 5 and 8; for the Jeffrey pine, 8 and 13. The numbers are part of the Fibonacci Series, which increases in a predictable pattern from 3 to 5, and from 8 to 13, etc., by adding the first two numbers to obtain the third, etc., beginning with zero.

All plants with an alternate or spiral arrangement of leaves or scales exhibit patterns which fit the Fibonacci Series. Even the flowers and fruits in the head of the sunflower have this arrangement.

Of the many thousand sequoia cones we observed, all but one have displayed the 3:5 ratio (Fig 23). The one exceptional cone has a 5:8 ratio which, while still in the Fibonacci Series, is atypical for this species. We do not understand fully the significance of this precise mathematical arrangement of whorls, so universal in plants. We delight, however, in pondering the unknown biological and physical forces which dictate to the developing cone scales so precise an array.

The seeds of the world's largest tree are surprisingly small. At maturity they are mostly 1/8-1/4 inch in length and are perhaps only three-quarters that in width. The tiny embryo is elongated in the direction of the long axis of the seed, which is flat, with straw-colored wings surrounding the embryo and aiding seed dispersal (Fig. 24). Each cone scale produces from four to seven seeds, and cones average about 200 seeds. One pound of seed contains an average of about 91,000 seeds (USDA 1948). More will be said about seeds under Cone and Seed Production, page 88.

Fig. 19. Living remnant of a severed trunk section. Severed from the parent tree by fires long ago, cambial and phloem tissues are fed through root fusion beneath the ground level. Remnant shown in this picture was devoid of bark and living tissues in 1902, is completely covered in 1971.

Fig. 20. Sequoia with buttressed trunk, Giant Forest, Sequoia National Park. This condition is common in the species although the one portrayed here is an extreme case. It has been suggested that the buttressed base is a supportive mechanism for trees growing in moist soils or on hillsides. Field evidence for such an explanation suggests that the condition is genetic. *Photo by* R. J. Hartesveldt.

Fig. 21. Giant sequoia cones, green and closed on the left, dried and open on the right. The cones, which mature at the end of the second summer, do not disseminate seeds while on the tree unless the cone stem is broken or until attacked by small beetle larvae. They are known to have remained attached in a green, growing condition for as long as 21 years.

Fig. 22. Lichen-encrusted sequoia cone. Within 4 or 5 years, growths of lichen begin to appear on some cones. Those cones which remain attached sometimes become so completely encrusted that eventual seed dissemintion is impaired.

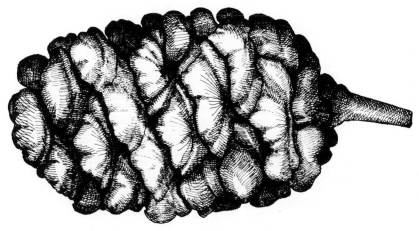

Fig. 23. Sequoia cone illustrating the 3:5 Fibonacci ratio. *Drawing by* Ivan Linderman.

Fig. 24. Giant sequoia seeds. Produced in prodigious numbers, the seeds of the world's largest tree are surprisingly small—91,000/lb—and proclaim the tenuous nature of this species' reproductive success. *Photo by* Shirley Fisher.

Nature of the wood

The sequoia, unlike most of its shade-intolerant associated trees, has soft and brittle wood. Generally, the taller trees in the early seral stage grow upward rapidly, thus maintaining their competitive position in the forest canopy, and the wood must be strong to hold the heavy crown aloft with minimal breakage. Obviously, the sequoia makes up in bulk what it lacks in tensile strength. Its dry weight—18 lb/ft^3—is considerably less than that of most forest trees. By comparison, ponderosa pine weighs 29.5 lb; Douglas fir, 32 lb; and canyon live oak, 53 lb/ft^3 (Peattie 1953).

The great brittleness of its wood (see Sequoia Lumbering Operations) may have been the sequoias' salvation. The reddish heartwood is made up of short fibers that render it soft and brittle by comparison to the wood of the coast redwood. Hence, it eventually fell into disfavor with the lumbering interests. Its use in lumber products, however, was generally where durability against decay was of greater importance than tensile strength (Noyes 1928). In contact with damp soil, it has few peers and an almost legendary durability. Peattie (1953) claims no signs of decay after 10,000 years.

The brittleness of the wood lay behind its almost unbelievable wastage during the lumbering days when as much as 80% of a felled tree became useless because of breakage. The older heartwood, especially when dry, breaks irregularly across the grain at almost any angle to produce an interesting variety of breakage patterns.

The sapwood is a light yellowish color and is coarse-grained in its early years of growth, when the annual rings are wide. Rings up to 10 and 12 mm wide (approximately 0.50 inch) are common in young trees growing in the better sites. As the tree grows in diameter, the wood cells of the innermost section of the trunk are changed in color by the deposition of chemicals which turn these once-functional cells a pinkish color. This area, now known as heartwood, is largely supportive in its role, and the chemicals which cause its darker color are believed to be the factor that makes the wood so durable.

In the coast redwood, Anderson et al. (1968) have identified chemicals believed to be the specific constituents that make the wood "unpalatable" to both insects and fungi. These have been named sequirin A, sequirin B, and polymeric phenolics. The giant sequoia, whose wood has not been so analyzed, apparently contains similar substances.

The heartwood of the sequoia, with its high tannin content, is not as immune to the activities of decay organisms as earlier writers have led us to believe. This belief is curious, if we consider how commonly heart rot occurs in the numerous remnant stumps in logged areas, and in the form of hollowed trunks of standing trees. Few, if any, studies have been directed at heart rot organisms in the giant sequoia. In fact, Bega (1964) lists only one fungus (*Lenzites saepiaria*) as a decay agent in this species; yet, for *Sequoia sempervirens*, he lists several, two of which are common. This suggests that further studies may eventually identify others, such as *Fomes* sp., in the sequoia. How the hyphae of the decay fungi enter the wood tissue of sequoias is not known.

Decay organisms do not seem to attack all trees: some are sound, while others are affected to a rather large degree. Some specimens are largely hollowed out by repeated fires, which have found the decay-softened wood an easy mark and have thus produced "telescope" trees with openings through the upper part of the trunk. The loss of so much supporting wood tissue weakens the tree and makes it much more susceptible to toppling, undoubtedly the major cause of death of old trees in this species. There is considerable evidence that, when the upper crown dies and the wood dries out, the limbs often become affected by a cubical brown rot. Such evidence has been found at virtually all elevations within the range of the species.

The thickness of the sapwood in relation to the heartwood is directly proportional to the amount of living crown. On trees whose crowns are full, there may be 3 or 4 inches of functional sapwood, but on trees whose crowns are reduced because of large fire scars, lightning, and other kinds of damage to the trunks, the sapwood may be reduced to a narrow band an inch or less in thickness.

Without the tannin content of the heartwood, sapwood on fallen logs usually decays within a few years where conditions are moist. The heartwood remains essentially unchanged for centuries, even where trunks have fallen and remain on moist ground, or are partially buried in it. Although John Muir believed that the wood might last on the ground for 10,000 years, no one knows just what its maximum durability might be under natural conditions. In 1963, three samples of wood were collected from old stumps or log remnants in Sequoia and Kings Canyon National Parks for radio-carbon dating by W. F. Libby and G. J. Fergusson at the University of California, Los Angeles.

Radio-carbon dating is based on the facts that carbon-14 is produced in the upper atmosphere, is radioactive, and has a half-life of 5570 years. When it is incorporated along with carbon-12 into the wood of a tree's trunk, it begins to lose its radioactivity, with half being lost in 5570 years. Thus the ratio of carbon-14 left with respect to the amount of nonradioactive carbon-12 gives a measure of when the wood was formed. If it is the last wood added before a tree dies, the time that has passed since the tree's death can be estimated by this method.

One of three sequoia specimens taken for this purpose from the Circle Meadow area of the Giant Forest was thus calculated to have been dead for approximately 2100 years ± 100 (Hartesveldt 1964). On the basis of such a small sample, we may assume that older specimens probably exist. Muir had hoped that such remnants might be found in forested areas between the extant groves, proving a greater continuous range in former years. None has yet been discovered, however, undoubtedly because the repeated fires would surely have consumed all that may have existed in the past.

Much of the earlier literature credits sequoia wood with low combustibility. While this may be true for the trunks of standing trees that are near full moisture content, the wood generally burns readily when dry. It is virtually without resin except where injury occurs to the trunk (Andrews 1958), and even then the amount of pitch is too slight to be much of a factor in combustion. Peattie (1953) lists the tannin content as the fire-resistant property. Certainly the bark is much more fire-resistant than the dried wood, and its tannin content is known to be high.

The wood of the limbs is especially brittle, probably because the annual rings are narrow. When upper limbs die by any cause such as fire scars interrupting the flow of nutrient solution from soil to crown, the wood dries out and becomes highly susceptible to breakage. Winters are often very destructive to these limbs, which may weigh a thousand pounds or more. Snow accumulation on the crown and winter storms take their toll, and occasionally limbs fall during the summer months, a hazard to visitors walking or sitting beneath the trees.

The wood fibers of the giant sequoia are so short that their value for paper pulp is slight. We do not know of attempts to utilize it for pulp in the United States, but in Hungary, where the tree grows rapidly in the better sites, its pulp has been used experimentally. While the fibers have proven too short to make sufficiently strong paper, further experiments are planned to use sequoia wood fiber as a filler, mixing it with fibers of other trees normally used in paper manufacture.

Longevity

Trees achieve long life in the absence of conditions or factors tending to weaken or kill them. In general, fire, fungi, and insects are the normal decimating agents which kill a tree directly or weaken it, thus hastening its toppling. Most trees have an identifiable age of increased susceptibility to the attentions of insects and fungi which shorten the tree's life span. We do not fully understand these relationships in the giant sequoia, nor can we identify for it an age of susceptibility comparable to that of other trees. The largest and the oldest-appearing trees continue to grow with apparent vigor, putting down annual layers of wood whose volume is about the same as in previous centuries. Indeed, if the giant sequoia remained free of fire damage and could otherwise remain upright, it seems that specimens might well live to the great ages sometimes predicted for them. And in these circumstances of old age, the reproductive capacity of these trees appears undiminished.

A common fallacy about trees is that size is directly proportional to age. The assumption is basically sound, but fails to take into account the very different average annual growth rates dictated by environmental conditions, especially the availability of soil moisture. It is difficult to comprehend the logic sometimes used to estimate great age, or the strength of the contentions proffered to the public. This belief even misled John Muir, who said, ". . . the largest trees are always the oldest and therefore are found upon ridge tops isolated from fire by rocky barrens or by streams" (Wolfe 1938).

Probably no aspect of sequoia life history has been so disputed as its believed antiquity. Diameter has commonly been the basis for age assumptions and they were often calculated from the ring-width of nearby cut trees that were possibly growing under different ecological circumstances. The accuracy of such ratio-and-proportion calculations has been in doubt almost since the first estimates were made. In reference to a calculation by Torrey, a comment was made that "Its enormous size is owing to its continued rapid growth rather than to any very extraordinary age" (Anon. 1854). The suggestion was ignored and subsequent calculations ignored this simple but well-founded explanation.

The exact age of trees is uncertain even from the ring counts of stumps;

calculating the age of standing, living trees presents a much more difficult situation. Trees are almost never cut at ground level so that early growth rings are not recorded at stump height. Furthermore, under certain climatic growth conditions, annual rings may not be represented at average stump height or at the height at which increment borings are normally made. Yearly additions to trunk growth typically begin in the crown area and proceed downward until growth is retarded or stopped by autumn climatic conditions. When radial trunk growth is retarded or stopped by a short summer and an early fall, rings at breast-height level may be absent.

Yet, such tenuous age estimates for standing specimens are still common in the literature. Increment borings are possible for short depths only into the trunk of a tree, and the greater the diameter, the less the accuracy of prediction. Claims of increment borings striking the center ring of a large tree should be completely discounted. The standard increment borer is only 15.75 inches long, and specially ordered instruments are only up to 3 ft in length, while ours is only 25 inches long. Furthermore, the chronological and geometric centers of most trees are seldom if ever at the same point. Chances of hitting the chronological center are remote at best, even if an increment borer of that length were available.

For the giant sequoia whose climatic conditions are not greatly variable over a long period of time, missing rings are known to be relatively uncommon. Schmeckebier (1912) states that sequoias never fail to add an annual ring, a statement later refuted by Gillette (1930) who found missing rings in a large specimen. Nevertheless, age-dating by ring count remains more accurate than any other method known for the giant sequoia.

Excessive age figures were derived early in the sequoia's human history, were passed from one writer to the next, and tenaciously held onto, some even surviving until recently. Without a doubt, the simple application of ratio-and-proportion arithmetic yielded many of the earlier figures, ranging from 5000 to 10,000 years. The botanist Willis Linn Jepson pointed out the fallacy of this method many years ago, when he established that a sequoia stump in the North Calaveras Grove, whose age by ring count was 1300 years, would have been 6480 years old by the ratio-and-proportion method of estimation (Lewis 1955). The General Sherman Tree, likewise on the basis of being the largest, has been widely heralded as the oldest living thing on earth.

Muir (1894) reported counting more than 4000 rings on the stump of a large specimen in the Kings River Forest (Converse Basin), a figure widely repeated by others in subsequent writings. As no one has ever been able to locate said stump, or any other with a ring count even close to that number, the report remains unverified. Even the Ellsworth Huntington Expedition into the Converse Basin, after counting rings on more than 450 stumps, failed to locate such a long-lived specimen.

At this writing, 3200 years of age is the oldest count on record. The stump count was made by A. E. Douglass, the well-known dendrochronologist, before 1920. But in spite of such knowledge, some still hold to much older figures for the greatest age, and a recent author claims one specimen to be 6000 years old.

The age of the larger specimens continues to evoke considerable interest. The park visitor often inquires about it, and the answers are not always easy. Age varies greatly with growth conditions within a site. Trees growing where soil moisture is readily available throughout the growing season will produce wood tissue at a rate approaching twice that of a tree the same size in a site where the soil moisture regime is poor.

A relatively recent method of calculating a living sequoia's age is a modification of a method reported by Spurr (1952); it takes into account the tendency of annual rings to become thinner with increasing age while maintaining a rather steady state of wood production. The larger the radius of the trunk becomes, the thinner the rings required to maintain the average growth.

By this method, age is most easily calculated by establishing the basal area of the trunk's cross section at the height at which one or more increment borings are made; then plotting it as a regression curve against time by adjusting the radius as derived from the cores for each 25- or 50-year period back to the innermost ring on the core. During the earlier years of growth, the basal area pattern is curvilinear, but then becomes approximately a straight-line function as the tree becomes older and the photosynthetic increment is evened out over many years (Fig. 25). The basal area pattern in these average circumstances, then, is straight enough in most specimens to allow useful calculations of age that are much more reliable than the older ratio-and-proportion method. With the straight-line assumption, we can establish the growth pattern of a living giant sequoia for the last foot or two of radial growth by one or more short increment borings, which provide the necessary figures to establish a basal area-to-age-slope when graphed. With the slope established, we can use a straightedge to project the basal area line toward the zero basal area level, keeping in mind the early years' curvilinear growth pattern. This better insures that calculations will include the all-important site quality inherent in the steepness of the charted slope. The steeper the slope of the growth pattern, the more rapid the growth, and the more likely for the tree to have optimal environmental conditions. In studies to date, the steepest slopes we have calculated are those of the General Sherman and General Grant trees, the world's two largest living organisms.

To facilitate predictions by this method, 100 complete cross-sectional growth curves were plotted from records taken in the Converse Basin by Ellsworth Huntington in 1911. The derived curves not only portray a vast range of growth conditions but also show that not all the growth patterns have followed the straight-line assumption earlier suggested. A few seem to reflect a continuously improving availability of soil moisture, perhaps as the roots extended outward and intersected more reliable sources of soil moisture. This, of course, complicates the estimation of age. For bottomland specimens, where soil moisture has been more reliable, the growth patterns are fairly steady, and calculations are apparently accurate within 5-10% of the known age.

The results of age dating by this method indicate the need for some rather drastic revisions of sequoia age estimates. According to an average of three cores taken above the butt swell of the General Sherman Tree, this largest of all trees is less than 2500 years old. In 1931, it was cored by Douglass, who calculated its age at about 3500 years by another method (pers. comm.). Estimates of the General Grant Tree, the second largest in the world, now give it less than 2000 years. The Grizzly Giant, fifth largest, is perhaps only 2500 years old, whereas

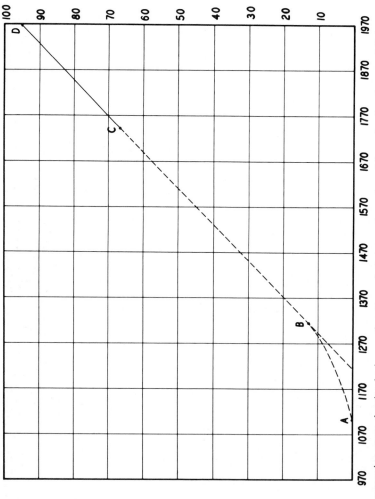

Fig. 25. Basal area regression curve showing basic growth pattern of giant sequoia, and used for estimating the age of living specimens. The solid part of the graphed line represents the basal area increment over the period of years represented by the core removed from the tree. The dashed line is a continuation of the straight-line function already plotted. During the earliest years of growth, basal area increases to present a curved pattern and is thus the most difficult part of the curve to assess. Age estimations, however, probably are more reliable than by other methods applied to living, standing trees. *Line drawing by Win Stiles.*

Fig. 26. Sequoia burl, Mariposa Grove. Burls are not uncommon on trunks of the giant sequoia, although less so than on the coast redwood. The growths, often as large as a washtub, are now believed to be caused by a soil bacterium. Although sometimes referred to as cancerous growths, they are not known to kill the trees. *Photo by* National Park Service.

earlier estimates based upon size and its unusually rugged and craggy appearance placed it at 3800 years. Cores which we removed from the Wawona Tunnel Tree after it fell in 1969 indicate that its age was close to 2200 years.

The giant sequoias' reduced age has brought shocking disappointment to many, and a final recognition that the bristlecone pine is truly the king of sylvan antiquity. Actually, this effects a change only in superlatives; the world's largest trees are the world's fastest-growing trees. They are growing on sites of optimum quality.

Refinement of this method of age calculation aims toward establishing a computer program which we hope will permit more accurate age predictions, perhaps within 5% of the age measured by short increment borings.

Meanwhile, 3200 years is the oldest known sequoia record based upon ring count. Findings of false and missing rings have been rare in sequoias, so that the 3200-year figure must be reasonably accurate. That older specimens will eventually be found is a good prospect. Furthermore, assuming that a continuing management program will prevent fire damage and falling, we believe man may eventually discover whether this species actually has an age of susceptibility to diseases and insects. Such a determination is, of course, many generations in the future.

Sequoia burls

Burls (Fig. 26) of considerable size are far less common on giant sequoia trees than on the trunks of the coast redwood. They occur at varying heights on the trunks up to about 100 ft and may be 3 ft or more in diameter. Unlike the redwood burls, those of the giant sequoia lack the ability to sprout foliage when cut off and placed in water.

The cause of burls in sequoia was somewhat of a mystery until Martin (1957-58) conducted experiments in Germany using burls that occurred on the stems of relatively young nursery stock. In these experiments, he isolated a soil bacterium, *Agrobacterium tumefaciens* (Smith and Townsend) Conn., which when injected under clinical conditions into the stems of uninfected specimens, always produced burls. We do not yet fully understand the mode of introduction into native specimens at many feet above ground level. However, an early account relates that a falling sequoia splashed mud and stones up to 100 ft on the trunks of neighboring trees. Conceivably, soil bacteria could have entered the stem through wounds caused by the flying rocks. This same bacterium is recorded as a crown gall organism on both giant sequoia and coast redwood seedlings (Bega 1964).

These limited observations on the occurrence of burls or galls do not preclude several other causes such as genetic, physiological, or other factors.

Other large trees

Man has favored the giant sequoia because of its size and age, symbols of strength and durability, but many claims have been made for other great trees.

Apparently, these other species have suffered similar inadequate measurement and, like the sequoia, have shrunk by today's standard measures.

Actually, comparing diameters of tree trunks raises some difficult questions: what is accepted as a trunk, and is the trunk a single stem or the fusion of several? Past comparisons have been notably careless, or perhaps intentionally vague. We know or strongly suspect some of the largest trees to be fused, yet we must give credit to their remarkable size even though comparisons with single-stemmed specimens are not really valid.

Other species of large trees, some either taller or greater in diameter than the giant sequoia, are listed below. The sequoia, as a single-stemmed tree, remains undisputedly the largest tree on earth in trunk volume, and only the bristlecone pine has been proven older.

Coast Redwood. *Sequoia sempervirens* (Lamb.) Endl.

Family: **Taxodiaceae.**
Native habitat: central to northern California, into southern Oregon.

The only really close contender for volume size with the giant sequoia is its cousin, the coast redwood. Ecologically, the latter is quite different from the sequoia and grows considerably taller in its foggy habitat along the Pacific Coast. Many specimens considerably exceed 300 ft, and one specimen in the northern range is nearly 370 ft tall. With trunk diameters commonly 10-12 ft but rarely exceeding 16 ft, total volume is considerably less than in the giant sequoia. The oldest recorded specimen is just over 2200 years of age, hardly a contender for the longevity record, but yet no youngster.

Baobab. *Adansonia gregorii* F. Muell.

Family: **Bombacaceae.**
Native habitat: Australia.

Although the largest specimens have 30-ft diameters, they are seldom more than 40 ft tall; a few, however, have been recorded up to 60 ft. The claim that this strange tree is more than 5000 years old seems debatable, as it produces no annual rings. The wood is reportedly very soft.

Douglas fir. *Pseudotsuga menziesii* (Mirb.) France.

Family: **Pinaceae.**
Native habitat: western North America; California north into British Columbia, east to the Rocky Mountains.

Although the Douglas fir has been occasionally recorded as the world's tallest tree, it probably ranks third or fourth, following the coast redwood, eucalyptus, and giant sequoia. The Douglas fir grows up to 220 ft, far less than record measurements of the other species mentioned. Diameters rarely exceed 10 ft, and claims of 17 ft are unsubstantiated. The tree is important as timber; no species in North America is cut in greater quantities than the Douglas fir.

Ceiba or Kapok. *Cieba pentandra* (L.). Gaertn.

Family: **Bombacaceae.**
Native habitat: Central America.

This handsome tree with huge basal buttresses grows to more than 12 ft in diameter above the butt swell, and up to 150 ft tall. Measurements around its buttressed bases have undoubtedly caused the tree to be claimed as the world's largest.

Eucalyptus, Mountain Ash, or Peppermint Gum. *Eucalyptus regnans* F. Muell.

Family: **Myrtaceae.**
Native habitat: Australia and Tasmania.

This species of eucalyptus overtops the tallest giant sequoia if its earlier height measurements are accurate. On Mount Baw Baw in Gippsland, Australia, is a specimen 326 ft tall, and one near the Styx River in Tasmania is 322 ft tall. The larger diameters are from 6 to 9 ft. Claims of 450-ft heights are fairly common, and Robinson (1882) places the tallest at 600 ft.

Dragon Tree. *Dracaena draco* L.

Family: **Liliaceae.**
Native habitat: Canary Islands.

Much of the earlier literature describes one specimen as impressively large. The tree which blew down at Teneriffe in 1868 was 45 ft in circumference, or 14.3 ft in diameter, and 70 ft tall. Claims that it was 6000 years old have no support in scientific literature.

Tule Cypress or Ahuehuete. *Taxodium mucronatum* Ten.

Family: **Taxodiaceae.**
Native habitat: Mexico.

A trunk of this species at El Tule, near Oaxaca, Mexico, has a circumference of 162 ft, or a diameter of 51.6 ft. This diameter is considerably greater than that of the largest giant sequoia, but botanists generally believe that this specimen is composed of several fused trunks, and that the comparison is therefore invalid. Another famous specimen, the Montezuma Tree, in Mexico City's Chapultepec Park, has a diameter of 14.3 ft and is 200 ft tall.

Kauri Pines.

Family: **Araucariaceae.**
Native habitat: New Zealand and Australia.

Queensland Kauri. *Agathis robusta* (C. Moore) F. M. Bail. Native to Queensland, Australia. Maximum diameters are recorded as 7-9 ft, and heights up to 160 ft.
Agathis palmerstonii F. Muell. Diameters up to 10 ft.
Agathis australis Salisb. One specimen, now destroyed, at Mercury Bay, New Zealand, measured 23.8 ft in diameter, and the first branch was 80 ft above the ground. Estimates, on unknown basis, put its age at 4000 years.

Fitzroya. *Fitzroya cupressoides* (Molina) Johnston.

Family: **Cupressaceae.**
Native habitat: Swampy areas in southern Chile.

Specimens are reported up to 15 ft in diameter and up to 240 ft tall, with some age estimates exceeding 1000 years.

Jaquitiba Tree. *Carinaria excelsa* Casar.

Family: **Lecythidaceae.**
Native habitat: Brazil.

The Jaquitiba, a relative of the Brazil nut tree, is recorded as having diameters up to 23 ft and being 150 ft tall.

Bo-tree, Peepul, or Pipal Tree. *Ficus religiosa* L.

Family: **Moraceae.**
Native habitat: India and Ceylon.

As its scientific name suggests, this tree has religious significance. Vishnu, an Indian deity, was supposedly born in the shade of a bo-tree. Like its relative, the banyan, it usually has numerous trunks. One specimen on the Narbudda River in India measures 2000 ft in circumference around its 650 trunks. Another specimen was brought to Ceylon from India in 188 B.C., so that it was 2161 years old in 1973.

Sweet or Spanish Chestnut. *Castanea sativa* Mill.

Family: **Fagaceae.**
Native habitat: Europe, from Great Britain to Spain and southern Italy.

The largest specimen recorded was at the foot of Mount Etna in Sicily. Named "Castagno del Cento Cavalli" (Chestnut of a Hundred Horses), it was still alive in 1935, but is now dead and destroyed. The *Encyclopedia Britannica* mentions its having a circumference of 190 ft in 1780, and *Chambers Encyclopedia* of 1836 gives the circumference as 204 ft. Tiemann (1935) and William Steere of the New York Botanical Gardens, in a personal communication, report that this otherwise amazing trunk was again due to several sprouts fusing into one. Other large specimens are reported in Sicily, and England claims a tree with a 15-ft diameter in Gloucestershire.

We have not included here other species of impressive proportions, such as the sitka spruce and Western red cedar, because no claim was ever made for them as the world's largest. (See Menninger 1967 for an excellent account of the world's larger trees.) Certainly, the issue is far from closed, although the giant sequoia seems to have no serious competitor for the title of largest in volume.

3
Distribution of the Giant Sequoia and its Relatives

Origin

The origins of most living organisms are lost in antiquity, lost in strata of ancient rocks buried in deep and inaccessible places; obscure and small beginnings therefore have escaped discovery. The paleontological record of the sequoia line stretches back perhaps 150 million years to the Jurassic period. Conifers which were probably ancestral to these ancient sequoias are found as early as the Devonian, some 300 million years ago.

The two closest living generic relatives of *Sequoiadendron* are *Sequoia* (coast redwood) and *Metasequoia* (dawn redwood) (Stebbins 1948). These trees have a history in the rocks much like that of the giant sequoia. All three probably had a common ancestor. Fossil evidence shows that the genus *Sequoia* occurred in most regions of the Northern Hemisphere and, interestingly, also at the extreme south of the Southern Hemisphere. There are fossil records from Chile, southern Australia, and Antarctica. According to Martin (1957), continental drift explains this unique distribution. Now increasingly accepted by geologists, this hypothesis would explain the present wide separation between known *Sequoia* fossils. The alternate hypothesis is that ancestral sequoias migrated southward to reach the continents' southern tips (Berry 1924). As the rocks in between have no fossil evidence supporting this idea, continental drift is a most plausible possibility. It too, however, raises some difficult questions, because the continents apparently started to drift apart in the early Mesozoic, long before the first sequoia-like fossils appear (Dietz and Holden 1970). Recent evidence (Emberger 1968) indicating that the South American fossils are *Taxodium* and not *Sequoia* would eliminate the controversy.

Metasequoia fossils found in rock formations throughout the Northern Hemisphere begin with the Cretaceous, about 125 million years ago (Emberger 1968). During the Eocene, some 40-60 million years ago, these trees, along with *Sequoia*, grew in the region that is now Yellowstone National Park. At Amethyst Cliff there are remains of 18 successive forests, each killed and buried in turn by volcanic materials (Dunbar 1960). These are spectacular remains, for many stumps still stand erect, and one diameter measures some 14 ft. By Pliocene time, *Metasequoia* was restricted to the Asian subcontinent and now lives only as a relict species in central China. For many years the fossil remains of this genus were mistakenly identified as either *Taxodium* or *Sequoia*, until discovery of the living *Metasequoia* resolved the confusion (Chaney 1951).

The earliest close relatives of the giant sequoia were probably *Sequoia reichenbachii* and *Sequoia couttsiae*, which appear as fossils through much of the Northern Hemisphere in Cretaceous and Tertiary age rocks. They are present in Greenland, Alaska, Canada, and England (Chaney 1951). Although no doubt they are related to the giant sequoia, their morphology differs sufficiently to show that they are not its immediate ancestors (Axelrod 1959). The oldest fossil sequoia considered directly ancestral to the living giant sequoia, in Idaho, is from the Miocene. This species not only closely resembles our giant sequoia but was associated, according to the fossil records, with plants not easily distinguishable from those of present sequoia communities (Axelrod 1962, 1964).

The most recently discovered North American fossil in presumed direct lineage with the giant sequoia is at Trapper Creek in southern Idaho. These remains show that it grew some 400 miles northeast of the present groves on the Sierra Nevada's western slope in California (Axelrod 1964). The species is called *Sequoiadendron chaneyi*. Other finds of this fossil in western Nevada bring the giant sequoia's ancient range closer to its present one. Some four known localities are within a radius of about 100 miles not far southeast of Reno.

Only a few million years ago the giant sequoia was on the east side of the Sierra and probably was growing at an altitude of about 3000 ft (Axelrod 1959). How did it cross the Sierra, and which natural forces enabled it to do so? What possible geologic and climatic forces split the groves into their widely spaced northern elements, yet left the southern belt more or less continuous? These are the major questions raised by the giant sequoia's relatively recent history.

This fossil form of sequoia, ascribed to the same genus as our present giant sequoia, is therefore regarded as its closest ancestral form. It occurred in western North America and reportedly also in Europe, where it existed as late as the Pleistocene (Martin (1957). We will discuss primarily its migration from the more central continental United States to its present range in California.

Plant forms of ancient fossil communities compared with those in their modern counterparts indicate that they occupied similar environments. We can interpret the association of certain fossil plants with *Sequoiadendron chaneyi* remains as representing a low-elevation, relatively moist community. The Idaho community, in part, consisted of maple, dogwood, oaks, and Douglas fir much like present closely related species. Axelrod (1964) has suggested that the annual precipitation was 45-50 inches and was well distributed throughout the year. Temperatures were probably moderate in the summer and cool during the winter. Overall, the climate was temperate in contrast with today's.

The two important climatic changes concurrent with the Sierra's rise were the reduced summer precipitation and the increased range of annual temperature. These apparently preceded the rise of the Sierra sufficiently to force further evolution of the ancestral giant sequoia while it migrated in a southwesterly direction. Increasingly severe winter temperatures would favor the southward migration, while diminishing summer rains would also favor the westward migration toward the Sierra Nevada. If this general movement to the southwest occurred during the Pliocene, it would have allowed the giant sequoia ample time to reach the Sierra's eastern margin long before that mountain range began rising to its present heights of more than 14,000 ft.

The giant sequoia's passage across the Sierra Nevada was probably not over an isolated single route, but possibly via several low passes serving as access routes to the west. The present groves' proclivity to extend both up and down stream courses strengthens this belief. If true, the foregoing might help explain the disjunct or disrupted distribution of the present sequoia groves. It is still uncertain, although frequently assumed, that formerly a continuous belt of this species existed in the Sierra Nevada. Comparing the known localities of the fossil giant sequoia in Nevada, and considering the position of the groves on the Sierra Nevada's west slope, we can visualize the possibility that they may always have existed in a disjunct pattern (Fig. 27).

Present distribution

Almost since the giant sequoia's discovery, many different explanations were offered for its greatly restricted and interrupted range. The disadvantage of early observations was that only about a dozen groves had been discovered at the time. The larger and better-known groves were often the ones in the seemingly better sites, while some of the groves discovered at later dates were smaller and often removed from the normal courses of human travel. Undoubtedly, the marginal environmental requirements of these groves should supply the reason for the disjunct range of the species. The last of the groves was discovered in 1933.

There are now 75 named community units known as "groves" in which the giant sequoia is but one member. These groves, listed in Appendix VI, are taken from Rundel (1969). The land comprising these groves is an area of some 35,607 acres (State of California 1952). In none of them does this species grow in a pure stand, although in certain limited localities it is overwhelmingly predominent. Such areas as the Senate and House Groups in the Giant Forest and the Sugar Bowl in the Redwood Mountain Grove of Kings Canyon National Park are always popular with the park visitor because they are nearly pure stands (Fig. 28).

The term "grove" is still inadequately defined for geographic delineation. Guidelines should be adopted and the necessary changes in geographic place names should be made to eliminate confusion over multiple groves with a single name, and multiple names for what is really a single grove. For instance, we logically use one name, the Redwood Meadow Groves, to designate four separate units of sequoia trees in the Redwood Meadow area of Sequoia National Park. They are all in the same drainage and in close proximity. In Sequoia National Forest, three grove names are assigned to one unit of contiguous sequoia trees. This is also true in Kings Canyon National Park, where lobes of the large Redwood Mountain Grove are named Buena Vista Grove and Big Baldy Grove, although they are nowhere detached from it and are all in the Redwood Creek drainage system. We recommend that the Redwood Mountain Grove designation include the smaller segments. Where two groves spill over a drainage divide as a narrow belt that widens out with decreasing altitude, they often bear separate names despite their continuity. The Garfield and Dillonwood groves are good examples of this dichotomy, but apparently cause less confusion because two separate drainages are involved. In the Sierra Nevada, the individual groves are scattered over a 260-mile narrow belt nowhere more than about 15 miles wide, and generally less. The range is from $35°51'$ N to $39°03'$ N and is restricted to the western slope at elevations averaging about 5000-7500 ft, depending upon the latitude, direction of exposure, position on the slope, and proximity to subsurface moisture (Blick 1963). The map of grove distribution (Fig. 26) suggests clearly what many people postulated earlier, that the severe winter climate at the higher elevations and at its northern limits on the one hand, and the aridity at the lower elevations and at its southern limits on the other, acted to limit the distribution of this species (Wilson 1928). Its narrow, discontinuous form alone suggests, moreover, that the species possesses a narrow tolerance range during the period of regeneration. Before this aspect was clarified in relatively recent times, Blick (1963) felt that there must be climatic unity throughout its range, at least within the groves' restricted areas and the few isolated individual situations where sequoias are found. His assumption is undoubtedly rather close to the truth, although climatic data from the various groves are few indeed. Muir (1878), Wulff et al. (1911), and Shinn (1889), among others, have also based seemingly accurate analyses of the disjunct range on climatically regulated factors, but in very broad generalities without considering the stage of sequoian life cycle in which the limiting factors are strongest. Sequoias have been so well planted and cared for outside their natural range that, once beyond youth, their future is pretty well assured. Irrigation of many of these specimens, however, introduces an artificial factor that negates their comparison with trees occurring as natural populations. The reproductive stage of most organisms is usually the most vulnerable, and so it is with the giant sequoia. We will discuss this later in some detail under the Life History of the Giant Sequoia.

The cause or causes for the very wide gaps between the northern populations will probably never be completely explained. Despite their discontinuity the groves as a whole are distributed in the form of an elongate, narrow belt which suggests strongly that at some time in the past, possibly during both pre- and post-glacial times, the groves may have been more continuous than they are now. But field evidence of their former occurrence in the present gaps is lacking. John Muir was the first to note that there were no sequoia-wood remnants to be found anywhere between the groves, an observation which is valid today. Groves probably became isolated long ago, because phenotypic (appearance) attributes peculiar to individual groves suggest that mutations have occurred following

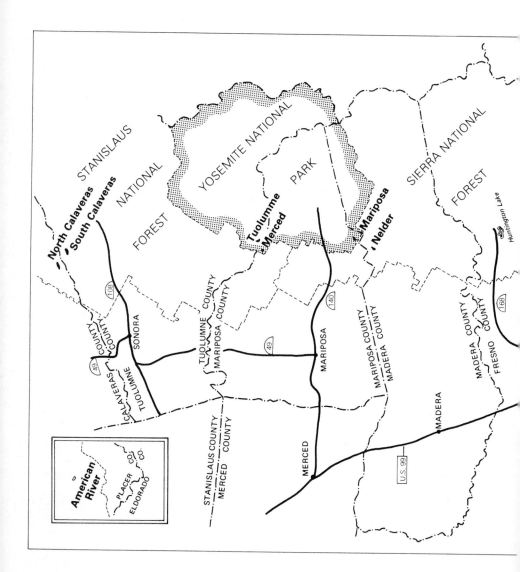

Fig. 27. Present distribution of the giant sequoia. The sequoia is limited today to more than 70 isolated units known as groves that cover a 260-mile stretch of the Sierra Nevada mostly between 4500 and 7500 ft elevation. In Nevada, the proximity of sites where fossils of *Sequoiadendron chaneyi* have been found is shown.

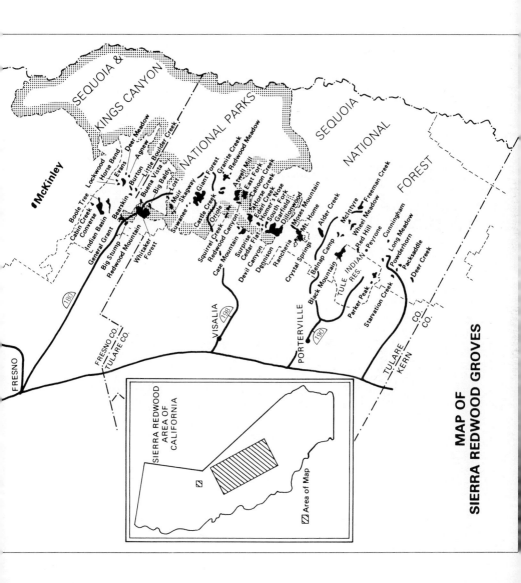

MAP OF
SIERRA REDWOOD GROVES

Fig. 28. The Senate Group, Giant Forest, Sequoia National Park. The very nature of the ecological requirements of the giant sequoia precludes its growing in pure stands. Small areas approximate a pure condition as shown here; such conditions, however, are rare. *Photo by* National Park Service.

isolation. A good example is the bark's spiral growth pattern common to many specimens of the Mountain Home Grove (Fig. 13).

Three main hypotheses have been offered to explain the great isolation of the northern groves: (1) that seeds by fortuitous dispersal reached distant favorable terrain and there established new populations; (2) that slow climatic changes narrowed and ultimately disjoined a once more continuous range; or (3) that there were several migrational routes across the Sierra Nevada. The latter seems more logical for a species whose seed dispersal pattern, under normal circumstances, is usually not much more than twice the height of the tree. But even the rationale of these hypotheses poses difficult questions when we consider that the northernmost Placer County Grove is farther than 60 air miles from its nearest neighbors, the Calaveras Groves, and that it had only six living sequoias when discovered. There are also two downed sequoia logs in this grove, but they offer little clue to its survival pattern throughout Pleistocene and Recent times. The total lack of natural sequoia reproduction there suggested that the range was indeed being pinched out at the northern end, and most observers offered the frigid winter climate as the prevailing reason. Yet, temperature measurements there by a maximum-minimum thermometer indicate that winter lows are about the same as in the southernmost Deer Creek Grove. Perhaps environmental conditions, inadequate for a long period, provided limited reproduction and seedling survival. This grove is well advanced in plant succession, a result of prolonged absence of fire or other disturbances. Whereas the almost total lack of downed sequoia trees apparently contradicts this assertion, the relative lack of fire may best explain the existence of this small remnant population.

Wulff et al. (1911) suggest that the cooler climate of the Pleistocene Epoch may even have reduced grove populations to a single tree, which could have served as a nucleus for the present groves. The observations of several early workers may yet lead toward a plausible hypothesis, especially if the results of studies by Rundel (1969) support them.

Of paramount importance is the availability of sufficient soil moisture during the sequoia's growing season, a function of both precipitation patterns and soil texture, which Barry accurately identified in 1855 as mostly sandy loam. Donaghey (1969) recently indicated a new factor in soil-moisture relationships; the heat from wildfires destroys soil organic compounds and causes wetability of the soil.

John Muir was perhaps the first writer to single out the role of soil moisture. He found that medium soil moisture is optimal for sequoia growth.

> The sequoia is never found in any valley exposed to the rush of floods, nor on any hillside so steep and unporous as to shed its soil and rain. It grows always where the deep sandy or loamy soil is capable of holding the winter moisture all the year, or where the rock is full of innumerable fissures and is shaded and cool and moist" (Wolfe 1938).

Even though he failed to indicate the necessity of sunlight for seedling development, his assumptions are essentially correct, and many writers have repeated them in modified ways. Invariably, these modifications involve the effect of climatic differences, soil type, depth of organic layer, leaf litter, shading, etc.

Recent investigations, curiously, do not bear out the belief that rich, deep soils are a necessity for sequoia growth. Observers have tended to compare forest soils to agricultural soils. While crop plants need nutritionally rich as well as moist soils, trees depend mainly upon available soil moisture. The grayish podzolic soils of the Sierra are less than impressive to the serious farmer. Furthermore, many people tend to grossly underestimate the complexity of soils. By and large, Sierran podzolic soils are relatively thin and not abundantly nutritious. With clay a minimal soil constituent, the total moisture-holding capacity of these soils is limited by the amount and distribution of precipitation, subsequent density of vegetation, temperature and relative humidity during the growing season, and the wetability factor of the soil. Sequoias show a strong tendency to favor drainageways where the requisite degree of moisture content is constant. Yet the drier slopes also support sequoia growth wherever the trees can become established (Wulff et al. 1911). Contrary to popular belief, then, soil depth and richness are clearly secondary to soil moisture availability. Sequoia distribution within groves strongly reflects its affinity for soil moisture; a crown that may weigh a ton or more seems to demand it.

Muir (1911, 1912) was a proponent of the thought that sequoias created their own moist environment.

> It is a mistake to suppose that water is the cause of the groves being there. On the contrary, the groves are the cause of the water being there. The roots of the Big Trees fill the ground forming a sponge which holds the water. The Big Tree is a tree of life, a never-failing spring all through the hot, rainless summer. For every grove cut down, a stream is dried up.

Perhaps Muir failed to understand the magnitude of transpiration, i.e., the vegetation "pumping" soil moisture back into the atmosphere. It is true that forest vegetation regulates the yearly flow of water, thus modifying the distribution of runoff and moderating the extremes. Forest trees play an important role in cycling water from the ground back into the atmosphere. Removal of the transpirational pumps, namely, the trees, has often converted a dry forest into a swamp.

The patterns of growth- and site-selectivity all bespeak the species' affinity for high soil moisture and reflect the effect of temperature and relative humidity perhaps more than does precipitation alone. The ratio of evaporation potential to precipitation as an environmental factor is important, and its recognition has produced the widespread belief that the sequoia grows best in protected locations where the average annual precipitation is from 45 to 60 inches (Schubert 1952).

Rundel (1969) amplified this interpretation somewhat. He found that sequoia stands on northerly slopes have greater density than on slopes of other aspects, although the total number is generally less. It is perhaps perplexing that these trees, admittedly with an affinity for abundant soil moisture, are much more numerous on westerly and southwesterly slopes, which are potentially the drier ones because of the sun's more nearly direct rays. Thus, for example, relatively moist drainage bottoms and meadow margins, although small in their total acreage, support dense stands of sequoias. Even rocky slopes support some 3% of the total sequoia population in the Giant Forest. Contrary to the records of

John Muir, large specimens are fairly common on slopes exceeding $30°$, and we find some on slopes approaching $45°$. We conclude that, regardless of a grove's geographical position, this species favors avenues of surface or subsurface drainage. Although surface drainage patterns are obvious, subsurface drainage may be too obscure for visual identification. The Grizzly Giant in Yosemite's Mariposa Grove, a good example, grows on a low ridge which appears well drained, but an apparently abundant subsurface flow of soil water is undoubtedly a major reason for the tree's great size.

Evaporation potential is partly a function of temperature. Since temperature decreases with increasing latitude, average temperatures in the north are the same as at higher elevations in the south. Thus, the mean altitude of sequoia groves in the Kaweah Basin to the south is 6600 ft, whereas it is 5400 ft in the northernmost grove. In the northern groves sequoias are found mostly on south-facing slopes; in the southernmost, on north-facing ones. Altitude and direction of slope, then, indirectly reduce water loss from the trees while maintaining an optimum temperature regime for growth.

The stream drainage channels are also channels of cold air drainage, especially if they descend from high mountain peaks, so that the value of available moisture must be pitted against the limitations of winter survival when temperatures may drop to sub-survival values. The same drainage channels, however, transport cones and seeds that are carried downslope where grove extensions form long, narrow fingers and occasional detached outliers.

In the Mariposa Grove, flooding, not too many years ago, carried seeds along a tributary of Rattlesnake Creek, and today there are numerous thriving young sequoias mostly at high flood level on either side of the creek. No parent trees grow above them, although some are so close to the drainage divide that chickarees might have carried the cones into the other drainage basin to eat them.

Perhaps the best-known and most classical grove extension is along the South Fork of the Kaweah River below the Garfield Grove. A dozen sequoias line the river bank at elevations as low as 2800 ft—one specimen growing on a gravel bar in the river channel, a most unlikely site (Fig. 29). The altitude is the lowest known in the world for a naturally seeded giant sequoia. An increment boring indicates that this tree was seeded in the middle 1880s, when a torrential flood also floated huge sequoia logs through the town of Visalia some 40 miles to the west in the San Joaquin Valley.

Muir (1911, 1912) first explained the sequoia groves' disjunct distribution as the result of glacial ice flowing through the canyons and completely destroying the trees and their habitats there. Muir had overestimated the Pleistocene glaciers' extent in the Sierra, so that today his hypothesis is largely discounted. He had based it on the finding that, in the more southerly part of the range, the groves are in pairs separated by drainageways. Yet none of these pairs is separated by a drainage which contained glacial ice during the Pleistocene Epoch. If the ice age were an influence, it is more likely that cold air drainage down some of the longer canyons was a strong influence in separating the trees into groves. Although three of the groves are growing on glacial outwash, none is recorded on glacial till.

We know little of how winter cold affects sequoia distribution. While the tree

Fig. 29. Giant sequoia on gravel bar in the South Fork of the Kaweah River, west of Sequoia National Park. This is the lowest elevation at which a naturally seeded giant sequoia exists. Its age corresponds well to the date of a flood in this basin during the 1880s. Curiously, the highest elevation naturally seeded giant sequoia is located about 15 miles distant on Paradise Ridge in Sequoia National Park. *Photo by* R. J. Hartesveldt.

is not nearly as frost-hardy as other tree species associated with it, this seems to pose little problem for it within its native range. Winter temperatures in the groves seldom reach 0°F and when such lows do occur, deep snow usually covers and protects the tender young seedlings. Temperatures in the intervening drainageways often fall to zero and below, especially when the stream's headwaters are on the slopes of high mountain peaks. The confusing part of the temperature relationship is that specimens planted in the eastern part of the United States are severely frost-bitten or killed by temperatures no lower than −15°F. Yet, in Europe, specimens not only have survived this temperature, but are surviving in Poland, Austria, and Hungary where it has dipped to as low as −32°F. Possibly the differences between the two continents lie in the soil's condition at time of death. In the Sierra, generally at least 3-6 ft of snow, and occasionally much more, protect the soil. Schubert (1957) records snow 29 ft deep in the Giant Forest during the winter of 1905-06, with isolated drifts still 12 ft deep in the early part of summer.

Soil type is probably less a controlling factor in the present distribution of sequoia groves than many earlier writers realized. Sequoia groves are mostly on granite-based residual and alluvial soils. Three groves are on glacial outwash, one is on metamorphosed basalt, and parts of others are on soils derived from schistose rock. Soil texture, however, does not vary much. Soils, generally very sandy, are low in their clay fraction, which nevertheless plays the most significant role in nutriment retention. Furthermore, we should point out that sequoias cultivated in various parts of the world are growing vigorously in clays, gravels, peaty soils, and even alkaline desert soils in Spain, all drastically different from soil types in their native Sierra Nevada. Soil type alone apparently has insignificant influence on the distribution of these trees.

Soil moisture availability

Although soil moisture availability has long been thought to play a significant role in the natural distribution of giant sequoias, it remained for Rundel (1969, 1971) to refine and amplify this broad hypothesis into a more meaningful explanation. In study transects which crossed grove boundaries, he obtained substantial proof that soil moisture was more available within the perimeter of the grove than outside, and that often the difference was marked. He used an experimental device known as a pressure bomb to measure moisture stress in the xylem tissues of sequoias and other trees and found convincing evidence that the stress was much greater outside the groves than in trees within the groves. The sensitivity of the sequoia seedling to moisture availability will be further discussed in the section of the species' life history.

Having identified moisture stress as the major limiting factor in sequoia distribution, Rundel delved into the post-Pleistocene climatic changes that may have influenced the present fragmented distribution of groves. There is good evidence that approximately 8000 years ago the climate of the earth began to warm, making the Sierra Nevada drier than it had ever been. Rundel called this the "Altithermal Period." He postulates that with increasing soil moisture stress, reproductive success declined, the old trees died and fell, and new ones either were not forthcoming or else grew in insufficient numbers to maintain the former extent of the stands. With this trend, their range of distribution shrank and the drier ridges and slopes became untenable for sequoia existence. Thus the process of fragmentation into the mesic sites which are the present groves was intensified, especially in the southern part of the range.

Senescence

The implications of his altithermal hypothesis led Rundel to still another study, which strengthens his contentions. He notes a great diversity in sequoia age-class distribution among groves, some groves comprising all age classes and a few being almost devoid of the younger trees. These various age-class distributions reflect a continuum of progressive development for sequoia which Rundel divides into four sequential stages and designates as follows:

1. The adolescent stage, or one in which trees of younger age classes are abundant.
2. The mature, steady-state stage, or one in which a wide range of age groups is well represented and in which the population size and age distribution are likely to remain static.
3. The senescent state, or one in which the population size is expected to dwindle for lack of replacement stock.
4. The decadent stage, or one in which only older individuals remain.

Without the benefit of Rundel's groupings and terminology, Aley (1963) predicted that, barring environmental changes over time, some groves will disappear.

As warming trends create increasingly xeric conditions, the isolated "islands" of sequoias that were trapped in the slightly less mesic sites were seriously threatened. Moisture stress, which seems to become critical within a rather narrow tolerance range, will probably tip the scales against both germination and seedling success if warming trends recur.

Certainly the term "senescent" does not apply to existing trees which are producing cones and viable seeds at the normal rates.

The above might well lead to the assumption, which Rundel verifies, that the adolescent stages are rare at present. Mature, steady-state groves, however, do occur—for example, in the large Giant Forest and the Redwood Mountain Grove. On the other hand, the groves in general may be regarded as senescent. They are apparently unable to maintain their present proportionate number of larger specimens. Muir Grove (Sequoia National Park) and South Calaveras Grove are good examples of the senescent stage.

Groves in the decadent stage are few, small, and rather isolated. Rundel cites the Powderhorn Grove as the prime example in which reproduction is virtually nonexistent and where only 10% of the population falls within the 1 to 5-foot-diameter class. In these circumstances, without factors favorable for regeneration, the giant sequoias constituting this grove will probably disappear, however slowly.

Stability of groves

Rundel's altithermal hypothesis seems to support the long-held and wide-spread belief that the giant sequoia not only has stagnated, but is headed for extinction. However, not all grove boundaries are static or shrinking; some are measurably expanding, though slowly. This is evident in the Lost Grove, in parts of the Muir Grove, the Giant Forest, and in South Calaveras Grove. In the Lost Grove, the uppermost trees on the slopes are considerably smaller and younger than the next adjacent trees below them. Increment borings in several of the trees yield growth patterns clearly showing that the smaller, younger trees began their growth at a time corresponding to a growth-release pattern shown in the larger and older adjacent trees downslope. This correspondence very likely represents the occurrence of a fire, probably in 1872 or 1873, according to release patterns from the older trees. The younger trees are more than 100 ft up-slope from the larger specimens which perhaps supplied the seeds. Because the Lost Grove is a small one, its percent of expansion is fairly large. Although this expansion has not been well studied, we find similar evidence in the other groves mentioned above. The percentage of additions to these much larger groves would, of course, be less.

The future of sequoia's total range will depend, then, upon climate and modifications by fire and other disturbances. If warming and drying should resume, however, most certainly grove perimeters will shrink and the total population of giant sequoias will be reduced.

Sequoias elsewhere

With the giant sequoia's discovery, it was to be expected that people would want to grow specimens in their yards, gardens, and public parks for ornamentation and as scientific curiosities. This horticulture began just a year after Dowd discovered the Calaveras Grove when a John D. Matthew sent a packet of seeds to his father at Gourdie Hill, near Perth, in Scotland. The seeds arrived there on 28 August 1853, the first to be shipped from the New World, and they were quickly planted. Other seeds and seedlings arrived in Europe the same year. Many of the seeds had been collected from the "Mother of the Forest" in the Calaveras Grove following that tree's unfortunate divestment of bark.

The British, with their characteristic fervor for gardening, raised many of the seedlings in their nurseries. At the outset, one-year seedlings sold in England brought the handsome price of £10 each (about $50 at the 1850 exchange rate), so that for a time their use was rather restricted to the wealthy for planting on the larger estates. Saunders (1926) stated that no other species of tree ever introduced into England had caused such excitement or had been so costly. Today, Alan Mitchell of the Royal Forestry Commission makes the statement (pers. comm.) that there is scarcely a hilltop or mountain peak in Great Britain from which a sequoia cannot be seen. They grow rapidly in that country, especially in the more humid regions of Scotland. A handsome specimen of some

8.5 ft dbh and 150 ft tall, the largest tree in all Great Britain, grows at Leod Castle north of Inverness.

It is estimated that in Europe there are perhaps as many as 10,000 sequoia trees. They are abundant in France, Germany, Switzerland, and the Low Countries, and easily identified as the tallest trees projecting themselves above the general tree-crown canopy. The most northerly are in coastal Norway, where the Gulf Stream lowers winter temperatures and cold climate is not a limiting factor. On the north shore of the spectacular Sogne Fjörd, in the yard of an ancient church in the town of Leikanger, at 61°11' N latitude is the northernmost specimen. Planted in the 1880s, it is now nearly 4.5 ft in diameter.

Progressing south and east across Europe, sequoias are increasingly fewer. Yet they grow well in Czechoslovakia, Hungary, Romania, Bulgaria, and along the Black Sea Coast of the USSR. They appear to be limited by continental cold air masses in Poland, northern USSR, Finland, and Sweden. Of the several that were introduced into Poland, only one has survived the frigid winter weather, a specimen growing near the city of Szezecin in the western part of the country.

In southern Europe, the seasonally arid Mediterranean climate inhibits growth unless summer watering is provided. Although there are several specimens in Yugoslavia, Italy, and Spain, the trees have not survived climatic conditions in Greece and Albania. In southern France, specimens are found more commonly at higher elevations where more mesic conditions prevail. By far the largest specimens in all of Europe are those in the palace grounds at La Granja, Spain, northwest of Madrid. In a warm climate and with regular lawn watering, the larger specimen is 13 ft dbh and 130 ft tall, while the smaller of the two is more than 10 ft dbh and 133 ft tall (Fig. 30). These two specimens were planted in the late 1800s. Because they grow in the open, they have retained their branches down to the ground and display a form that is rarely seen in its native habitat.

Specimens are also known to be growing in Turkey, Egypt, Lebanon, Israel, Cyprus, Japan, South America, Australia, New Zealand, and in British Columbia, Canada. In the Southern Hemisphere, they seem to be indifferent to the reversal of the seasons and grow vigorously, particularly in New Zealand.

The sequoia's successful existence in such diverse and widely scattered environments abroad has provoked many to ask why its natural range is so restricted. This logical question fails to take into account its nurture by man and the fact that nowhere outside of its native Sierra Nevada has the giant sequoia ever been known to re-seed itself by natural means. Yet even in the Sierra, wherever the necessary conditions for natural re-seeding are fulfilled, the early seedling stage is always the most vulnerable to environmental vicissitudes.

However unique the ecological relationships within the perimeters of extant sequoia groves, probably the only plant exclusively found in these groves is the giant sequoia itself, and even the combinations of plants and animals associated with it vary from grove to grove, resulting in different biotic interrelations. We will treat this complex subject in more detail later.

But first, what is ecology? What major ecological principles apply to the life of this fascinating tree?

Fig. 30. Giant sequoias in the palace grounds, La Granja, Spain. The largest sequoias in Europe
—possibly the largest trees in Europe—are 10 ft and 13 ft (left) in diameter. Planted in the 1880s, they
have grown rapidly with constant lawn-watering and have grown at a rate greatly exceeding those
known in their native Sierra Nevada. *Photo by* R. J. Hartesveldt.

4
Ecological Concepts

Like most living organisms, the giant sequoia does not live alone; it is but one member of a complex association of plants and animals, and its continued existence depends on its environment's physical and living components and their dynamic interactions. The study of these interactions is ecology.

The roots of ecology, a relatively young science, are a body of facts generally included in what has been popularly called natural history. But, as venerable as natural history is, its main concerns have been qualitative, while modern ecology tends more to quantify the relationships between living things and environment. The word ecology is derived from the Greek word *oikos*, which means "house or household," and *logos*, which means discourse or study of. We can divide ecology into three major aspects: (1) the components and their structure and function; (2) the dynamic energy-based activities of organisms; and (3) the changes occurring over time through the interactions of organisms and environment.

A basic concept in ecology is that of the ecosystem, which includes a given area's biological community of organisms and the interacting components of the physical environment—the soil, atmosphere, and the phenomenon of weather. Ecosystems vary greatly in size and complexity. A pond, for example, may be considered an ecosystem, or we may consider the entire earth's surface as the dynamic system of life with its indispensable support systems of air, water, energy, and minerals. Functionally, in any ecosystem we can study either its living components or its nonliving factors. All the interacting living organisms within a given ecosystem constitute its living component or biotic community.

Within each community, each kind of organism plays a different role. Some produce food from the sun's energy; others are herbivores living upon this food, while still others consume the herbivores, and so on. Green plants are the primary producers, inasmuch as they begin the long sequence in the energy chain with its first step, the elemental fixation of solar energy. The herbivores, or animals deriving their sustenance from plants, are known as primary consumers, while the carnivores, which feed upon other animals, are called secondary and tertiary consumers. In sequoia forest communities, the giant sequoia is one of the major primary producers. The chickaree, or Douglas squirrel, is a primary consumer which feeds upon the cones of sequoias; and the marten, which preys upon the chickarees, is a secondary consumer. Upon the death of any member or portion of an individual of the biotic community, decomposers such as bacteria and fungi utilize the remains as food and eventually convert the organic matter into inorganic nutrients—water and carbon dioxide—all of which is potentially recycled for use once again by the sequoia plant community's many members.

The animals of the community interact mainly along food chains where one form of life feeds upon another. All food chains start with a producer, a plant that is green or at least autotrophic, so that the producer's form and abundance greatly influence the subsequent dependent organisms in the food chain. Food chains are rarely isolated from one another because most consumers feed on many different organisms; in this manner, food chains are interwoven into food webs. The complex and varied interdependencies of food webs tend to bring stability to the community's dynamic food relationships. Simple ecosystems are more prone to greatly oscillating population numbers than complex ecosystems; thus man should be cautious in exterminating certain species within a community for he may well simplify the system and thus disrupt the dynamic balance of nature which the diversity provides.

The major interactions in the biotic community involve production and transformation of food. The pattern varies from ecosystem to ecosystem, but its basic design derives from the flow of energy and the cycling of elements and nutrient materials. The science of ecology is built on the premise that energy flows unidirectionally through the community, eventually to be lost, while nutrients or minerals are used over and over again.

The giant sequoia, capturing energy through photosynthesis, utilizes it to maintain itself and to supply two major food webs. One web involves the herbivores, namely, insects and vertebrates, which feed directly upon certain tissues of the living tree. The other major web involves organisms which decompose the dead parts of the tree fallen on the ground—cone and branch debris—or the dead tree itself. Insects and fungi are important decomposers. In forest communities in general, the decomposers rather than the herbivores utilize most of the energy captured. But only as this dynamic process keeps up with the demands of the main producer can the community remain relatively unchanged. Studies suggest that the giant sequoia and its decomposers are in balance because around trees that are probably at least 2000 years old the soil is still not depleted of its vital nutrients (Zinke and Crocker 1962). The constant "rain" of twigs, cones, and branches and their subsequent decomposition by soil organisms maintain this dynamic balance by constantly returning nutrients to the soil.

The general pattern of food relationships is best explained by the pyramid of numbers concept. Simply stated, this means that green plant producers outnumber the primary consumers that feed upon them, primary consumers outnumber the predators that feed upon them, and so on up the food chain. The pyramid of numbers is based upon the pyramid of energy and is reflected also in the pyramid of biomass, or the total living (bio) weight (mass) of a certain group of organisms. For example, we measure biomass as the tons of sequoias in an acre, or pounds of insects feeding upon the sequoias. Under most conditions, the biomass of the producers is greater than the biomass of the herbivores, which is in turn greater than that of the carnivores. Thus we can observe that mountain lions are relatively few in contrast to numbers of deer, and that deer are far fewer than shrubs. What leads to these pyramids is the underlying inefficiency of energy transfer, which is roughly 10% in any step of the pyramid. At each transformation, much energy is lost, usually as heat, which the next link in the food chain cannot use. The energy pyramid always shows a decrease up the food levels from producer to consumer, but the pyramids of numbers and biomass are sometimes distorted by a surge of energy flow, which then subsides, from one level to the next.

In a forest community where most of the captured energy goes to decomposers, little activity is apparent because only a few active predators enliven the scene. Therefore, in a sequoia forest, most of the activity is in the subtle decomposition underfoot, inaudible as one walks across the forest floor. The decomposers are busy utilizing ancient sunlight to run their lives and returning to the soil the nutrients and products of photosynthesis which long ago were picked up by the roots and built up by the leaves of the giant sequoia and its associates.

One or two factors such as water quality and quantity, or temperature, or topography, often dominate the physical environment of a given community. Through the long evolutionary process of natural selection, forms of life have become adapted to varying habitats, each having major unique characteristics such as the dryness of deserts or salty wetness of salt marshes. Ecology divides the factors which affect life into two major categories, the climate and substrate. The climate is determined by great world forces which shape the movement of air masses and winds, the precipitation (its timing and amount), and the duration of hot or cold periods, all of which are functions of solar energy. The substrate may be the dominant factor such as in the marine environment, but usually on land it merely modifies the climatic effects. For example, high mountain ranges such as the Sierra Nevada profoundly influence the climate to the east, inducing a great desert in its rain shadow. On the western slope of the Sierra, climatic conditions combine with soils and topography to produce a favorable habitat for the giant sequoia.

Only a short distance from native groves in the Sierra, limiting factors apparently restrict the spread of the sequoia (see "Soil Moisture Availability"). At the lower elevations, the factor may well be the amount of available soil moisture or the high temperatures, while at higher elevations winter cold may be critical (Beetham 1962; Rundel 1969). Each species of organism can tolerate extremes of physical conditions only to certain limits. Thus, the maximum and the minimum values of a specific condition such as soil moisture are very important in the survival of a species. Average conditions are considered in ecology, but the extremes which an organism can tolerate mainly determine the size and distribution of the population of that organism. This law of tolerance applies as well to all factors upon which the organism depends, so that an organism with a wide tolerance range for most factors may be severely limited by having a narrow tolerance range for just one factor. The law of the minimum is another fundamental idea: just as a chain is only as strong as its weakest link, so an organism's presence and numbers are often determined by the needed ingredient that is in the shortest supply. Organisms with a wide tolerance range for all the necessary factors tend to be widely distributed.

In general, the early reproductive stages of an organism have the narrowest ranges of tolerance. The narrower this range, the more offspring that organism tends to produce. A single giant sequoia may produce several million seeds during its lifetime, yet most will not germinate, and only a few of the resulting seedlings will survive to become mature trees.

An additional ecological concept is the carrying capacity of the total environment, i.e., that the environment's resources can sustain a certain density. Thus, on an acre of Sierran soil there may be about 15 sequoias more than 3 ft tall. The conditions prevalent in this grove, then, permit an average number of 15 sequoias per acre, and this figure is the density value for that particular population. Other groves may sustain as many as 35 per acre under a different set of circumstances. The carrying capacity may vary from grove to grove or from time to time in the same area. Most populations of organisms seem to have reached the optimum number that can survive in the particular area in which they are found.

A very significant phenomenon is the periodic invasion of new species of plants in most plant communities. Although changes of this sort may be due to several phenomena, the one of greatest relevance is known as ecological succession. Successional changes occur when one assemblage of plants alters the soil and light regimes to such an extent that the plants' own progeny cannot compete successfully with the more tolerant invaders, which replace them. The different stages, named seres, vary greatly from one climate to another. In climates where rainfall is up to 30 inches per year or more, trees tend to dominate the later seral stages, replacing herbaceous plants and shrubs. Inasmuch as plants are the foundation of food webs, the kinds of animal life likewise change with each new assemblage of plants. Periodic interruptions by such phenomena as fire tend to return the community structure to an earlier seral stage in which there is often an abrupt invasion of shrubs, herbs, or shade-tolerant trees typical of that particular stage.

A prolonged period without disturbances produces a long-enduring community which terminates the process of change. This terminal stage is called the climax community; it comprises an assemblage of plants that can tolerate the conditions which they themselves create and can reproduce their kind in full shade and root competition. Soils develop to maturity concurrently and, barring climatic changes, the climax species can hypothetically continue to reproduce without end.

Because of variations in topography and soil, a given locale may exhibit several long-established, interspersed plant associations which may appear as a variety of climax communities. These variations are due mainly to differences in the substrate and not to the general climate of the region. Thus forests of trees growing in deep soils may be adjacent to shrubby communities growing on rocky substrates or next to a wet meadow of small herbaceous plants. The subdivisions of forested areas are sometimes called subclimaxes, and it is often assumed that even the rocky areas and meadows will eventually give way to the forest community of that particular locale.

Before the advent of western civilization, forested climax communities were probably less common than they are today. We know that fire came frequently to most forests, favoring certain plants and discouraging others. The maintenance of such a community is often called a fire climax. Some ecologists place the giant sequoia, whose reproduction is favored by fire, in this category. The larger sequoias, while affected adversely by fires, resist heat better than the other trees of their community, and many have persisted through numerous fires, standing today in forests which have largely progressed to the climax state. Such relicts are unique among plants, being able to persist for more than 3000 years and, in a sense, standing ready to replenish their kind when the proper conditions arise. Fire is the most widespread and frequent agent producing an environment favorable to the revitalization of the sequoia forest community. And so succession is repeatedly set back and the sequoia is favored over most other species until it produces conditions of too much shade and leaf litter for its offspring to tolerate.

The giant sequoia and its associate plants form, in the Sierra Nevada, a fascinating mosaic, unique among all forest communities on earth.

5
Life History

Reproduction

To continue as a living species, a higher plant must succeed in community competition at the most precarious point of its life history, which for land plants, at least, is usually the period of reproduction. A plant's reproductive success requires the following exacting sequence during this period:

1. The production of sufficient viable seeds.
2. A dependable method of seed dispersal.
3. A suitable substrate for germination.
4. Climatic conditions conducive to germination of the seeds.
5. Adequate light and soil moisture for seedling survival.
6. Survival of enough seedlings to maintain the species.

The responses of plants to environmental factors vary greatly with the genetic make-up of the species; the more exacting these requirements and their timing, the more tenuous the plants' reproductive success.

The giant sequoia is a classic example of reproductive fragility in the plant world, eloquently expressed in its restricted and much interrupted natural range, the relative stability of grove boundaries, and the diverse age-class structure within individual groves. Many of the groves have produced little or no progeny within the relatively short period since the beginning of western civilization in California. The much more extensive range of sequoian ancestors has led several persons to believe that the species may be nearing extinction, much like the dinosaurs of the past. Here rests an interesting parallel: the sequoia and the dinosaur represent the largest developments of a land organism within its kingdom in the earth's history.

One of the most misunderstood facets in the sequoia life cycle is that of its reproductive requirements and the sequence of events which lead to the successful perpetuation of its kind. Until now the story, fragmented and erroneous, has been passed without question from one generation to the next by amateur and scientist alike. Only recently, following an extensive series of objective studies, have the ecological relationships of the sequoia life cycle begun to be well understood.

Cone and seed production

The reproductive sequence generally begins in mid- to late winter, when the tiny staminate (male) cones literally cover the outer branchlets of the crown. At the height of pollen dispersal, golden clouds of this pollen or male reproductive cells may be seen drifting about on the slightest breeze or staining the snow with their yellowish tint. This great abundance of pollen simply ensures reproduction, other conditions permitting. Such safety in numbers is typical of organisms faced with low reproductive success.

At the time of pollination, the female cone is only about the size of a grain of wheat and is hard, with a pearly gray tint (Fry and White 1930). In the first summer after fertilization, the developing cones begin to produce chlorophyll, which colors them bright green. At the end of the first growing season, the cones are usually more than three-quarters their full size and the cone scales are very soft and fleshy. From the flattened apices of the scales project slender hair-like bracts, which identify the cones as immature. The seeds, including the area occupied by the embryo, are now a light straw color, and generally cannot germinate—although, in an experiment at San Jose State University, a single first-year seed successfully germinated on wetted filter paper in a petri dish. Because first-year seeds have little opportunity to be disseminated onto the ground, their role in regeneration is very much limited. At the end of their second growing season, the cones attain maturity and generally produce viable seeds.

By late summer of the second growing season, the cones approximate their full size. The cone scales are somewhat woodier in texture, the hair-like bracts will have now fallen away, and the cone is usually a dark forest green. Maturity of the seeds is clearly indicated by the dark brown, longitudinal stripe which runs through the flat oval wing and marks the place where the embryo lies.

With maturity, sequoia cones behave differently from those of most other conifers, neither turning brown nor in any way commencing to disseminate their seeds. Rather, the cones remain attached to the stems in a green, active photosynthetic state, and they increase slightly in size each year so that the cone scales, becoming bulbous, give the older cones a rather knobby appearance. There is good evidence that the vascular connections between the cones and the seeds remain intact as long as the cones remain green on the trees. Cones remain in this state rather commonly for 8-12 years and at least one green cone was determined to be 22 years of age by Buchholz (1938). After 4 or 5 years, cones may begin to support a growth of foliose lichens, which sometimes completely cover them (Fig. 22).

We determine the age of sequoia cones just as we determine the age of a tree's trunk, namely, by counting the annual growth rings in the peduncle or stem of the cone. A clear cross-sectioned cut with a razorblade or knife will suffice to expose the rings for counting. The first 2 years' rings are large enough to be seen with only slight magnification, but the later ones are often extremely narrow and difficult to distinguish (Fig. 31).

The phenomenon of green cone retention poses some interesting questions. Perhaps foremost is the situation in which mature, viable seeds are retained in a moist cone where summer temperatures are surely within the range required for germination. What, then, prohibits germination of the seeds in these circumstances? Experiments indicate that it may well be the function of the reddish, crystalline-like substance found between the cone scales. This substance, often referred to as red cone pigment, is in a liquid form at the time the cones are green. It is an amorphous, water-soluble compound, like the blackened exudate found on scarred parts of sequoia trunks, and makes up about half of the seeds' weight. The function of this pigment has been much debated over the years, in part because green cone retention was not understood. In the early part of the century, analyses indicated that the pigment was very high in tannin, and therefore many assumed that its role was to prevent insect and fungus attack. Fry and White (1930) felt that the pigment helped maintain the seeds' viability over the years. Beetham (1962), after soaking the seeds in a solution of cone pigment for 2 months, found no apparent advantage or disadvantage to seed viability or to the resulting seedling. She did find that planted seeds which had been treated with an 85% solution for 2 months were very slow to germinate,

Fig. 31. Cross section of sequoia cone peduncle showing annual rings. At maturity, sequoia cones do not open and shed their seeds. They are retained as living entities for as much as 21 years. Age of living cones may be determined by counting the annual rings in the peduncle. *Photo by* R. J. Hartesveldt.

but that the total final germination was very near that of the controls.

Martin (1957-58) obtained a rather different result from similar experiments in northern Germany. Although his studies concur with Beetham's in showing that seed germination time increased with increased concentration of the cone pigment extract, he found that in concentrations of 30% and more the seeds failed to sprout at all. Thus, he reasoned that the pigment's role was to arrest germination of the seeds within the cones through the establishment of a reverse osmotic gradient. He further reasoned that when the cones opened, the liberation of the seeds occurred only when rainfall had dissolved and washed away the cone pigment.

Martin reports identification of the pigment chemical as tannin glucoside ($C_{21}H_{20}O_{10}$). In fungus cultures treated with the extract, however, not even its highest concentrations inhibited their growth. Such results do not necessarily negate the possible role of the pigment as a fungal preventive. Recent studies also indicate that at least two species of insects feed regularly within sequoia cones, the pigment apparently not deterring them in the slightest. Clearly, further investigation is necessary to clarify the exact role of the pigmenting chemical.

Because the pigment is soluble in water, naturalist John Muir made ink of it and wrote numerous letters with the fluid. Letters written 60-70 years ago are still clearly legible today. The Forest Products Laboratory in Madison, Wis., analyzed this substance for its potential as commercial ink, but samples, submitted to the Carter Ink Co., clogged pens readily because of gummy accumulations that attended the evaporation of the water (Kressman 1911); thus nothing ever came of it.

The other major question in cone retention is over just what finally triggers the browning of the cones to permit seed dispersal. Ring counts on the penduncles of browned cones removed from living trees show that the drying process usually commences after the 5th or 6th year of the cone's life on the tree, although it may often start only several years later. This great variation among individual trees largely eliminates genetic time-switches and climatic variations as causative factors. Stecker (1969) discovered that cone drying resulted from the activities of a small cerambycid beetle, *Phymatodes nitidus*, which feeds upon the cone flesh. This subject will be considered in greater detail under "Seed Dispersal and Cone Fall."

Beginning age of cone production

Estimates of the age at which sequoias begin to produce cones also vary greatly in the literature, perhaps because authors have used different standards. While some have given the species' average age at which cones begin to appear, others have been specific for individual trees, and some give the age of abundant cone production. Still others cite the time at which cones bearing viable seeds are produced. For instance, Harwell (1947) sets an age of 200 years for the beginning of cone production. Clarke (1954) gives 175-200 years; the U.S. Department of Agriculture (1948), 125 years; Cook (1955), 70 years; Metcalf (1948), 50 years; Wulff et al. (1911), 24 years; and Anon. (1960), 11 months

(Fig. 32). This represents a ratio of estimate of 218:1.

This great reported variation is interesting because we have a long record of sequoias that have borne cones at an early age. The first such reports came out of England, where proud gardeners probably watched their precious newly imported specimens with intense interest. The *Gardener's Chronicle* (London) (Anon. 1859) reported a 4.5-ft specimen of Wellingtonia bearing cones, and Muggleton (1859) records a cone on a 36-inch specimen. Numerous other reports of cones borne at an early age came from throughout northern Europe in the following decade. None of these earliest cones bore viable seeds, however, which raised considerable curiosity until it was discovered that sequoias begin to produce ovulate cones several years before staminate cones, so that pollen was not at first available for fertilization in Europe. When staminate cones eventually did begin to develop, so did viable seed. Brown (1868) records fertile seed produced for the first time in England on a specimen that he felt could not have been more than 10 years old. Undoubtedly, some of the cones removed for seed viability tests were first-year cones which bore only immature seeds.

We have experimented with seeds taken from trees estimated to be within 10- to 14-year range that had been planted by the U.S. Forest Service on the McGee Burn in the Converse Basin of Sequoia National Forest. Cones removed from near the tops of several 12- to 15-ft specimens yielded a total of 220 seeds. These were placed in petri dishes for germination. A total of 64 seeds, or 29%, germinated, a viability percentage which compares favorably to that of seeds taken from trees several hundred years old. (Hartesveldt et al. 1967).

The specimen recorded by Anon. (1960) as producing a cone at 11 months was perhaps influenced by unnatural growth conditions at the Argonne National Laboratory in Illinois. It was subjected to an abnormally long daily photoperiod of 16 hours for its entire 11 months, plus a controlled temperature regime. The seedling was only 16 inches tall when its leader shoot began to swell and formed a cone which eventually arrested the growth of the terminal shoot. A lateral branch took over the leader shoot role, and the cone and its shoot became lateral. While this specimen was unusually young and small for cone production, such cones are not uncommon in nature on trees 6-10 ft tall and perhaps 8-10 years of age. The cone's tip usually bears the continuation of the leader shoot. Although tests have not been made, it has been generally assumed that these cones bear no viable seeds.

Sequoias of all sizes and presumably of all ages are prolific bearers of cones and viable seeds. We know of no age beyond which the tree's reproductive capacity stops or even diminishes. Even severely damaged trees continue to bear abundantly.

Cone abundance

Because the crown is so high and the foliage so dense, it has been difficult at best to obtain reliable estimates of the total number of cones on mature trees. Recently, with an elevator rigged in a 290-foot specimen now known as the Castro Tree in the Redwood Mountain Grove of Kings Canyon National Park, Steckler has made in-crown studies which may now permit more accurate

Fig. 32. Sequoia cone on 11-month old potted specimen, Argonne National Laboratory, Illinois. Perhaps the youngest sequoia ever to produce a cone, this specimen was subjected to an abnormally long photoperiod of 16 hours of light per day. Although fairly common on natural specimens in the field, these cones seldom attain maturity and are assumed to produce few if any viable seeds. *Photo courtesy of* Argonne National Laboratory.

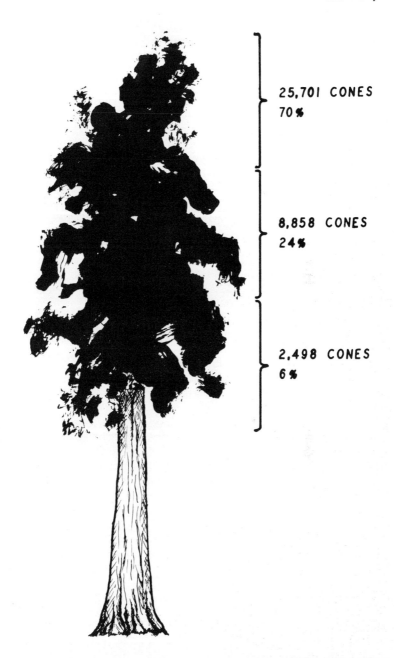

25,701 CONES
70 %

8,858 CONES
24 %

2,498 CONES
6 %

CONE-LOAD DISTRIBUTION IN THE CASTRO TREE
TOTAL CONE-LOAD - 37,057

Fig. 33. Diagrammatic view of cone-load distribution in mature giant sequoia. *Drawing by* Win Stiles.

estimates than those made from the ground by Shellhammer. These studies indicate that previous estimates of cone-load and number of seeds dispersed yearly have been greatly in error. Almost certainly, earlier authors have also misunderstood the life span of living green cones and the ratio of green cones with viable seeds to browned cones with none.

According to these in-crown studies, a large sequoia tree might be expected to contain at any given time about 11,000 cones, of which perhaps 7000 would be closed, fleshy, and photosynthetically active. The remaining 4000 cones would be opened, brown, and largely seedless, although Fry and White (1930) record viable seeds remaining in cones 16 years after the latter have turned brown. An average of 1500-2000 new cones are produced in the average year. Occasionally, optimal weather conditions greatly increase the production of new cones. For instance, in 1970, the Castro study tree produced 20,697 new cones. Each year somewhat fewer older cones, both green and brown, are felled by wind, rain, and snow than the previous year. Variations in total cone-load are very probably genetically controlled, and certainly controlled by site location; very large specimens growing on favorable sites may bear more than 40,000 cones at one time, while those on the poorer sites may have as few as 6000. The upper part of the crown of any mature tree invariably produces a greater abundance of cones than its lower portions (Fig. 33).

A correlation apparently exists between the number of new cones produced each year and the quantity of available soil moisture during the winter and spring months. The cones produced in wet years are more numerous and yield seeds of greater viability than those produced in dry years.

Seed viability

While Fry and White (1930) record the average viability of sequoia seeds as only 15% of the total crop, our experience shows that 35% is a more representative figure. The actual percentage of viable seeds produced varies with such factors as the tree's topographic site, the cone's age, its specific location in the crown, and the seed's position within the cone. Large seeds usually are more viable than small ones.

Initial studies show that rocky slopes and ridges are definitely more advantageous for seed viability than flattish bottom lands with deeper soils. Our experimental plots in the Redwood Mountain Grove have trees on the rockier slopes yielding seeds with 54% average viability, whereas in the flats along Redwood Creek the figure is 32%.

In preliminary studies with cones of various ages, it was found that seeds which retain their vascular connections with the cone continue to grow. This is partially borne out by the viability statistics in Table 2 derived from both snap tests and actual germination tests in petri dishes. The snap test involves breaking the seed across the embryo and noting its color. If it is an off-white color and the embryo completely fills the embryo case, it is most likely viable. However, if it is snow-white and shriveled, or brownish, the seed is not viable (Clark 1907).

On the basis of a previous assumption that the seeds of the living cones grow and perhaps increase in size and viability, the decrease in viability following the

TABLE 2. Germination for sequoia seeds of various ages.

Age of seeds and cones	Viability by snap test	Viability by germination
2 years	26%	20%
3 years	25%	32%
4 years	27%	33%
5 years	50%	52%
6 years	32%	41%
7 years	25%	32%
8 years	34%	27%

fifth year appears inconsistent. However, the beetle-feeding activities mentioned earlier provide a plausible explanation.

Within individual cones, the seeds' germination was 26% in the basal portion (nearest the peduncle), 59% in the central portion, and 36% in the apical region. Perhaps this variation is due to effective vascular connection between the seeds and cone scales, which in turn may also control the size of the seeds produced. This, however, is yet to be verified.

Studies indicate that cones produced near the tops of the trees tend to be smaller than those lower in the crown, and that the larger cones produce a higher percentage of viable seeds. Metcalf (1948) records large cones with seeds showing a 75% viability, a figure which Stecker has verified in cones from the crown of the Castro study tree.

The older cones cluster along the branches' main axes, back from the growing tips; the newest cones are in groups of 2-19 at the very ends of the main branches and are often surrounded by dense new foliage; the mature cones of various age classes are distributed proportionately between these two extremes. Cones from the last 3- or 4-year age groups, that is, ages 1 through 3 or 4, are about equally represented on a branch. About 65% of the living cones are up to 5 years old, 25% are 6-10 years old, and up to about 10% are 11-20 years old.

Seed dispersal and cone fall

Over the years, writers have quoted others who said that a mature sequoia tree sheds close to a million seeds a year, a figure derived by unknown methods and which the in-crown studies show to be a gross overestimate. Ground-level calculations, however, were undoubtedly difficult because of the dense foliage obscuring many of the inner cones. Certain assumptions are necessary to obtain a more realistic figure of annual production.

We can assume that the average number of cones opened or otherwise lost per year probably equals the average number produced. Then, according to the given average of 1500-2000 new cones per year and an equal loss due to browning and falling, and if we assume 200 seeds per cone (see page 88), the mature sequoia would disperse between 300,000 and 400,000 seeds per year. This means a potential seed dispersal of from 200,000 per acre per year to perhaps as many as 2 million.

Dispersal takes two different forms: seeds may be distributed from tree-top level as the cones either open upon browning or are eaten by chickarees on the limbs of the crown; or, the cones may be cut or otherwise fall to the ground, where they dry out and spill their seeds upon a relatively small area of the soil or leaf litter surface. Each has advantages and disadvantages. A very important point here is that a high percentage of sequoia seed is dispersed by the activities of animals.

The chickaree (Fig. 34), inhabits many trees in the Sierran forest region. Outside sequoia groves, the chickaree feeds commonly on the seeds of the sugar pine, white fir, red fir, ponderosa pine, incense-cedar, etc. But in sequoia groves where sequoias displace some of the other tree species, this handsome little squirrel also feeds on the fleshy green scales of the younger sequoia cones, much as people do in eating the flesh from artichoke bracts. In the process, the seeds, too small to have much food value for the squirrel, are dislodged and, if the cone is eaten on a high limb, they are scattered over the ground. Dispersal from this height has the potential advantage that wind drift may extend the species' range.

In circumstances not fully understood, chickarees will cut innumerable cones from individual trees, dropping them immediately to the ground. They may cut cones from individual trees for 6 or 7 years in a row, thus changing the cone-load factor for a considerable period. Shellhammer (1966) observed a lone chickaree which cut down 539 green sequoia cones in 31 minutes. There are many records

Fig. 34. The chickaree, or Douglas squirrel, is now believed to play a significant role in the reproduction of the giant sequoia. This small rodent is apparently more interested in the flesh of the cone scales as a source of food than the tiny seeds. In the process of feeding upon the cone scales, many seeds are spread upon the soil surface. *Photo by* Tom Harvey.

of large cone cuttings in a single day or during a season, one of the most amazing being that of Fry and White (1930). In 1905 they recorded a single chickaree cutting cones which, when gathered up, filled 38 barley sacks and yielded 26 lb of seeds. Calculating 91,000 seeds to the pound and 200 seeds per cone, we obtain a figure of nearly 12,000 cones.

Once the cones are cut, the chickaree caches them away as future food. Because the cones are edible only when green and tender, the storing must be such as to maintain this condition over the longest possible time. Many chickarees will bury the cones individually in the leaf litter and duff, or in caches of six or seven cones where space permits. In places, often in the bed of an intermittent stream where the soil is moist or bog-like, they will store hundreds or even thousands of cones in impressive piles. Sometimes the space between a fallen sequoia log and the ground is used, or the base of a hollow tree may be packed tightly with cones. The chickaree, returning in fall and winter to eat, usually spills the seeds onto the ground in the relatively small space where it feeds. This wastage certainly contributes to the sequoia's potential regeneration, although without the advantage of wind dispersal or of shallow burial in soft, friable soil following a fire. However, seeds properly placed during this feeding process are in good cold storage throughout the winter and so are ready for spring germination. The many cones not eaten by chickarees eventually dry out and spill their seed contents too.

In late summer and autumn, especially on warm days with a breeze, sequoia seeds flutter to the ground in an almost constant rain. Their small oval wings help insure that the slightest movement of air will carry them away from the parent tree, perhaps as much as 600 ft. The already mentioned feeding activities of the beetle, *Phymatodes nitidus* (Fig. 35), causing the cones to turn brown, probably bring about much of this seed fall.

Stecker (1969) discovered this beetle high in the crown of the Castro Tree during the summer of 1968. In virtually all the browned and dried cones, tiny insect emergence-holes were found. These insignificant indications of insect activity, having somehow eluded discovery by science until then, gave the first evidence that browning was not simply a natural aging of the giant sequoia's cone tissues. Dissection of thousands of these cones showed that the agent is a very small cerambycid or long-horned wood-boring beetle larva (*Phymatodes nitidus LeC*) and, furthermore, that it plays an important role in the giant sequoia's regeneration. The larvae's length is only 3-5 mm (1/8 to 1/5 inch).

Oviposition by the female beetle takes place at cone-scale junctures and occasionally along the cone stem or peduncle. Upon hatching, the larval borer chews its way into the cone's interior, obtaining nourishment from the carbohydrate-laden tissues of the cone scales. The mines are about one-third the diameter of a lead pencil and are packed with chewing and digestive waste, or frass, which in this case resembles a fine salt-and-pepper mixture. The vascular channelways or veins (two layers of them in each cone scale of giant sequoia) are often severed during this feeding, which diminishes water conduction to the ends of the cone scales. At first one scale will brown, and then others, as they dry out, following the direction taken by the feeding larvae.

As the mining turns the green, fleshy tissues into a sun- and air-dried cone, the flesh shrinks, creating gaps between the cone scales. And so, the cone's hold

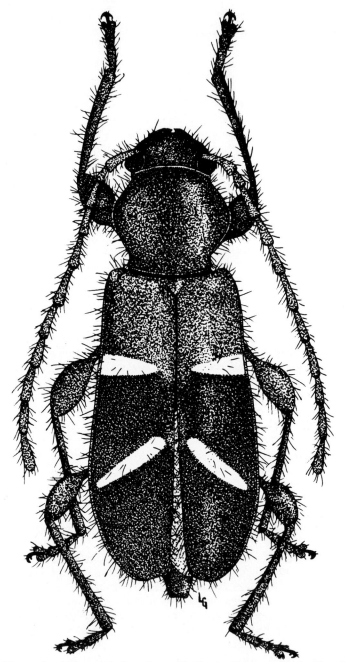

Fig. 35. *Phymatodes nitidus,* a long-horned, wood-boring beetle, responsible for dissemination of some of the crop of sequoia seeds from tree crown levels. The larvae of these beetles feed on the interior flesh of green cones and eventually sever enough vascular connections to kill the cone. This results in the opening of the cone and eventual dispersal of the seeds. *Drawing by* Loren Green.

upon the seeds is relaxed and dispersal follows. Seeds thus released from the tree's top, which also has the greatest cone load, can be carried to considerable distances by even relatively light winds.

Normally, *Phymatodes* does not eat the seeds although it may damage some of them in its feeding pathway. As mentioned earlier, browned cones do not necessarily drop their seeds immediately upon opening, but rather drop them slowly over the years as the vascular connections are severed.

The beetle larvae average 1.4 individuals per cone in the cones attacked, and Stecker has occasionally noted as many as eight in a single cone. About one-quarter of the 39,508 cones in the Castro Tree are "browns," or cones on which *Phymatodes* has fed. If this is more or less representative for mature sequoias, this tiny insect deserves considerable credit for spreading the sequoia's seeds. It seems that each species' well-being depends on some reciprocal arrangement of services.

Chickarees, interestingly, seem to prefer cone flesh when the cones are between 2 and 5 years old, infrequently cutting 1-year cones, but for some reason seldom eating them. As *Phymatodes* is apparently most prevalent in cones 4 years and older, there is really little competition between these two animals. This further insures that seeds of all age classes are shed. The sequoia, the chickaree, and the cone beetle may someday reveal a fascinating coevolutional story because without the two animal organisms, as well as frequent fires, the giant sequoia might not exist today.

We know that the chickaree prefers the larger seeds of other conifers, and that it feeds more heavily upon the cone flesh of sequoias in years when the other food is in poor supply. If a fire destroys a large percentage of the other tree species, chickarees provide added assurance by eating sequoia cones and dispersing the seeds at a time when the seed bed is a soft, friable mineral soil. Fires also speed the rate at which cones will dry out and scatter their seeds to the ground. In essence, this is a back-up mechanism insuring seed release and rather heavy seeding of sequoias after a fire.

While animal activities cause most of the seed dispersal, cones do fall during wind and ice storms and because of heavy loads of wet snow. The proportion of this kind of seed-fall has never been measured. Certainly it is locally heavy, but occurs so irregularly that its overall role in regeneration may be slight in comparison to animal-influenced release. Some cones find their way into streams and are carried considerable distances, extending the range of the species. (See details in sections discussing present distribution.)

What happens to a cone and its seeds if not cut by a chickaree or opened by the feeding of *Phymatodes* is a minor question. Note that, although the oldest known cone in a green, growing condition was 22 years of age, the longer the cones persist on the tree, the less viable their seeds; hence, increased length of cone retention does not benefit the species. Furthermore, the older cones frequently become so encrusted with foliose lichens that the seeds are less able to fall free, even when the cones finally open.

Seed viability loss after dissemination

Whereas seed viability in green mature cones may be as high as 75%, snap tests of seeds taken from the surface of the soil indicate an average viability of between 1 and 2%! This markedly reduced reproductive potential seems due mostly to the sun's direct radiation and to desiccation resulting when radiant energy is converted into heat at the soil surface. When kept dry and out of sunlight, sequoia seeds are known to maintain their viability for many years.

In tests, a viability of 40% dropped to 10% when the seeds were exposed to sunlight for 10 consecutive days, and 0% by the end of 20 days. Although this reduction in viability is proportionate to the size of the seeds, the average sampling of seeds tested shows clearly how vulnerable is this stage of the sequoia's life cycle. Thus man, by changing the tree's environment, can either aid or retard its reproduction rate.

Effect of animals on seeds upon the ground

Contrary to some earlier reports, animals do not greatly disturb sequoia seeds on the ground. Insect damage to the embryo is probably the most serious effect noted to date, but we do not know whether this occurs before or after loss of viability by radiation and desiccation. Vertebrate animals apparently rarely eat the seeds on the ground. Repeated tests by Howard Shellhammer and by Beetham (1962) both in and out of sequoia groves have shown that animals favor sequoia seeds least among the seeds of sugar pine, ponderosa pine, Jeffrey pine, red fir, white fir, and incense-cedar. Usually, if sequoia seeds are placed on the ground in piles, squirrels, chipmunks, mice, or shrews merely kick them about and leave them uneaten.

Conditions for germination

For germination to occur, the giant sequoia requires the necessary physical conditions, but also the proper sequence of events. Perhaps even more uncertain is the survival of the resulting seedlings.

Muir (1878) was very probably the original source of the idea that bare mineral soil is essential for the germination of sequoia seeds. This was a convincing story, which virtually all sequoia literature repeats without question. Yet, in some sequoia groves, there are extensive areas of almost bare ground within the seeding range of mature sequoias on which we find no sequoia seedlings year after year. In other instances, mineral soil plays absolutely no role in germination and small sequoia seedlings growing from rotting stumps and other masses of organic debris such as thick leaf litter. Normally, such debris holds too little moisture to permit continued growth; if the litter is too thick, the seeds' small energy package does not allow the seed roots to penetrate to mineral soil and, if germination does take place, the young trees often die aborning.

Mineral soil, then, is only one of several influences upon germination of sequoia seeds. Statistically, it is the most important substrate for germination, but is not an absolute requirement. The condition of the bare mineral soil, also affecting the survival of seedlings which do actually get started, may well be at least as critical, if not more so, for seedling survival as it is for germination.

To better insure germination, the soil's condition must be such that some sort of disturbance will loosen it before the distribution of seeds. The tiny seeds lack sufficient weight to become buried upon falling, except where the soil is very soft and friable. This perhaps explains the absence of seedlings on soil surfaces where the seeds may be unable to penetrate. When lying on the exposed soil surface, the seeds not only quickly lose their viability but also seem to germinate poorly even when the soil is moist. Fry and White (1930) claim that seeds pressed against the soil surface by heavy snow germinate well, but recent experimentation indicates that germination is greatest when the seed is completely surrounded by moist soil, as when burried. That seeds germinate on the surface is well documented; but again, survival is extremely low.

Disturbances of the soil may come about in any of several ways. Falling trees leave exposed and loosened soil in their root pits, and the skidding trunks on sloping terrain may "plow" up the soil and even bury some seeds. Avalanches of snow and floods of water contribute to the burial which favors germination. But fire is perhaps the most influential and certainly the most widespread of all the natural factors. In fact, there is a high probability that, without fire, the giant sequoia would not today be an extant species.

Fire burns the organic content of the uppermost horizon of the soil leaving temporary voids between the soil's particles, so that the tiny seed falling from the crown is often buried to a depth sufficient to insure its full contact with the soil and to eliminate potential radiation damage. Usually, the soft, friable surface condition of the soil after fire is short-lived; rainfall, wind, and gravitational settling of the soil particles result in compaction, which in turn reduces successful germination. We have also observed that the heat of fires speeds the cone's drying and that seed-fall during the days immediately following fires is greatly increased.

In recent years, of course, man's mechanical disturbances to the soil—as along roadsides, in areas of building construction and logging activity—have likewise created a receptive medium for seed burial, so that seedling growth is often extremely heavy and the degree of survival is high.

Other factors that influence germination, for better or for worse, are air temperature, soil moisture, light, mineral content of the soil, soil pH, soil type (texture), and depth of the seed in the soil. These, and other lesser influences, have been thoroughly investigated by Stark (1968) in the Sierra Nevada.

Stark's field experiments indicate that although germination actually occurs over a very wide range of temperatures, namely, from $30°$ to $92°F$ ($-1.6°C$ to $34°C$), optimum temperatures are most common during the months of April, May, September, and October. Soil moisture conditions and seedling survival are generally better in the spring than during any other season. High summer temperatures and the resulting desiccation of the soil greatly reduce germination.

Soil moisture content varies with soil texture and the amount and nature of the soil's organic matter. At field capacity, which is the maximum moisture that can be held against the pull of gravity, native Sierran soils, which are mostly sandy, probably store no more than 18-22% soil moisture by weight. This appears wholly adequate for the germination of sequoia seeds, and the high sand content insures good aeration in the soil, which is another requisite for successful germination. In flooded soils there is little oxygen available for the embryo's respiration and growth. Some seeding occurs along streams, but germination occurs only when floods deposit seeds high enough on the banks to escape the flooded soil conditions. Dry soils also reduce germination to the zero point, although the critical minimum level of moisture for this process is unknown.

Experiments indicate that sequoia seeds will germinate in full sunlight and also in the dark, but that optimal germination occurs during the growing season when the light is approximately one-half full strength of the sun. When stronger, light is converted into excessive heat energy and thus dries the soil. Again, fire plays an important role in preparing the seedbed by reducing the amount of shade. Under field conditions, sequoia seeds require between 40 and 60 days to germinate.

Whether natural chemical inhibitors affect the germination of sequoia seeds on the ground is not yet known. In preliminary studies at San Jose State University, germination tests subjected sequoia seeds to various solutions of chemicals normally found in soils and to solutions extracted from leaf litter (Morris 1967). There were no significant differences over those in the controls, indicating possibly that, in the natural state, physical factors influence germination more than chemical factors. Closely allied is the pH or degree of acidity or basicity of the soil. Stark (1968) found that a slightly acid soil (pH 6-7) produced the highest germination percentage at a temperature of $68°F$ and concluded that pH was not a limiting factor in natural sequoia habitats. She found that strongly basic soils (pH 9) stunted the seedling growth, but did not retard germination. It did, however, alter the color of the foliage to an intense blue-green.

Variations in soil texture are actually not very important in the sequoia's native Sierra Nevada where sand percentages are high and clay percentages characteristically low, a combination admirably suited to successful germination. Experiments of Beetham (1962) indicate that poor germination in clays, limestone, and peat soils indicates a relationship to insufficient moisture. Once established, seedlings transplanted to many other soil conditions grow well throughout the world. Sequoias have never re-seeded themselves naturally on these other soils, indicating this tree's special needs for successful reproduction.

We have already mentioned that seeds on the surface generally do not germinate because insufficient moisture is transmitted to the embryo. Burial of the seed is important, but the seed must not be buried too deeply. While seeds placed deeper than 1 inch may germinate, the developing shoot will seldom reach the surface and survive. The optimum depth, which seeds rarely exceed in normal circumstances, is about 0.25 inch (Beetham 1962).

Seeds will often become wedged in a small crack in the soil alongside a partially buried rock or piece of wood, which provides the necessary protection against radiation and proper soil moisture conditions. This is also an advantage in seedling survival, the next most delicate stage in the sequoia life cycle (Hartesveldt and Harvey 1967).

Conditions for seedling survival

> ... fire, the great destroyer of the sequoia, also furnishes the
> bare ground required for its growth from the seed. (Muir
> 1878, 1912).

To a very strong degree in sequoia reproduction, seedling survival is much more critical than is germination (Beetham 1962). Muir alluded to this in 1878, and numerous writers since have repeated it. Sequoia seeds can remain viable under a rather wide range of conditions, but once the seedlings commence their growth, they cannot survive beyond the range of a rigid set of environmental conditions. It is now suspected that the microenvironmental climate is the major restriction squeezing the species into the present isolated groves, and that it has limited the groves' expansion to relatively minor boundary extensions during the last century or so. Some believe that sequoias would doubtless flourish in many locations in the Sierra Nevada outside the existing groves if stock were only introduced. According to this hypothesis, extension of the range is limited by a subtle environmental barrier and one that was poorly understood until the recent outstanding work of Rundel (1969).

Because of the small amount of food stored in sequoia seeds, the newly germinated seedlings must become rapidly self-sufficient. Fry and White (1930) state that the earliest stage of germination (extension of the radicle or primary root) takes place beneath the snow, and that the seed roots are as much as 1 or 2 inches long before the snow melts. This may affect the survival of the emerging cotyledons, or seed leaves. As soon as the protective seed coat is shed from the new leafy shoot, a root system must be functional to supply the cotyledons with the necessities for photosynthetic activity, and because sequoias apparently produce few, if any, root hairs, root length becomes the more essential.

Considering the many hazards offsetting this species' great reproductive potential, we may surmise that survival of seedlings is tenuous. Muir (1878) records that not one seed in a million germinates, and that not one seedling in 10,000 attains maturity. These figures, widely repeated, may be figurative rather than literal, but the frailty of the species during this stage is no myth.

The newly germinated seedlings are, like those of all plants, tender and soft because of the yet small deposits of cellulose and lignin and are susceptible to a variety of decimating factors even before the unfurling crown is pushed above the soil surface. Some seedlings seem more predisposed to survival than others. For those that die, the cause of death is not always obvious, especially if the roots are affected. Furthermore, the decimating factors may be subtly and confusingly interrelated. Seedlings derived from the larger seeds may have the advantage of a larger and more rapidly growing root system from the very beginning and, therefore, a better chance for survival. However, our studies indicate that even the heartiest of seedlings may die in areas where others of apparent lesser vigor will survive.

Probably the most extensive cause of sequoia seedling death is soil desiccation downward to the full depth of the root system. Harvey suggests other possible causes are damping-off, intolerance to shade, flooding, heat canker, root fungi, soil ectocrines, burial by leaf- and branch-fall, insect depredations, grey mould blight, being eaten by birds and mammals, trampling, and various other disturbances by animal life, including man. Many of these are probably more serious threats where there is deep duff and litter. Fire, on the other hand, in removing the duff and litter reduces some of the danger.

Desiccation of the soil is generally more prevalent in disturbed open forests, e.g., following a fire. It is related to the length of time the sun strikes the mineral soil surface during the day, to air temperatures, relative humidity of the air, and to some extent the color of the soil surface. Fire has been the most common natural agent influencing the above factors and, in some cases, it also darkens the surface with its char. The increase in sunlight, so necessary to the survival of sequoia seedlings, is also the factor which may dry the soil to the permanent wilting point and bring about the seedlings' death. And while the litter layer is an insulation against soil moisture depletion, it undoubtedly harbors the damping-off fungi and other pathogens (Martin 1957-58). Obviously, sequoia reproductive success lies somewhere between the two extremes. But nature is generally not much given to continuous provision of optimal conditions for survival of any one species, and where sequoias fail, other plants with adaptations more suitable for the immediate set of conditions may succeed.

Beetham (1962) has amply demonstrated that seedlings grow best in full sunlight where the soil is protected by at least a light layer of leaf litter. Where litter was absent, she found soil temperatures 25-35°F hotter and increased death rate of seedlings by heat canker. Hartesveldt et al. (1967) recorded surface temperatures in July up to 157°F on char-darkened soil in the Redwood Mountain Grove at 1:45 p.m. by means of a tiny thermister, which records the temperatures of a literally paper-thin layer at the soil surface. The threshold temperature for the death of most protoplasm being less than 150°F, not surprisingly several seedlings were found dead with the blanched and sunken symptoms of heat canker on the stem just above the mineral soil level. Despite the very high temperature of the soil surface in this open situation, many seedlings in the same vicinity were not killed by the heat, a testimony to litter effectively moderating temperature extremes.

By far the greatest mortality occurs where soils dry out to below the seedlings' average rooting depth, which is rather common during periods of prolonged though not necessarily excessive high temperatures and low relative humidity. In experimental manipulations, Hartesveldt et al. (1967) found that more than 90% of the seedling mortality occurred under these conditions. Death began within a few weeks after germination, continuing at a much reduced rate in the following years. At the end of 3 years, surviving seedlings will usually have root systems that penetrate the soil to beneath the level of midsummer dryness, or about 14 inches.

Beetham (1962) reported that optimal growth of sequoia seedlings occurred in soils with moisture contents at or near field capacity, or about 20% for most Sierran soils. She further determined that the soil moisture content at the time of seedling death by desiccation is about 5.2%. Seedling survival was found to be critical in the low range of soil moisture in studies of Hartesveldt et al. (1967) in which desiccation was the most frequent form of seedling death.

However, those same studies revealed that relatively slight variations in soil moisture in the lower range may make the difference between survival and death. It was found that seedlings growing next to partially buried rocks, limbs, etc., definitely had a greater advantage in being taller, more branched, and surviving better than their nearby counterparts whose stems were surrounded only by soil. This may be a response to better soil moisture conditions beneath the partially buried objects, perhaps due to the deflection of drying winds and the interference of direct solar radiation at the soil surface. Together, these factors reduce the rate of evaporative moisture loss from that portion of the soil surface where the objects occur.

We should point out that Sierran soils are notably poor compared with those measuring up to agricultural standards, and limitations to seedling growth apparently do not relate to low nutritional levels in the field (Beetham 1962).

One of the more difficult forms of seedling death to assess is that from reduced light brought about by canopy shading that may starve the plant. Although Baker (1949) lists sequoia as having intermediate tolerance to shade, Beetham (1962) indicates clearly that it is very sensitive to low light intensity. This is supported by the fact that sequoia seedlings are seldom found in areas densely populated with taller vegetation. A striking example of death influenced by shading was found by Hartesveldt (1963) in Yosemite's Mariposa Grove. At the end of a 25-year period, of the several thousand seedlings established there and recorded on a park map dated 1934, only 13.8% remained alive in a 1959 resurvey of the same area. Hundreds of dead saplings, twisted and contorted in dense shade, demonstrated the effect of the heavy overtopping crown canopy composed largely of white fir (Fig. 10). Soil moisture appeared adequate in the areas in which the young sequoias had died. Undoubtedly, excessive shading may be coupled with another agent such as root fungi or poor soil-moisture conditions. In marginal circumstances, young specimens barely maintain life and grow so sparingly that measurement of yearly increment is difficult. In fact, Metcalf (1948) records a 25-year old specimen as having a stem just 0.50 inch in diameter.

Excessive moisture is a factor which limits gas exchange at the root surface because it usurps the pore space normally occupied by gases. Low soil oxygen content reduces root respiration which reduces water intake and photosynthesis, eventually to the point of cessation. This is probably a common cause of seedling death along the edges of meadows where seeds of sequoias are often scattered abundantly, but where seedlings seldom survive. Although the situation has not been thoroughly studied, the general lack of trees within the wetter meadows is expressive of the sensitivity of most tree species to wet soil. Moreover, dead sequoia snags are occasionally found in wet meadows in which the meadows have formed after the tree had become established in a more mesic situation. Large sequoias often fall across drainageways, forming a dam which impedes water drainage and creates wet meadows. Meinecke (1927) recorded the death of large sequoia trees by this means in the Giant Forest.

Where sequoias do become established in moist areas, the degree of moisture definitely affects their growth, and even large specimens have died where the soil moisture has become excessive.

Soil dampness promotes the incidence of damping-off, a disease which fells the seedlings by attacking the stem at the soil level. Any one of several soil fungi can be causative agents in this disease. Damping-off has long existed in forest nurseries among virtually all types of trees, and the giant sequoia is no exception. Another disease affecting juvenile sequoias is a root rot caused by the fungus *Sclerotium bataticola* Taub. found in damp, dark areas. Gray mould blight was recorded by Martin (1957-58) on sequoia seedlings in Germany, and we later observed it in the Giant Forest and in the Redwood Mountain Grove. The affected leaves appear "cemented" together by the fungus, which completely destroys their photosynthetic capabilities. Long burial under wet snow in winter and spring is the probable cause. For overall seedling survival, however, it is only a minor problem.

The depredations of insects and vertebrates on sequoia seedlings have been exaggerated because of the statements by Fry and White (1930), which we have not been able to verify. Their observations in the park nursery at Ash Mountain, outside the tree's natural habitat, possibly led to the contention that no other conifer is attacked in its infancy by so many destructive agencies. They further state:

> Birds, such as finches and sparrows, are attracted to the green tops for food. Cutworms destroy many of the plants by cutting them off near the ground. Large black wood ants levy a heavy toll by cutting off the plants and dragging them to their nests. Rodents, such as ground squirrels and chipmunks, destroy many of the plants by eating off their tender tops.

Insect depredations on seedlings do occur, but they appear minor and are almost wholly limited to first-year seedlings' tender tissues. Damage may also be accentuated when sequoia seedlings predominate among foods available, as they may after a fire. In weekly post-manipulation examination of hundreds of dead seedlings, from 3.4 to 17.5% per year showed signs of insect feeding. The tender epidermis on the stem was commonly eaten away from the crown downward to the ground level, or else the stem was girdled. In a report of ours (Hartesveldt et al. 1968), Stecker identified this damage as the work of a camel cricket (*Pristocauthophilus pacificus* Thomas), a nocturnal feeder, in its first and second instar stages. Occasionally, the larvae of a geometrid moth (*Sabulodes caberata* Gn. and *Pero behrensarius* Pack.) were feeding upon the seedlings' leaves, but the few resultant deaths would qualify it as relatively unimportant.

There is some indication that tops of new seedlings are eaten off by birds or mammals, but the number is certainly insignificant, as is the number of those uprooted by rodents or by deer hooves. Compared to desiccation losses, animal losses are negligible.

Sequoia seedlings probably seldom die by winter freezing within their native range. Temperatures here rarely reach $0°F$ and, at times when such lows are most likely, seedlings are generally well insulated by snow and are not much affected. Beetham (1962) lost seedlings planted above 9600 ft in the Sierra where low winter temperatures prevail. Low temperatures are more a problem in nurseries (Wulff et al. 1911) and where seedlings have been introduced into cold climates in other parts of the world.

Seedling density

The density and rates of growth of young sequoias vary considerably with the circumstances of seed distribution and seedling survival. Where fire has created optimal conditions for seedling establishment, there may be as many as 25-50 seedlings, and reportedly even more, per square foot. Such densities, however, are usually limited to relatively small areas because of either an irregular seed dispersal pattern, or spotty soil receptivity, or both. In areas where fires have heated the soil surface, the high temperatures seem to favor both the seedlings' survival and increased rates of growth.

DeBano and Krammes (1966) have discussed water-repellent soils and their relationship to fire; more specifically, Donaghey (1969), experimenting with soils from sequoia groves, has demonstrated that incineration of soils increases both their wetability and soil moisture retention. This better explains sequoia seedlings' survival and growth in burned areas. On recent experimental and prescription burns in Kings Canyon National Park, seedlings have been especially abundant in soils severely burned by the combustion of dry downed logs, and their resulting elongated pattern conforms to the position of the log (Fig. 36). This high seedling survival under burned-out logs possibly explains the remarkably straight rows of even some mature sequoia trees.

Competition, of course, increases with density, and mortality thins out the trees continuously as their crowns expand and compete for light. Being very intolerant of shade, the young trees without sufficient light are killed, or at least the lower portions of their foliage die away.

The juvenile stage is commonly a narrow conical spire where site conditions are optimal and where growth is therefore rapid (Fig. 11). When sequoias are virtually the sole species established in a given area, the slender crowns are well-fitted for maintaining dense stands for many years since the conical form assures that the sun will reach part of each crown. The 10-year olds portrayed in Fig. 37 at Cherry Gap, Sequoia National Forest, are from 6 to 15 ft tall, and such stands are much too dense for a man to walk through with comfort. Although the supply of subsurface drainage water is highly dependable, this density obviously cannot long continue because the light factor will soon become critical for the smaller trees. Those which now dominate the others in height will almost assuredly be the eventual survivors. Of the 126 saplings in this small grouping, probably no more than four or five will survive to mature size.

The sapling stage

In areas of high site quality, vertical growth of young sequoias is commonly as much as 1-2 ft per year, and rapid growth continues until the trees are 100 or more feet high.

The trunk grows rapidly in thickness at the same time, the growth layers of vigorous specimens being as much as 0.50 inch thick or more. Both radial growth and growth in height reflect photosynthetic success. Radial growth decreases slowly with size and age although total additions of wood, spreading over a greater circumference, may remain essentially the same.

At this stage, cone production is usually well advanced and the vigorous spire-topped trees may be heavily laden with cones of several years' production.

As the spreading bases of the crowns begin to compete for light, not only does the foliage begin to die back, but within several years' time the limbs are self-pruned through shading and give the tree a more mature appearance. In its native habitat, topographic and soil conditions rarely restrict nearby competing vegetation to such an extent that a sequoia maintains its branches down to the ground level. Specimen trees in municipal parks and other open situations show this characteristic much more commonly than in their native range (Fig. 30).

Maturity

As vertical growth slows, elongation of the lateral limbs continues at an increased proportional rate so that the crown's sharp spire gradually gives way to the rounded form of the mature tree (Fig. 16). If the tree is more than 200 ft high, it has, in all likelihood, solved its light problem and, barring the catastrophies of intense fire, lightning, snow-loading on the crown, and blow-down, now stands an excellent chance of surviving to old age. No other tree in its native Sierra Nevada overtops the crown of the taller sequoias. Thus, its upper foliage, which is still intolerant of shade, has a dependable, uninterrupted supply of sunlight for its photosynthetic needs.

By this stage in the sequoian life cycle, the total number of large, mature specimens has been considerably reduced by fires and other decimating factors. In the Redwood Mountain grove we studied, the mature trees varied from 5 to 8 per acre. Elsewhere, in localized situations, the density may approximate 15-20 per acre such as the Senate Group in the Giant Forest and the Sugar Bowl group in the Redwood Mountain Grove. Nowhere has the sequoia ever been found as a pure stand.

Old age

The characteristic form of the older trees is one of irregular, craggy, and sometimes grotesque crowns which often reveal the dead upper part of the trunk, or "snag-top" (Fig. 38).

Although lightning has been suggested as the reason for these dead tops, it now seems more probable that they are the result of fire scars at the bases of the trees which have a diminished translocation of water upward from their roots. The few large, old specimens still maintaining symmetrically rounded crowns invariably have small fire evidence, usually only a superficial char on the bark. A study of 100 snag-top sequoias in the Giant Forest revealed that each of them had one or more basal fire scars burned through the bark into the wood tissue (Hartesveldt 1965). The severance of the effective connections between the root system and the crown may well have deprived the crown of a portion of its requisite supply of moisture and nutrients (Rundel (1971), and it seems logical that the portion with the longest supply route would be the first to suffer. Scars at the bases of snag-tops are from 15 to 96% of living specimens' total circumference and there is a general correlation between the size of the scar and the size of the dead snag at the top.

It is very probably impossible to find a sequoia in the mature or later stages

Fig. 36. Counting seedlings in trough of burned sugar pine log. The seedlings are too small to be evident in the photograph, but author Ron Stecker and wife Phylis recorded young seedlings in the soil heated by its combustion. Records indicate that seedling survival is better in situations where soils have been heated to a high temperature. This could well be one of the reasons behind the straight lines of mature sequoias.

Fig. 37. Sequoia reproduction in area burned by fire of 1955 in Cherry Gap area of Converse Basin. Of the 126 saplings in this small group, few will survive. *Photo by* H. Thomas Harvey.

Fig. 38. "Snag-top" sequoia, indicative of old age and injuries to the base of the trunk. Older sequoias have felt the ravages of fires over and over again. Where burn scars interrupt the flow of soil nutrients, often the uppermost portion of the tree dies back. *Photo by* R. J. Hartesveldt.

Fig. 39. The Black Chamber, Giant Forest, Sequoia National Park. This tree is a living remnant of its former 18-ft diameter, with 96% of its former circumference burned away. Yet the tree is growing radially at about the same rate as an uninjured tree of similar size in optimum site condition.

Fig. 40. Lightning-topped sequoia, Giant Forest, Sequoia National Park. In contrast to the "snag-topped" sequoias, those struck by lightning have had at least the upper third of the trunk broken away. Lightning seldom kills mature sequoias in the Sierra Nevada. *Photo by* R. J. Hartesveldt.

that does not bear the black char marks of fire. Various authors have strongly suggested that fire has been a normal factor in almost all Sierran environments since the time forests existed there. The degree to which a tree is burned or spared probably depends on its topographic location with respect to other vegetation, the relationship to fuel accumulations, and other factors which would similarly influence the intensity of the often-repeated fires. The burn scars of individual trees are probably due more often to the cumulative effects of many fires, not all necessarily intense, than to single fires.

Prior to the Western innovation of fire prevention and suppression, both the incidence and size of forest fires were greater than now. The intensity, however, of fires then was probably less. With repetitions of fires at rather regular intervals, fuel could not accumulate to proportions that would support today's dreaded crown fire holocausts. Each fire cleaned up the previous accumulations of fuel on the ground, and although other trees' crowns may have been badly damaged, sequoias, because of their size and fire-resistant bark, had a substantial survival advantage. Individual, standing, dead sequoia snags are common and show clear evidence of having been burned to death. But such dead snags are rare in a given locality, and nowhere cover a large area, suggesting that intense crown fires were less frequent in the past.

In the snag-top study referred to earlier, fire scars were found just about in any conceivable location on the trunks observed. They varied from surface scorching to deep "cat-face" scars only at the base to longitudinal scars often running the full length of the trunk, and to hollowed "telescope" trees. Of the basal scars, analysis showed that approximately 90% were decidedly on the trunk's up-hill side. In the field, the reason becomes quite obvious. Cones, limbs, and other combustible debris, as it falls to the ground, is generally carried downhill by the pull of gravity and it comes to rest against the barriers formed by the trees' trunks. Thus, even light ground fires smolder longer in these collections of fuel and sear slowly through the bark and into the wood tissues.

The resulting scars on the up-hill side become somewhat concave just above the ground level and the cavity presents a greater storage space for new accumulations of falling fuels. Therefore, not only do later fires have a greater fuel supply, but the concave surfaces also tend to accentuate the effects of subsequent fires as they reflect the heat like an oven. And the larger the scar, the more pronounced the effects of each successive fire.

Despite their cragginess and "imperfections" in old age, the trees remain mystically beautiful and enchanting. They are by now the largest members of their community and they dominate the tree-top horizon in such a manner that the species can be identified easily by an observer many miles away. These are the specimens of trees that prompted the establishment of the parks that now preserve them and are the trees which are most prominent in the interest of the visiting public.

Contrary to popular belief, these old veterans have not stopped growing, nor have they necessarily even slowed their rate of growth. Green foliage proclaims that photosynthesis is still on-going, and this, in turn, implies continuing yearly increments to the trunk diameter, no matter how large the specimen. Although the annual ring width is narrower, the radius of the tree becomes continually greater so that the amount of wood added each year is proportionately the same as when the tree was younger and is more or less maintained continually.

The ring width at this stage may vary from 0.50 mm per year to 1 mm for trees in well-watered sites. This means that during each 24 years the world's two largest trees, the General Sherman and the General Grant, will add about 24 mm (1 inch) to their radial growth, or 48 mm (2 inches) of diameter. Even the fragmental trunk of the Black Chamber in the Giant Forest is adding 1 mm of radial growth yearly, despite 96% of its circumference having been destroyed by fire, as is most of the trunk (Fig. 39). Here is the quintessence of tenacity of life for which this species is so well known.

Unlike other plants and animals, the sequoia does not seem to lose its reproductive ability with old age. The very largest specimens (not necessarily the oldest) have crowns that are loaded with cones containing viable seeds. Difficult as it is to determine the age of living trees without considerable effort, it is likewise difficult to assess any slowing of cone production due to aging. But, over our years of observation, we have found no indication of such slowing. The five largest specimens of sequoias in the world all bear moderate to heavy cone-loads and germinable seeds. Likewise, the remnant crown of that hopelessly "crippled" Black Chamber is loaded with green cones.

That lightning affects the tops of tall sequoia trees is well documented by observers fortunate enough, from our point of view at least, to have been near one of these natural lightning rods when it was struck. Fry and White (1930) describe a dramatic horizontal bolt of lightning striking a trunk with a 16-ft diameter in the Garfield Grove. Surely it was the sight of a lifetime, the bolt knocking out a 20-ft segment from the middle of the trunk and dropping the crown which, oddly, caught up in the split of the trunk below. They further report that the trunk sent out new growth and may be presumed alive today. The Giant Forest seems to have a higher incidence of lightning strikes on sequoias than most of the other groves, perhaps because it is so close to the edge of the great "plateau" on which it is located. In several trees broken off near their middles, the lower branches have taken over the crown's sole function (Fig. 40). Recovery for these stricken trees appears reasonably well assured.

Former National Park Service employee Ralph Anderson recalls vividly one of his earlier days in the service when he was stationed in Yosemite's Mariposa Grove. During a summer thunderstorm, a bolt of lightning struck the dead top of the Grizzly Giant, dislodging several hundred pounds of wood and dropping them literally at his feet. Although this incident may have strengthened the assumption that snag-tops are created by this means, it must be recognized that where bolts of lightning have hit the living parts of trees, the entire upper portion was often broken away, perhaps because of the great heat affecting the moisture within the stem. The Grizzly Giant's dry top, dead many years or even centuries, was perhaps a poor conductor of electricity, resulting in a relatively small portion of wood being torn loose. Fry and White (1930), perhaps the longest continuous observers of the giant sequoia, record only two specimens actually killed by lightning.

Differing from most other tree species, the sequoia seems to have no known age of senescence. There is no record of mature sequoias ever having died from disease or insect depredations, afflictions common to other species of trees in their old age. If the sequoia could be kept from falling over or being burned to death, we can imagine that our descendants, a millennium hence, may see a General Sherman Tree approaching 40 ft dbh.

Death

With advancing old age, the thick, resin-free bark of this tree is doubtless a definite asset to its longevity and survival. Fires that kill or severely damage other species and younger sequoias may be of far less consequence to the relict larger sequoias which have survived many successional sequences of these associated species. Occasionally, however, a fire has been severe enough to kill all the foliage on more than one specimen in a given locality. Stricken, charred trunks remain witness of these fires for many centuries before they disintegrate. Seldom are more than two or three such snags found in close proximity, which suggests that crown fires were less prevalent before the advent of Western Civilization.

Sometimes lightning strikes will set fire to the dead wood of a snag-top specimen. The wood, which may have been drying for a thousand warm Sierran summers, holds the fire very well, contrary to popular opinion and despite the limbs' size. We watched such a fire in the top of a large sequoia in Redwood Canyon in the summer of 1966. Charles Castro of the Sequoia National Park Forestry Division had climbed into its crown via a nearby fir tree to spray water onto the burning portion, unreachable from the ground. From our vantage point, and with Castro as a reference, the burning limb seemed about 3 ft in diameter, hardly a good prospect for a continued blaze. Just such a fire in the Giant Forest Lodge cabin area burned away the entire crown and upper part of another large sequoia in 1959. Again, the fire was burning well above the reach of water streams, and there were no adjacent trees suitable for access into its crown even if Castro had already developed his unique fire-fighting method. The tree, which burned for 2 weeks and disconcertingly dropped firebrands amongst the cabins, is now but a dead snag to about one-third its original height.

Old sequoias most commonly die by toppling. Because of the wood's brittleness, this virtually assures death, although an occasional specimen has retained green leaves for several years after falling, which perhaps indicates that the fall did not sever all its vascular connections. One unique tree in the Atwell Grove that fell many years ago is still growing vigorously, with seven lateral branches giving the appearance of a candelabrum.

Fire is probably the greatest contributor to death by falling because it creates gaping fire scars at ground level which weaken the tree's mechanical support. The extreme weight of the big trees coupled with their shallow roots increase the effects of this weakening, especially in leaning trees. Other causative factors are water-softened soils, undercutting by streams, snow-load on the crown, uneven reloading with moisture, wind, heart-rot, nearby falling trees, perhaps carpenter ants cutting galleries in the bark and dead wood near the trunks' bases, and, of course, various combinations of the above.

We mentioned the finding that 90% of the fire scars in trees growing on slopes were on their up-slope sides. It is not surprising, then, that 90% of all fallen trees seen during that survey were found to have fallen up-hill, toward the side with the least support. Likewise, sequoias on the edge of wet meadows tend strongly to fall into the meadow because of the greater weakness associated with the softened saturated soil, and, in addition, because of the heavier foliage on the more illuminated side. Trees in these soft substrates also may come to lean because of wind pressure or snow-loading on the crown. If they survive, their off-center of gravity still continually subjects them to ever greater strains. Yet many of them, such as the immense Grizzly Giant leaning about $17°$ from the vertical, marvelously remain standing for centuries. The large, tenacious roots obviously provide sufficient anchorage to prevent their fall.

The lean of the famous Tunnel Tree in Yosemite National Park was surely part of its undoing, to say nothing of the tunnel cut through it in 1881 which weakened the tree much as a fire scar would. Unfortunately, this tree was chosen because of its large fire scar which lessened the work required to carve the tunnel. The Washburn Brothers were paid only $75 for the task (Russell 1957). Less wood had to be removed on the up-hill side, and the tree had a decided lean in that same direction.

Examination of its remains revealed a failure of the wood on the leaning side, which was also the one with the least wood support. The tree probably collapsed between February and May 1969 when, very fortunately, park visitors were not lined up bumper to bumper awaiting their turn to park in the tunnel and take the traditional photograph to be found in almost all geography books for nearly a century (Fig. 41). Because of the unusually heavy snow during that winter, the crown may well have borne 1-2 tons of additional weight which the wood could not support. No evidence supports the idea that its collapse was due to excessive trampling by people, the possible effects of which had earlier caused considerable concern (Hartesveldt 1963). Of course, the cutting of the tunnel is looked upon today as a sort of vandalism, and the tree very likely would still be standing had the tunnel never been cut.

Curiously, although averse to vandalism to our irreplaceable natural objects, many people held the Tunnel Tree in near reverence. In both Yosemite and Sequoia National parks, visitors have most often asked, "Where is the tree I can drive through?" Despite this question's humorous association for rangers in Sequoia National Park, the announcement of its falling was greeted with great sorrow.

Its fall marked the end of an era in Yosemite that many will remember fondly. Letters have often inquired when and where the next "tunnel tree" would be cut. Of course, it will not be, at least not in the national parks and forests or other public lands because laws hold federal agencies responsible for the preservation of these near-immortal trees. Not far north of the Grizzly Giant in Yosemite's Mariposa Grove is the tunneled California Tree, which in many older photographs bears the name "Wawona" over its portal. This was a useful ruse perpetrated by stage drivers in the spring of the year when the upper part of the grove was still deep in snow and the real Wawona Tree was inaccessible. Delighted passengers failed to notice that the two trees were really quite different. To assure better preservation, this tree has long been accessible only by foot.

One rather frequent form of toppling difficult to explain occurs during the warm summertime when the air is still. Records on individual trees are few, and

Fig. 41. The remains of the Wawona Tunnel Tree following its collapse in 1969. After surviving 88 years of traffic passing through its well-known tunnel, it was felled by the rigors of winter. *Photo by* R. J. Hartesveldt.

so cannot tell us whether all or most of the fallen trees were leaning ones. If they are leaning, why haven't they gone down at some earlier time? Just what finally gives gravity the advantage after many centuries and brings the trees down? The late Willis Wagener, formerly of the U.S. Forest and Range Experiment Station at Berkeley, proposed some initial hypotheses and submitted them to us a few weeks before his death. To follow up these hypotheses, projected studies in the Giant Forest will consider leaning trees, excessive loss of water by transpiration on warm, dry days, and the shock of recharge weights as more humid conditions return. We hope these studies will bring determinations of and predictions for "accident-prone" specimens, and prevent such tragedies as that of August 1969 in the Hazelwood Picnic Grounds, Sequoia National Park when a woman was hit and killed in a bizarre falling of two trees on the windless day.

The chapter on the characteristics of old age may never be finished, at least for many generations to come. Continual protection and surveillance, improved age-dating for living trees, and extensive studies can determine whether there really is an age of senescence or a time when sequoias become more susceptible to debilitating diseases and insect depredations.

Man's interest does not necessarily end when a tree lies prostrate on the ground. To many, a downed tree appears even larger than when standing—witness the countless visitors scrambling over the remains in any sequoia park, and the photographs of cavalry troops, horse-drawn carriages, and automobiles standing atop the fallen logs for comparison. Long after death, these trees command admiration.

Decay

For science, the giant sequoias' slow rate of decay has raised several perplexing and still unanswered questions. The heartwood is particularly resistant to fungal attack and even the sapwood on some specimens is slow to decay. Many fallen trees appear today essentially as they did when photographed as much as a century or more ago.

The heartwood's unusually high tannin content, discouraging both fungi and insects, was first advanced as an explanation during the 1800s, and the Forest Service later gave it credence (Sudworth 1908). The hypothesis is still generally accepted (Schubert 1962). Detailed chemical analyses of substances from the coast redwood indicate that perhaps other organic substances deposited in the heartwood are also the retardants in this species (Anderson et al. 1968; Balogh and Anderson 1965, 1966). Similar studies have not been made on the giant sequoia but, considering the relationship of the two trees, we can reasonably assume that related repellents are likewise in its wood.

Perhaps the most interesting remaining question is how long the fallen trunks remain undecayed. Muir (1878) postulated that the trunks would last about 10,000 years and that their charred remains should be found in areas outside the existing groves. Such remnants, if they occur, would be a clue to the earlier distribution pattern of the species, as would the trenches in the ground made by the great impact of the trunks in falling. At this writing, no such remains to substantiate Muir's hopes of nearly a century ago have been found. Perhaps the pits or trenches have been eliminated during the milennia that erosive forces have been at work and that the log remnants would have been consumed by repeated fires. Contrary to some earlier opinions (Clark 1937; Schwarz 1904; Blick 1963), sequoia wood burns readily and individual dry logs have been observed to burn completely within a week. Furthermore, if the range were once continuous, fires must have burned repeatedly and erased every last vestige of their presence.

Some small indication of the wood's durability is indicated by carbon-dating of three wood specimens mentioned on page 56.

There is one species of tree known to be more ancient than the giant sequoia in its living state—the bristlecone pine. This five-needled pine ranges over six southwestern states, including southeastern California, although it is not found in the Sierra Nevada. Specimens growing in the White Mountain Range have been analyzed and one specimen is recorded at 4900 years of age by ring-count determination (Fritts 1969).

By cross-dating tree rings from these ancient pines and carefully accounting for missing of duplicate rings, an absolute chronology of nearly 8200 years has been assembled. This chronology has been useful in correcting the carbon-14 determinations which have apparently varied in their rates of production in the atmosphere within past ages (Renfrew 1971).

6
Sequoia Community Interrelationships

Structure of sequoia communities

While the interdependence of associated organisms is clear, the boundaries of what should be recognized as biotic communities are often difficult to determine and arbitrarily set.

Two major systems of community classification apply to the mountainous regions of western America. Merriam's Life Zone System recognizes that plants and animals vary in form and kind with increasing altitude, and that these assemblages are essentially in bands or zones of varying width along the mountain slopes. Originally based upon temperature zonation, this concept has limited usefulness. However, the recognition of indicator organisms for each zone may serve the fundamental concept that physical factors have selected various life forms, and that these factors, mainly temperature and precipitation, vary directly with altitude and, to a lesser extent, with aspect of the slope. Very much similar to the Life Zone concept is the plant belt system of Storer and Usinger (1963), which identifies the Sierra's plant associations in horizontal belts from the lowlands upward to its crest. Along a transect crossing such belts one would encounter the Great Valley, the Foothill, the Yellow Pine, and Boreal belts in that order.

Another system common in California is that of plant communities, such as Munz and Keck (1959) proposed and described. They recognize 29 such communities in California, each based upon the kinds of dominant plants found in association with one another. Some basic vegetation types are important here: marsh, grassland, chaparral, and coniferous forest. The latter category includes some nine recognized plant communities that range from the redwood forest in the mild coastal climate to the bristlecone pine of the much colder region of the high mountains. Under this classification, the giant sequoia is an element of the yellow pine forest community. Storer and Usinger's plant belt system places sequoias with the Yellow Pine Belt, and the Life Zone scheme, in the Transition Zone.

Because of its large bulk or biomass and tallness, the giant sequoia is clearly a dominant in its association. However, since no vascular plant species is found only in association with the giant sequoias (Rundel 1969), there is no such thing, strictly speaking, as a giant sequoia community, even though sequoia groves do qualify as biotic communities of interacting plants and animals.

The sequoia community, much like other forest communities, is stratified, or layered. The uppermost layer is the vegetation of the canopy, comprising the crowns of the giant sequoia and of other tree species such as the white fir (*Abies concolor*), sugar pine (*Pinus lambertiana*), ponderosa pine (*Pinus ponderosa*), and often, at lower elevations, the incense-cedar (*Libocedrus decurrens*). At higher elevations, it may include the red fir (*Abies magnifica*). In the more northerly groves, Douglas fir (*Pseudotsuga menziesii*) is also a part of the canopy, although uncommon in the Mariposa Grove, which is essentially that species' southern limit.

The understory vegetation includes trees of lesser stature, including the young of these species in the canopy layer, and shrubs. Of the tree species, white fir is today the most abundant of these saplings. In the earlier stages of succession, we find California black oak (*Quercus kelloggii*) and occasionally canyon live oak (*Quercus chrysolepis*). Two shrubs, perhaps the most common in the groves, that can tolerate the low light values at the lower strata of this forest are mountain whitethorn (*Ceanothus cordulatus*) and chinquapin (*Castanopsis sempervirens*) (Rundel 1969). The California hazelnut (*Corylus rostrata*) and a small tree, the Pacific dogwood (*Cornus nuttallii*), also survive well in the more shaded parts of the forest, and the northern part of the sequoia range has still another tree in the lower story, the western yew (*Taxus brevifolia*). The latter occurs only in the North Calaveras Grove, which is roughly the southern limit of its range.

At ground level, a wide variety of perennial plants characterizes the ground cover. Here, highly efficient photosynthesis is a necessity even though low productivity is the rule. These ground plants apparently can make maximum use of the minimal light penetrating to their level. They are rich in chlorophyll and generally have broad leaves so oriented as to expose the greatest possible surface area to the light.

The ground-cover plants vary greatly from grove to grove in kind and abundance, especially the annuals and biennials, and with the stage of plant succession. However, certain species are commonly associated with the giant sequoia in the large southern groves. The trail plant (*Adenocaulon bicolor*) is an associate not only of the giant sequoia but also, in the coastal mountains, of the coast redwood. Also common to many sequoia groves are sweet cicely (*Osmorhiza chilensis*), white hawkweed (*Hieracium albiflorum*), and a wood violet (*Viola lobata*). These four ground-cover plants are most abundant at about 5% of full sunlight in the Redwood Mountain Grove (Hartesveldt et al. 1967)—a good indication of their ability to survive on shaded forest floors. Seedlings of white fir are similarly abundant at this low light level.

In areas subjected to the physical removal of the understory or its destruction by prescription burning, two major changes occurred in the ground-cover plants. Harvey found that some of the species, such as trail plant and hawkweed, decreased considerably where the ground-level light averaged 25% of full sunlight following manipulation. Other plants increased in abundance as their light requirements became more nearly optimal.

Small-leaved ceanothus (*Ceanothus parvifolius*) sprang up around the perimeters of burn piles where the fire, heating the seeds, had enhanced germination. It is known from other studies (Sweeney 1956) that, in many of the chaparral species, heating the seeds changes the seed coats so that they admit water and initiate germination.

Two types of plants increased abundantly most likely because of the disturbed ground cover and exposed mineral soil. Small, delicate annuals, such as gilia (*Gilia giliodes*) and a popcorn flower (*Cryptantha affinis*), proliferated following manipulation by fire. The thin-stemmed primrose (*Gayophytum nuttallii*) also increased greatly. The second group, the perennials, likewise grew strikingly in number. *Phacelia mutabilis* and gooseberry (*Ribes roezlii*) showed a dramatic 10- to 20-fold increase after fires and after other physical manipulation of the ground and vegetation. Each of the above plants is part of the typical giant sequoia forest community.

The most conspicuous streamside plant within sequoia groves is the western azalea (*Rhododendron occidentale*). It is especially attractive in the spring, with its large, irregular, flamboyant, white flowers, and again in the fall when its foliage turns reddish. On the flood plains and gentle slopes, bracken fern (*Pteridium aquilinum*) and a tall lupine (*Lupinus latifolius*) literally carpet the forest floor. In spring and early summer, the bright purple flowers of the lupines against rustic red sequoia bark is a sight to treasure.

Within the areas studied, we find approximately 65 species of plants in the sequoia forest plant community, excluding the strictly riparian species. Although the species combination varies from grove to grove, the larger groves probably have close to that number. Appendix II contains the names of vascular plants mentioned in the text.

Plant and animal relationships

With the exception of insects and possibly some other invertebrates, animal life in the groves is very much like that found throughout the Transition and Canadian zones in the Sierra at elevations from about 4000-9000 ft. The mixed conifers support a delightful wealth of vertebrate life, much of it ubiquitous throughout the Sierra.

There is no reason to believe that any particular species of vertebrate is exclusive to the groves, even though one animal, the chickaree, depends strongly on the sequoia for food. And since no vertebrate is known to nest or roost exclusively in it, the sequoia adds little to the wildlife habitat of which it is but one constituent. The groves border on nonsequoian forest communities, as well as on wet meadows, dry rocky outcrops, open grassy meadows, dense shrubby areas, and many other types of vegetation or ecological situations depending upon local environment and the stage of plant succession.

Animal populations, then, vary with location and time according to the available food and other requisites of life provided by plants, and such a variety precludes complete and detailed analysis. What follows is a synthesis of our studies in the Redwood Mountain Grove and Whitaker's Forest, and observations which we and others made in other groves as well. It mostly describes the faunal characteristics of the typical giant sequoia grove.

Appendix III contains the scientific names of the vertebrate animals mentioned in the text.

Vertebrates

Birds are the most abundant and obvious vertebrate animals within the sequoia forests, and the composition of their populations does not vary much from north to south within the range. As Kilgore (1968) has pointed out, " . . . the bird species which are found in the surrounding forests, without either species of sequoia, make up the sequoia forest avifauna." He attributed this to bird communities' greater correlation with the growth form of the forest vegetation than with a dominant species of plant.

The most typical birds in the associated nonsequoian coniferous forest are the yellow-rumped warbler, western tanager, mountain chickadee, brown creeper, warbling vireo, Oregon junco, Steller's jay, hermit thrush, golden-crowned kinglet, and solitary vireo. Within the groves, the species composition is very much the same, but the dominance of one species over another varies with the stage of plant succession. In the young mixed conifers which include sequoia at Whitaker's Forest, Kilgore (1971) found the following four species as dominants: western robin, Steller's jay, western tanager, and Oregon junco. In a nearby mature sequoia-mixed-conifer forest, Shellhammer (Hartesveldt et al. 1968) found the mountain chickadee and Oregon junco to be dominants, and the western tanager, jays, nuthatches, and flycatchers as subdominants. All the 12 common nonsequoian forest birds were present in these two sequoia areas, as were numerous other species.

Many birds tend to be more or less restricted to specific life zones, and hence the altitude at which a particular grove lies affects its avifauna to some extent.

Most of the 30 or more species listed in Table 3 are residents, breeding in and near sequoia groves. Over a period of time, one might count at least twice as many species if including the transients and occasional visitors.

The mammals of the sequoia forest communities are both common and numerous although, because many have nocturnal habits, park visitors see them much less than the birds.

The most common mammals are the deer mouse, gray squirrel, Douglas squirrel or chickaree, mule deer, golden-mantled ground squirrel, coyote, and black bear. They are found in virtually any Sierran forest.

The California ground squirrel, although normally much more abundant at lower elevations, is found as high as 6500 ft in the southern Sierra Nevada. It is relatively common in many of the groves, and appears to be more abundant in

TABLE 3. The more common birds within a typical giant sequoia grove classified by their feeding habits (Salt 1953, 1957; Kilgore 1968).

Feeding habit	Species of birds
Air-soaring (raptors)	Goshawk, Red-tailed Hawk, Spotted Owl, and various other owls.
Air-perching	Western Wood Peewee, Olive-sided Flycatcher, and various Empidonax Flycatchers.
Foliage-insect	Winter Wren, Townsend's Solitaire, Golden-crowned Kinglet, Solitary Vireo, Warbling Vireo, Nashville Warbler, Western Tanager, and Black-headed Grosbeak.
Foliage-seed	Steller's Jay, Cassin's Finch or Purple Finch, and, in lower elevations, Band-tailed Pigeon.
Timber-search	Mountain Chickadee, Red-breasted Nuthatch, and Brown Creeper.
Timber-drill	Pileated Woodpecker, Yellow-bellied Sapsucker, Hairy Woodpecker, and White-headed Woodpecker.
Ground-insect	Red-shafted Flicker, Robin, Hermit Thrush, and Oregon Junco.
Ground-seed	Mountain Quail and Rufous-sided Towhee.

the groves lying within the national parks. Some claim that this results from the higher number of visitors and the correspondingly greater destruction of rattlesnakes which previously preyed more heavily upon the California ground squirrels in these areas. Others claim that the squirrels have always been numerous there, so the argument is far from settled.

Most sequoia groves support populations of one or more species of chipmunks. The long-eared chipmunk occupies open, brushy, or rocky areas in the northern and central groves. In the same groves, the yellow pine chipmunk is found in open forest conditions. In the central and southern Sierra, these two species are replaced by the lodgepole chipmunk, normally found in groves in the Canadian Zone, and the Townsend chipmunk, usually restricted to those in the Transition Zone.

Occasionally, the golden-mantled ground squirrel shares a particular area with the chipmunks. Park visitors often confuse this squirrel with the chipmunk, but the former is considerably larger and lacks the stripes across the face which clearly identify the latter.

The one shrew which inhabits the dry forest floor of the Sierra's sequoia-mixed-conifer forest is the Trowbridge shrew, which is normally found in small numbers and, with its rather secretive activities, is rarely seen by visitors. This is true for most carnivores as well. While some visitors are fortunate enough to see an occasional coyote or even a bobcat, very few see the more elusive marten, the long-tailed weasel, or the mountain lion.

In the moist meadows and riparian communities throughout the Sierran mixed-conifer belt, one might find populations of mammals not normally found in the drier forested areas. The following mammals typify those habitats both within and outside of sequoian communities: vagrant shrew, water shrew, broad-handed mole, long-tailed meadow mouse, mountain meadow mouse, Botta pocket gopher, and raccoon.

Bats are more commonly seen during the evening hours, especially in the groves near the lower border of the Transition Zone. Although they are difficult to identify on the wing, the common species of bats in sequoia groves are as follows: little brown myotis, fringed myotis, California myotis, long-eared myotis, Yuma myotis, hoary bat, red bat, and big brown bat.

Only the hoary bat and red bat are tree-dwelling species, and may be found in the foliage of a grove in the daytime. The rest are cave-dwellers, or they roost in old buildings. All the bats are warm-weather visitors and migrate either into the Central Valley or southward with the onset of cold weather.

Of all the mammals in the sequoia forests, the chickaree or Douglas squirrel certainly plays the most significant role in the sequoia's life cycle.

The cold-blooded vertebrates constitute another varied group of animals not often observed by the average visitor. The term "cold-blooded," or its more recent synonym "ectotherm," refers to the amphibians' and reptiles' inability to maintain constant body temperature by themselves. Because they depend on mild climates and sunny areas, ectotherms are more numerous in the groves at lower elevations and the more open groves of the middle elevations.

The following reptiles and amphibians often inhabit the lower groves: Gilbert skink, western whiptail lizard, rubber boa, western terrestrial garter snake, and California mountain king snake.

Another group, more universal to most of the groves, regardless of elevation, includes: Eschscholtz's salamander, western toad, yellow-legged frog, western fence lizard, northern alligator lizard, and western rattlesnake.

One species, the sagebrush lizard, is found in the lodgepole pine-fir belt, chiefly in rocky, shrub-filled areas. Some sequoia groves, especially those protected by park status, shelter the rather rare western ringneck snake. However, most of these animals require either riparian or open, dry, rocky areas, and therefore are often missing from the larger groves. We might say that, in the large mature groves, the basic four are Eschscholtz's salamander, the western fence lizard, the alligator lizard, and the western rattlesnake.

The food chain

Trees, shrubs, and herbs are the sequoia community's primary producers. These, plus the fungi, provide the nutritive base for the rest of the community. The green, photosynthetic plants support an amazing array of invertebrates, mostly insects, which are in turn consumed by a large variety of birds and some mammals. The reptiles and amphibians, although mostly insectivorous, play a relatively minor role in the food webs of sequoia groves because of their low numbers and the rather unfavorable environment for their existence.

Birds and a few mammals usually dominate the animal world of a giant sequoia grove. Most of the birds are insectivorous almost throughout the year although some of them switch to eating berries in the fall. The birds and the insect parasites are major agents in balancing insect populations. Where birds enter an area with large and growing insect populations, their territories tend to become smaller and their numbers increase. Which bird species abound in any one year, then, depends to a degree upon the species of insects in abundance. After a fire, for example, there is often a decrease in some of the ground-dwelling birds such as the mountain quail, Nashville warbler, and hermit thrush, resulting from the reduction of nest sites and of some litter-dwelling food organisms. In contrast, the populations of flycatchers and robins increase, in part because they are behaviorally adapted to more open forests (Kilgore 1971). Following the more intensive ground fires, after logging, or amid an outbreak of various forest insects, there is usually a decline among mountain chickadees, nuthatches, creepers, woodpeckers, warblers, and tanagers. It is doubtful whether parasites and insectivorous birds together can contain insect populations at a sub-epidemic level, but they and other factors play a significant role in maintaining the balance.

A high percentage of the seeds of annual plants and many of the indigenous fungi serve as food for deer, and in particular for small rodents such as mice, chipmunks, golden-mantled and California ground squirrels, so that their populations increase when these seeds and fungi are plentiful. The larger population reduces the next year's food supply, and the undernourished animals become less resistant to disease and starvation, and probably more vulnerable prey.

Relatively few vertebrates utilize the giant sequoia for food or shelter. A variety of foliage-feeders, such as the vireos, kinglets, and warblers, and air-feeders such as the flycatchers capture insects from or near the tree's foliage. Wherever the bark is thin, maturing sequoias often show the damage of sapsuckers, sometimes over much of the trunk in specimens whose bark is genetically thin. Stecker has found fresh sapsucker damage near the very top of each mature specimen he has studied. Heavy damage to younger trees sometimes occurs. Where the bark is literally peppered with sapsucker holes, the upper portion of the crown dies because of interrupted vascular continuity. Hartesveldt (1965) reports a 2.5-ft diameter specimen in the Suwanee Grove, Sequoia National Park, which has no fire scars, but whose trunk is covered with holes nearly to the ground and is a dead, dry snag in its upper 4 or 5 ft. Curiously enough, no record seems to exist that humans have witnessed a sapsucker in this activity on sequoias.

The thick, fibrous bark of older giant sequoias is often drilled by woodpeckers and is used for nesting, especially by white-headed woodpeckers and occasionally by flickers and a few of the perching birds such as nuthatches. There are reports of certain rodents, for example, chipmunks, using the dust accumulated in these bark cavities for dust baths. Some believe that the pulverized bark, rich in tannin, repels such common ectoparasites as lice and fleas. Other birds, such as flycatchers, will utilize these holes and limbs as nesting sites. The giant sequoia, however, is never exclusively sought out for food or nesting. The vertebrate that comes closest to reliance upon the giant sequoia is still the chickaree.

The role of the chickaree

The chickaree, (Fig. 34) is far from an exclusive devotee of the sequoia groves; it is in fact a resident of coniferous forests extending from the southern Sierra and San Francisco regions northward through the Cascades into Canada and Alaska. Its close cousin, the red squirrel, ranges from eastern Washington southward and eastward across the United States and Canada to the eastern seaboard.

The chickaree does have a peculiar relationship, however, to the giant sequoia. The general habits of the sequoian and nonsequoian chickarees are very much the same except for their specific feeding habits. Anywhere within their range, these hyperactive squirrels normally harvest the cones of pines and firs for the seeds' food value, removing the cone scales with their sharp teeth and dropping them wherever they happen to be feeding.

Outside of sequoia groves, they often build nests of twigs, grass, fungus, and bark for winter protection from the elements inasmuch as they do not hibernate. Thus, they must store food for winter use before the time of snowfall.

The study by Smith (1968) and the studies underway by Shellhammer and others reveal chickaree's year-round territoriality and an ability to maintain it by calling and chasing. This territoriality breaks down for mating purposes, but as soon as the year's brood can fend for itself, it is chased off by the parents to set up territories of its own. Variations in certain aspects of the chickarees' behavior in association with giant sequoias are not yet fully explained. For instance, they seldom if ever build external nests in sequoia groves, yet they are common especially in the more northern areas within their range. We know little about nest sites within sequoia groves, but there is evidence that the hollowed portions of tree trunks are sometimes used. Chickarees have been observed stripping the soft, fibrous bark of young sequoia trees, presumably to line nests. Chickarees conspicuously strip the bark of some trees, especially the lower portions of the trunks. Probably the most significant variation in the behavior of chickarees in sequoia communities is that they make the soft flesh of green sequoia cone scales a major food item.

Observers have long assumed that seeds were the main quest of the chickaree in cutting sequoia cones. Yet within their kitchen middens, remnants of individual seeds that have been bitten through indicate that their consumption is more likely incidental to their proximity to the more nutritious cone-flesh being eaten.

The number of cones utilized in a year's time varies greatly, depending on the supply of alternate foods such as the seeds of sugar pine, white fir, incense-cedar, etc., as well as the air temperature and the animals' sexual condition. Often a chickaree will harvest far more cones than it can possibly eat before the scales dry out and become unpalatable. When living in a given sequoia tree, a single chickaree may cut and eat as many as 3000-3500 cones per year. They are opportunists, however, and will switch to other, more productive tree species when the cones are at an edible stage, even though green sequoia cones are still plentiful. They also utilize fungi, hazelnuts, and a variety of other foodstuffs, but in a dense stand of sequoias, green sequoia cones appear to be their major source of food. Their diet varies proportionally to the diversity of the forest they inhabit.

Several years' observation in the Redwood Mountain Grove, where both chickarees and sequoias abound, indicate that the density of chickaree populations may vary greatly from one year to another. During years of high densities, the territories may be as small as 0.6 acre, and each animal seemingly requires at least one large sequoia tree and a tree of another species nearby, such as a large white fir or possibly a sugar pine. They seem to prefer the former as a nest tree, possibly because it is more prone to insect attacks and diseases, and therefore to drilling by woodpeckers, thus providing more nesting cavities than does the typical sequoia. In high density years, the hills and valleys resound with the squirrels' frequent high pitched calls and scolding chatter. In years of low density their home range may cover as much as 25 acres, with their defended territory near its center. During such years, the chickarees are relatively quiet, the only occasional tell-tale signs of their presence are the many freshly chewed cones beneath sequoia trees.

The chickarees' territorial defense merits further explanation. Defense is a type of agonistic behavior that contains elements of aggression (i.e., attack), retreat, or submission. Successfully evolved agonistic patterns seldom involve much actual contact or injury, if any, but rather consist of retreat, bluff, and easy surrender. Establishing a territory is an important phenomenon which among others provides its owner enough food upon which to live, but loses much of its survival value if the animals must kill one another to obtain and then protect their defended territories. Hence, the chickaree has evolved a behavior that relies on threats, reminders, and challenges in vocal form. The interloper usually does the same, and there is thus a relationship of emotional display rather than one of physical violence. In this manner, mutual recognition and respect allow them to live and let live, a requisite for species' survival.

The chickarees' territories change constantly in a given forested area. A chickaree may live in one sequoia for 3 or 4 years and prune a substantial portion of its total green cone crop. If they were longer-lived creatures, they might conceivably strip a tree of its younger cones, but such is not the case. Most chickarees mate at least once during their lifetime and drive away their young when reared, forcing them to take up territories of their own. When the parent dies, its tree may remain vacant for some years until, by chance, another squirrel claims it as home base. This results in a more-or-less continuous alternation or "rotation" of territories, insuring a more uniform usage of the tree's food supply over a long time (Fig. 42).

The chickaree displays a decided preference for the younger green sequoia cones and generally eats only those that are between their 2nd and 5th years of growth. They seldom take the immature cones or those older than 5 or 6 years. The larvae of the beetle *Phymatodes* infest a high percentage of the older cones which are in varying stages of drying out on any given tree, and are perhaps too woody to be palatable to the chickaree. Cones stored by chickarees may remain

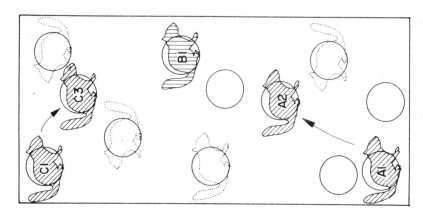

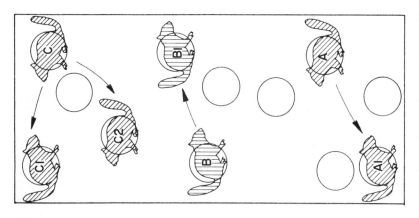

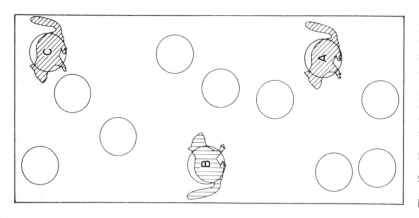

Fig. 42. Hypothetical "rotation" of chickaree territorial use of sequoia trees for cone harvest. Flesh of sequoia cone scales, not the seeds, appears to be the energy source sought. *Drawing by* Ivan Linderman.

green and edible for a year or more in the low, moist areas often used for storage. Those that are apparently cached in creeks are probably free-falls which have ended up in stream depressions quite by accident and most of which are unavailable for later use.

Some squirrels eat all their cones while in a tree's crown, and the seeds so released are spread over a greater area than those eaten on the ground (see "Reproduction"). Either way, seeds disseminated just before and during a snowfall may play an important role in sequoia regeneration. During most of the summer, the feeding of chickarees and beetles produces an almost constant fall of sequoia seeds, but many are lost to reproduction because of damage by insects, fungi, desiccation, and direct radiation.

Chickarees are small, very active mammals with very high rates of metabolism. Smith (1968) and others estimate that their basal metabolic rate is 1.76 times that expected from the weight-to-metabolism relation for most mammals. He suggests that, if the metabolic rate for most mammals were applied to chickarees, a male would still have enough energy to perform heavy labor 24 hours a day or to put on several grams of fat per day. A female could work just as hard and still supply energy to her young for their maintenance and growth. Chickarees do not hibernate and require considerable energy input every day of the year. In most parts of their range, they feed on large, high-energy conifer seeds, fungi, nuts, and berries. In the sequoia groves, however, the food is primarily the cone flesh, not the seeds.

Calorimetric or food value analyses of sequoia seeds and the outer cone material reveal that a chickaree would quickly starve to death eating sequoia seeds alone. However, they can and do eat enough cones each day to provide five or six times their basal metabolic rate. This figure was derived from cone counts around various trees multiplied by the average caloric value of a cone's eaten portion. The squirrels in our studies stripped approximately 3000-3500 cones per year, each cone yielding about 30 kg-cal. Thirty kg-cal equals the energy in two teaspoons of sugar, or a half slice of bread, or a medium raw tomato. While this diet may be greatly enriched by some sugar pine seeds in the fall, the cones are still the important overwintering food. Food that is four or five times their basal rate requirements appears more than adequate in the summer months, but not so in winter.

Red squirrels and probably chickarees have a rather high critical temperature of 68°F. The critical temperature is that below which the animal must expend energy beyond its basal rate to maintain a constant body temperature (Irving et al. 1955). This helps explain the correlation between temperatures and such evolutionary features in these two squirrels as nestbuilding, the caching of food underneath the insulating snow, daily foodgathering, etc., as well as the cutting of cones in large numbers and then making many trips to the ground to store them. But on this point, the chickarees of the Redwood Mountain and other groves begin to vary from red squirrels and chickarees from other areas. They expend great energy running up and down 300-ft tall sequoias. They apparently do not build large nests and, hence, probably expose themselves to the cold for the 20-25 minutes they take to eat each cone. This combination of food habits and behavior patterns in the long, cold winters may well push them to the limits of their adaptive abilities, and some starve or are weakened so that they fall prey to martens. Their life seems a biological compromise, with energy plentiful in the summer and often insufficient during the winter cold. Seldom, however, is a sequoia grove wiped clean of its chickarees—some of them are a bit stronger, healthier, quicker, more fortunately situated, or just luckier.

Some always survive to reproduce. In certain areas, they may have from four to five young and may breed a second time later in the summer, although apparently not in the southern sequoia groves, where they tend to have just one litter of from two to four young. Even so, they can build up rapidly in several mild years until the valley again rings with the territorial calls, and most sequoias are again having their cones cut. Not for long, however: an outbreak of plague, a long, cold winter, or heavier than normal predation, and down go their populations as the forest's complex ecological relationships bring them into bounds.

Invertebrate relationships

The invertebrate relationships of an ecosystem are very often relegated to a low priority of investigation unless there is clearly an economic reason to study them. Until recently, the giant sequoia was believed literally immune to insect attacks, and only 19 insect species were recorded utilizing the giant sequoia to complete one or more phases of their life cycle. Of the other invertebrates, virtually nothing is recorded except as they are related to commercially valuable tree species.

Although it may generally be assumed that invertebrates, especially insects, play significant roles in the interacting food webs of almost all ecosystems, some of the roles played remain unsuspected until such time as concerted studies are undertaken out of pure academic interest. Such was the story of the cerambycid beetle (*Phymatodes nitidus*), which probably plays such an important role in the reproductive life of the giant sequoia (see Seed Dispersal and Cone Fall).

The literature often states that insects have never been known to kill a mature giant sequoia. Although serious studies are lacking, this assumption may well be true. Actual observation suggests that insect depredations do not seriously affect sequoias after the second year of the seedling stage, and it is unlikely that insect attack alone causes their death. Yet many of these creatures contribute to the tree's loss of energy, and some to loss of structural support, all possibly aiding its eventual downfall. Damage or death of sequoias has been most noticeable not in native specimens in the Sierra, but where man has planted them in sites that were too moist. In such locations, aegeriid or clear-winged moth damage has been significant in trees 5-15 years old. A colorful metallic wood-boring beetle (*Trachykele opulenta*) may kill specimens damaged by road cuts or the undercutting of stream banks. The larvae of these beetles, which remarkably can mature solely within the bark, usually girdle the tree by feeding within the nutritious inner bark area.

Insects are highly important in promoting the decay of dead trees and nonliving parts of all trees, including the giant sequoia: they make passageways enabling decay organisms such as fungi and bacteria to gain entry and thus reduce the plant remains to soil humus once again in the ageless cycle of decay and growth. The openings they make beneath the bark and in the wood tissues also permit entry of oxygen and moisture needed for decay.

The *Phymatodes* story is but one part of an intricate food web around the sequoia cone. Several species of parasitic ichneumonid, braconid, and chalcid wasps prey upon the *Phymatodes* larvae, thereby helping to check their populations. In fact, these parasites' specific searching behavior helps to identify the early work of *Phymatodes* larvae, which is impossible to recognize from the exterior, which, in turn, is an aid to the researcher in his attempt to find the early instar stages. A few insects use the old emergence holes and pupation chambers of *Phymatodes* for their brood-rearing, one of the more interesting being a snakefly (*Aqulla assimilis*) that lays its pale-green, banana-shaped eggs in the pupation chambers. Upon hatching, these highly efficient predaceous larvae will seek out invertebrate animal life for food, either within the cone or underneath adjacent loose bark.

During a cone's first year, when it is soft and green, it may be attacked—not always successfully—by a small gelechiid moth (*Gelechia* sp.). Only 0.50 inch across the wings, this moth deserves an award for its persistence. The larva, roughly one-sixteenth of an inch long, bores into the cone scale junctures, at which point it is usually repelled by the reddish cone exudate. The dead "pitched-out" larva is often visible within this small transparent mass of resin-like pigment. Less than 10% of these moth attacks are successful and most attempts abort during the first larval instar. We can recognize the moths' work by the browning of only one or two scales, although occasionally some mature larvae will cause up to two-thirds of a cone to turn brown. Internal inspection reveals mines three times the diameter of those made by *Phymatodes*, as well as distinctive fecal pellets and silk webbing.

In its larval stage, this moth also causes double cones by feeding in the cone's axial core and splitting it in half. Each half bows outward and distorts the shape of the maturing cone into an apparent double cone. Such dry cones can be broken easily into halves with the bare hands, unlike genetically formed "doubles."

The gelechiid moths' activity corresponds to how large a cone crop a given year produces. The new cone crop in 1970 was approximately four times that of the years immediately preceding. In fact, the upper third of the foliated portion of the Castro study tree contained nearly as many new cones as those of all other age classes combined, so that their total number on this tree rose from about 19,000 one year to more than 39,000 the following year. Gelechiid moth activities increased considerably at the same time. In the 1969 study, 1 of 11 cones showed evidence of gelechiid moth damage, while the proportion in the 1970 crop was 2 to 5, and in the upper 30 ft of the crown, 1 of every 2 was affected.

Brown, dried-out cones remaining upon the tree also harbor a small community of insects between the cone scales. Common in this community is a small lygaeid bug (*Ischnorrhynchus resedae*), about an eighth-inch long, that hides in the cone's openings when not feeding upon the juices of seeds and nearby foliage. It generally moves to the cone's center when an observer comes within about 4 ft of it. Psocids, or book lice, are also numerous within the diminutive labyrinthine passageways of the cone scales. Possessing chewing mouth parts, they cause minute damage to seeds that the opened cones may still retain, although investigations in the Castro Tree indicate that few seeds are really harmed, those still attached to the opened cones maintaining as much as 75% viability. This may result from strong vascular connections between the seeds and cone scales.

Several insect relatives that are predators also use the cones as a hiding place or as protective cover. The most interesting are the tiny pseudoscorpions, less than one-sixteenth inch long, which very likely feed upon the smaller book lice (psocids) also residing within the cone. Mites, jumping spiders (attids), and crab spiders (thomidids) are other arachnids which also live and feed upon the invertebrates associated with these cones.

An insect whose populations are apparently increasing in certain sequoia groves is the carpenter ant (*Campanotus laevigatus*). These black ants, often half an inch long, are the largest in the forest and live in colonies within the bark and dead wood of living sequoias, and in stumps, logs, and dead trees. Two or more colonies may inhabit one tree at a given time. They normally feed at night, but are sometimes seen fighting during daylight hours. More conspicuous than the ants themselves are the open-ended galleries which may honeycomb the tree's thick bark to a considerable extent (Fig. 43), and on the ground beneath is usually a mass of reddish sawdust chewed out by the insects' strong mandibles. The tunneling is expressly to make brood chambers for their young, the wood or bark removed in no way serving as food. Colony chambers may be as long as 20 ft, and the tunneled area a few inches to several feet wide.

Seasonal park naturalist Jack Hickey, of Sequoia and Kings Canyon National Parks, has long had an interest in the carpenter ants, and his preliminary study of this insect, particularly in Giant Forest, may show a possible link between the ant population increase and human activities. The carpenter ant scavenges on both plant and animal debris, including the food tidbits spilled by park visitors. The National Park Service has arranged for the University of California, Berkeley, to conduct in-depth research on the carpenter ant's relation to sequoia trees.

The damage is largely to the bark and of little direct consequence to the "host" sequoia. Yet the galleries do offer possible entry routes for other insects and decay organisms which may somewhat increase decomposition, and, perhaps more important, they provide access for air that would hasten the drying of bark and wood and thus increase the latter's inflammability. Dried wood becomes more brittle and the affected tree may weaken in time, fall, and die. Although the tunneling is generally confined to the base or near the bases of trees, a sequoia had its top knocked out by another falling tree in the summer of 1969, breaking off very near the site of carpenter ant tunnels about 90 ft above ground level.

Fire is apparently the nemesis of these insects. Even light ground fires seem readily to discourage ant populations by reducing their food supply. It has been suggested that their possible recent upturn is related to plant successional trends in the absence of fire, resulting in increased natural food. Present studies may eventually confirm this interpretation.

Other insects that create interesting food web patterns, while far less important in the sequoia's life cycle, are yet highly significant in the local faunal interplay. An insect not previously recorded as feeding upon the giant sequoia is

Fig. 43. Galleries of carpenter ants in bark of giant sequoia tree, Giant Forest. Recent interest in carpenter ant activities in sequoias suggests a possible relationship with increased human activities. *Photo by* Jack Hickey.

a small green aphid (*Masonaphis* sp.) which is found throughout the larger trees, concentrated on the branches' tender tips in the lower third of the crown. It is also found on some of the seedlings along with another species of aphid. On a mature sequoia, these small sucking insects may number in excess of 100,000 individuals during late summer when they are at their peak. Each of the myriad tiny twigs on the tree may be host to ten or more per inch. Despite their juice-sucking activities, foliage discoloration is too slight to measure and photosynthetic reduction is believed to be almost insignificant. Nor do infested seedlings suffer from their feeding activities.

This rather large aphid biomass is preyed upon by the larvae of a syrphid fly (*Syrphus* sp.) that resemble elongate maggots. The visionless larvae find the aphids by probing randomly upon the branch tips where a female had oviposited her eggs among the aphids several days earlier. The larvae hang onto the narrow stems by means of posterior leg-like structures and thrust their bodies out into space after securing an aphid in their rasping mouths. Then the body fluids of the prey are sucked out. The effectiveness of the larvae in this blind search is borne out by research in which one individual was observed to have captured three aphids in one minute when the researcher removed the captive aphid by forceps each time one was caught. Normally, 3 minutes are required between captures.

The predaceous syrphid flies also have their problems in this complex food web and many of them end up as food for the larvae of ichneumonid and braconid wasps which parasitize them. If they achieve adulthood, they are often eaten by a robberfly (*Neoitamus affinis*). These latter flies, which are highly predaceous, wait in ambush upon the ends of the sequoia's projecting branches. They capture adult syrphid or "hover flies" that are ovipositing along the outer margins of the foliage. They usually return to the site of the ambush to devour their fellow fly relative. The food web continues as the robber flies, in turn, are chased as potential food by several species of birds within the tree's crown.

In all, 151 species of insects and 37 arachnids are known to be associated with the giant sequoia in the sense that they use it to complete some part of their own life cycles. This organic web in living and on downed sequoias is highly complex. For some insects, the tree serves mainly as an unusual "high-rise" location for courtship: horse flies (*Tabanus laticeps*), bee flies (*Villa*), horn tails (*Sirex areolatus*), and even the tiny chalcid wasps hover over the tops of the tall sequoias as if to amuse or taunt an entomologist. In reality, they use this landmark to consolidate themselves for mate selection, a phenomenon called "hill-topping" in insects. Appendix IV contains the scientific names of invertebrates mentioned in the text. There are several species and subspecies of the snail *Helminthoglypta* that are completely restricted to groves of giant sequoia trees in the southern Sierra Nevada (Rundel 1969). The relationship of the snail to the sequoias, however, does not appear to be established.

Although the invertebrate story for sequoia groves has been much increased within the last past few years, it remains fragmental. The sequoias that we studied intensively were all part of one large grove and were approximately at the same altitude. It seems reasonable to assume that studies at different altitudes and latitudes would further enlarge the scope and understanding of these relationships.

Finally, examination of the thick leaf litter layer beneath clusters of large sequoia trees reveals a rich invertebrate fauna co-acting with fungi, bacteria, and other decay organisms in the dynamic ecology of this layer and the soil. Studies in this area are almost totally lacking.

Competition within communities

In all biotic communities, each organism possesses its own distinguishing set of genetic traits. To be sure, there are similarities between one and another species but, like human fingerprints, no two are exactly alike. Thus, no two species of plants or animals react identically to a given set of environmental conditions, which insures that every species fills a specific niche in time and space, and the species' distinct genetic traits enable it to compete with other organisms present in that niche.

Green plants' success or failure in this competition depends also upon the availability of such essentials as solar energy, soil moisture, and nutrients. Competition within the plant world is strongly, but not exclusively, governed by the sunlight available at the photosynthetic or leaf surfaces. This is partly a function of stature, with the taller plants succeeding, and partly one of chlorophyll density within the leaves, as some shorter plants can compete successfully in reduced light. In both, the responses to light are inherited and determine vertical stratification of canopy levels as well as the sequences of plant assemblages over time. The new assemblages replace earlier communities as the plants' collective action and structure change the environmental conditions. Such sequential changes in plant communities are what we have called plant succession.

Plant succession

Plant successional trends are of two basic types: *primary*, which begins with the original breakdown of rock into soil materials to form a suitable substrate for the growth of higher plants; and *secondary*, or the sequential changes in plant communities following disturbances which destroy some of the plant cover, but which disturb the soil substrate less. For primary succession, it is sufficient to say that the soil base in sequoia groves is derived largely from granitoid and schistose rocks, and that it evolved over a very long period, antedating the giant sequoia's migration onto the western slope of the Sierra Nevada.

Secondary succession, however, recurs to some degree following such distrubances as fire, blow-downs, disease and insect epidemics, logging, etc. The degree of successional setback depends on the severity of the disturbance and the actual stage of succession at the time it occurs. The relatively short rotational sequence of secondary succession is of signal importance in succession theories and for vegetation management. Since disturbances such as fire appear to have occurred rather regularly in the natural sequence of events, the potentially long-enduring climax community was, in reality, somewhat rare in the mixed conifer forest of the Sierra Nevada before modern times. Fire was probably the most widespread and frequent disturbance; for the sequoia, it was perhaps the most beneficial factor leading to optimum conditions for reproduction.

With plant successional changes, there are recognized concurrent changes in both quantity and quality of the soil substrate. This is perhaps the more important in primary succession where sandy soils present a low cation exchange or nutritive capacity typical of soils low in the mineral clay fraction. Sierran granitoid soils, high in sand content, thus improve with age as the organic content increases. The humus performs a function similar to that of clay, enriching the developing soil, a factor of considerable importance in the seedling stage of many native plants. It plays a role in a plant's ability to compete with other plants in a community comprising several other species.

As soils increase in depth and organic content, this environmental change permits, through natural selection, other species of plants to invade, thus insuring also a change in the nature of both the litter layer and of the soil's humus content. The nature of the soil continues to change with each succeeding seral stage until at the climax stage of succession it comes into dynamic balance with the final breakdown of organic matter, and the soil depth becomes stabilized. Because of topographical variation, both plant successional and soil developmental sequences also vary greatly within short distances. This, coupled with set-backs by fire and erosion, forms both a mosaic of soil conditions and of plant community structure which thus gives the impression of a variety of climax plant associations. These are the often long-enduring sub-climax communities that typify the mixed coniferous forest region of the Sierra Nevada.

When intense fire sets back plant succession in the Sierra's mixed coniferous forest, the resulting plant community is usually dominated by a dense cover of shrubs. The species vary with the elevation and other geographical factors such as availability of soil moisture, steepness and aspect of the slope, depth of the soil, and, of course, the availability of a given species' seeds. Typical shrubs of this stage in the central and southern Sierra Nevada are deer brush, mountain whitethorn, small-leaved ceanothus, bitter cherry, manzanita, and wild gooseberry. These are usually mixed in a given locality, although one species may predominate, and may have an irregular sprinkling of herbaceous plants as well. There may also be a sparse and struggling overstory of almost any of the local tree species, perhaps relics not consumed by fire or those seeded into optimum sites. Ceanothus not only seems well adapted to fire conditions, but it and lupine, which is a legume, have mutual relationships with nitrogen-fixing bacteria whose activities enrich the soil with nitrogen. Here, then, is a predetermined system of fertilizing the tree seedlings and saplings which follow in the succession. It is during this juvenile state that nitrogen is most necessary for their successful growth.

Where fires have been so intense as to destroy most of the tree vegetation, including the seeds, the shrubby stage may be prolonged for years because of the slowness with which trees invade from the edges and by which birds and mammals occasionally distribute seeds. Usually shrubs cover the fire-scarred land rather rapidly, soon providing more satisfactory protection against soil erosion until trees once again dominate the community.

The influx of trees may be of any local species, although the shade-intolerant ones tend to predominate. Their general characteristics cause them to dominate the early portion of succession. Because of their sensitivity to shade, these trees mostly possess the genetic trait of rapid vertical growth, enabling them to maintain their photosynthetic "factories" in as much sunlight as possible. Only thus do they survive. Such traits produce characteristics that man values—tallness and straightness. Trees that grow tall rapidly generally grow straight, reflecting the mathematical axiom about the shortest distance between two points. Tall trees require additional strength to maintain their very high crowns. Over the evolutionary years, natural selection has provided strength to the wood of most of these trees, which is reflected in the quality of lumber they produce.

In addition, these shade-intolerant species lose their lower foliage early in life as the leaves are shaded out, a process which not only continues as the tree gains stature, but is aided by the self-pruning of dead limbs. Lumber cut from these trees has fewer knots, a plus factor in the lumber trade.

In the mixed coniferous forest, the ponderosa pine, Jeffrey pine, Douglas fir in the more northerly groves, and the giant sequoia all qualify as shade-intolerant, their genetic traits best insuring success during the period when sunlight can bathe their crowns. The assumption that sequoia, because of its size, is a climax stage species is clearly in error because it cannot reproduce itself in strong competition where shading may bring early death to many of its seedlings (see "Conditions for Seedling Survival").

Recalling that sequoia wood is relatively soft and light in weight, one may think it strange to include the giant sequoia in this early stage group. Of course, what it lacks in wood strength it makes up in sheer bulk, remaining indisputedly the tallest tree species in the Sierra Nevada. Its conspicuousness in climax communities composed predominantly of white fir does not identify it as a climax species, but merely as a relict which has continued to solve its light problems by keeping its crown higher than that of its associates. Indeed, if another species commonly grew taller than the sequoia, the latter would succumb because of its life-long shade intolerance. Thus, its genetically determined height has played a major role in the species' survival.

We pointed out that the giant sequoia was a prolific producer of seeds and that the conditions necessary for regeneration were rather exacting. Wherever fires, intense or not, burn through sequoia groves, they set back plant succession and to some degree help regeneration of sequoias and other early-stage trees. The sequoia's successful reproduction depends on distribution of undamaged seeds and success in seedling development. Because its competitive strength is roughly commensurate with that of the other early-stage trees, neither the sequoia nor the others have much opportunity to develop into pure stands, and rarely does one species predominate. Furthermore, where successional setback has been only partial, as it was so commonly because of past oft-repeated fires, other species that are somewhat more shade-tolerant also seed in, and provide additional competition for, the less tolerant species. The majestic sugar pine, largest of all pines, and the California incense-cedar seem to fall more properly into this category. Whereas sugar pine is generally spaced out, the incense-cedar often forms dense thickets which to some are not very aesthetic, restricting other more desirable species' reproduction, and furthermore clearly presenting a fire hazard. Like the sequoias, if they survive the hazards of their early years, they may grow into mature trees more pleasing to man. The old sugar pines are second in size and grandeur only to the giant sequoia and are the delight of visitors.

Where sequoia forest communities have escaped fire for a long period, the shade-intolerant species have multiplied greatly. The white fir appears to be best fitted for such an existence, and we find its seedling offspring surviving under the most shaded circumstances where other species are struggling or dead. Early photographs of sequoia groves indicate that white fir was considerably less abundant than it is now. Hartesveldt (1962), in an analysis of nearly 200 photographs taken in the Mariposa Grove between 1859 and 1932, noted an openness of the forest that is now scarce. In fact, the young white firs' preponderance today completely blocks many of the same views. These photographs further show that shrubs such as mountain whitethorn, manzanita, and bitter cherry were all more abundant in the past. Vankat (1970) has noted similar vegetational changes in the Sequoia National Park region that have resulted from the practices of early western man, especially grazing of domestic animals and practices of governmental land management agencies.

The changes just described were apparently caused by the advancement of plant succession attending man's highly successful campaign to prevent fires and to extinguish them as quickly as possible. This result, a stunning surprise to many, has created problems, some of which we have already discussed.

In the same context as the value of lumber of early stage trees, the climax species, white fir, is low on the scale. With no serious problem of light to solve, it does not attain the stature of others. Nor does its wood have the same degree of tensile strength; also, an unpleasant odor renders the wood less desirable as lumber. However, neither of these factors is directly related to its successional position. Tolerating shade, the lower foliage remains alive longer and, even when the leaves die, the dead limbs remain on the trunk, many of them remaining on old trees. This characteristic guarantees dry loose knots in the wood, again a liability for lumber use, and presents a somewhat cluttered view and obstacles to hiking. For the forest manager, it means increased fire hazard right to the ground level, and, in addition, the dense thickets of young white firs with their pitchy limbs and foliage can carry flames readily and rapidly at certain times of the year into the crown canopy.

While a serious problem for man, these features may be a well-ordered part of the natural diversity of life forms caused by successional stratification in time. We might regard them as ensuring that the earlier-stage plant species will again appear and not become extinct. While this may seem a bit contrary to older beliefs that fires are undesirable, it does make good sense if we can but screen out our own peculiar value judgments. Man has singled out and favored a few plants and animals to which he attaches monetary, practical, and aesthetic values. In attempting to increase their number, he has created circumstances that sometimes have actually reduced them. In fire prevention, man has inadvertently favored the less valuable tree species to the detriment of those with greater monetary value, so that the more valued early-stage trees have tended to disappear from the scene. Hypothetically, then, the sequoia could cease to exist sooner than if he (Western Man) had never entered the scene simply because of his well-intended protection of the sequoia.

It was stated earlier that man has had a tendency to see plant communities as assemblages of individuals at a given point in time. The comprehension of plant succession, although a step in the right direction, does not even necessarily imply an understanding of the community in its dynamic, sequential state of being. If one can visualize the entire spectrum of biota succession as an *individual entity*, as opposed to a static assemblage of plants, then perhaps there can be a closer appreciation of nature without the distracting value judgments of man. In nature, no one organism may be assigned greater or lesser value since each is only a functional part of the whole.

With dry limbs extending to or near the ground level, wildfire has an increased opportunity to destroy the dense canopy of the climax stage trees and permit the sun's rays to reach the ground. This, in turn, ensures that the shade-intolerant seedlings will have a better chance to survive to reproductive maturity. Again, because of the same dry limbs, even slow-moving ground fires can easily climb up the "ladder" into the crown of white firs which, though not necessarily destroyed by the flames, appear to be highly susceptible to desiccation and eventual death as a result of the heat. Thus, at least a partial opening of the crown canopy may result. While substantiating evidence is elusive, observation suggests strongly that these do occur. Following fires, there is generally an influx of those plants which were scarce in the later stages of the natural cycle of events, but were abundant when similar conditions prevailed earlier in the cycle.

Such knowledge becomes an advantage to man and aids greatly in the understanding of some of the problems inadvertently created out of ignorance of basic ecological principles. Man's changing attitudes toward the obvious implications of this knowledge, especially the fire relationships, will be discussed in the last pages of this book.

Where fires of lesser intensity burn through sequoia communities, the successional set-backs are also of a minor nature. The fewer trees of the upper crown canopy that are destroyed, the poorer the opportunity for shade-intolerant plants to reestablish themselves. With the disappearance of thick accumulations of leaf litter, small-seeded annuals increase greatly, but the shade-intolerant herbs such as the orchid (*Goodyera oblongifolia*) continue to maintain their populations at about the same levels as before. The giant sequoias will often germinate in great numbers after a light fire, but their chances for survival are much less under these more shaded conditions. Furthermore, the lightly burned soils remain more nearly unwettable than where incineration has been moderate to intense, and are therefore less satisfactory for seedling survival.

The undesirable changes due to the advanced state of plant succession as a result of fire control were clarified by Hartesveldt (1962) in a study on the effects of human impact upon the giant sequoias and their environment.

Human impact

At the outset of the reservation of our scenic treasures as national parks, very little concern was expressed over the deterioration that might occur from use by excessive numbers of people. The population of the United States was small in 1864 when President Lincoln signed into law the bill that set aside as a park the Yosemite Valley and the Mariposa Grove of giant sequoias. Because of the primitive means of transportation at the time, the demand for the use of such wild areas was but a tiny fraction of today's demand. The concept of ecology had not yet been formulated and the Congress and general public alike were simply and understandably not attuned to the concept of such problems, let alone to begin planning for them. The wording of the acts which established the various parks did mention preservation from impairment of the primary value being set aside, but it is wrong to assume that ecological connotations were the basis for the wording. Vandalism and thoughtless damage were doubtless the intent expressed in the acts. One person, however, had the imagination to project his thoughts far into the future and to foresee that the hundreds of visitors of his day would be the millions of a future day, and that mass use was likely to bring about changes of an undesirable nature to the park values.

His name was Fredrick Law Olmsted, creator of New York City's Central Park. He was selected as the first chairman of the board of commissioners of the new Yosemite Grant, operated as a state park. In 1865, having visited his new domain and interpreted the legislation that created the park, he issued a report that served as the basic guideline for management policy for the new park. In war-torn 1865, he showed rare understanding of the natural biotic communities, predicting the changes that we have now long recognized in popular park areas. Olmsted felt that the value of the parks would increase with growing population, and that from the very beginning, protective park management should serve posterity. Olmsted wrote (1952):

> An injury to the scenery so slight that it may be unheeded by any visitor now, will be of deplorable magnitude when its effects upon each visitor's enjoyment is multiplied by these millions. But again the slight harm which the few hundred visitors of this year might do, if no care were taken to prevent it, would not be slight if it should be repeated by these millions.

The full text of Olmsted's report is a literary masterpiece.

Not too surprisingly, in view of the then scarce ecological understanding, Olmsted's prophecy fell on deaf ears. His manuscript, too, was lost for many years.

In spite of some individuals' subsequent concern over detrimental changes, no overall policy advocated study or even careful observation to detect and rectify them. Apparently, it was only in 1933 that park biologist George Wright first included recommendations for such a policy in his book (Wright et al. 1933). Although not much came from Wright's ecologically oriented philosophy of park management, the thought persisted, and a publication of the U.S. Department of the Interior (1940) suggested ecological investigation as essential to the proper management of the biotic communities of national parks. Unfortunately, World War II delayed the implementation of such management programs for a good many years.

In an early, isolated instance, the National Park Service and other administrative agencies expressed concern over the effects of excessive tourist travel on the sequoias in the Giant Forest and in the Mariposa Grove, two of the most heavily used groves. This led to the employment of Dr. Emilio P. Meinecke, a Forest Service plant pathologist, who conducted a short survey in each of these areas to assess the damage done to sequoias and recommended ways to rectify the situation.

Meinecke's studies (1926, 1927) were disappointingly brief considering his findings and strong recommendations. The major point in each of his reports concerned physical damage to individual trees and the physiological damages he assumed to have occurred. There was no mention of community changes due to successional trends in the absence of fire, or of the relation between fire and sequoia regeneration. He was explicit, however, in his feeling that continued heavy use of sequoia groves was a threat to their future and that trees in the most severely compacted soils very likely would die. He did recommend restoring the parks to their original conditions, but without concrete suggestions for attaining the goal.

The two Meinecke reports, though not supported by extensive studies, were a beginning and led eventually to a 3-year study by Hartesveldt (1962) on the effects of human impact upon the sequoias in the Mariposa Grove. The results of this and subsequent studies in Sequoia and Kings Canyon National Parks shed considerable doubt on the old philosophy of noninterference by man to preserve specific biotic communities and their components, such as the giant sequoias. Moreover, they showed that Meinecke's fears were not well founded: human impact on sequoia communities was proven, but in forms not previously suggested.

Investigations revealed that soils were severly compacted in areas of heavy human foot traffic. Depending upon the weight of the body and the size of the foot, the latter's force in walking represents a pressure of 5-20 psi of ground surface. In areas where auto traffic had been permitted for years, the compaction was severe and the old roadways traveled by stagecoaches and wagons with narrow- and steel-rimmed wheels were still so densely packed after more than 35 years of abandonment that few woody plants had become established. But these narrow bands of compacted soil covered relatively small percentages of the larger sequoias' rooting areas.

In some regions with no pathways to channel visitors, the soils compacted by human traffic constituted as much as an acre of land. Around such popular trees as the Grizzly Giant, compaction greatly reduced water infiltration and the soil's capacity to absorb excessive surface flow. Such accumulated surface water created drainage channelways which then became gullies of erosion as volume and velocity of flow increased. In several places erosion had exposed the roots of sequoias to a depth of a foot and more, threatening the trees' future stability. Likewise, accumulations of water on impervious pavement had created similar channels to the side, some of them 3 and 4 ft deep. Yet to this date, no giant sequoia is known to have fallen as a result of this channeling.

Compacted soils were definitely shown to restrict penetration by roots, an effect that Meinecke believed very important. However, field studies of sequoia growth patterns revealed no sequoias tending toward death as a result, but rather an increased average annual growth rate of almost all sequoias growing in such soils. The soil profile of areas subject to extensive foot traffic showed a soil moisture regime almost universally more favorable than that in untrampled soils. Compaction to a degree restrictive to root penetration generally did not extend much below 6 inches in depth. The compacted layer seemed to form a protective cap which helped maintain the moisture level deeper down. Another important factor was the reduced competition for soil moisture by smaller plant species. The abrasion resulting from human trampling had largely eliminated these plants and consequently reduced most species' reproduction. Considering the relatively small volume of soil sufficiently compacted to be restrictive within a sequoia's rooting zone, very possibly the improved soil moisture at greater depths more than offsets the losses within the compacted zone. Whether affected trees adjust their feeder roots to greater depths, as has been suggested, is yet to be determined. Most significant is the fact that no record exists of a giant sequoia having succumbed due to compacted soil.

Changes in the chemical relationships of soils because of severe trampling fail to show any significance in statistical comparisons. The total organic content of the uppermost—or A_1 soil-horizon—has changed but little even in those areas where trampling has virtually eliminated the leaf litter layer. Reduction of basic soil nutrients was also light. The increased soil moisture at depths less than about 5 inches would undoubtedly have proven significant had a statistical comparison been made. Although these changes were of no consequence to the larger sequoia trees, they did have a profound effect upon the smaller herbaceous plants and seedlings of both trees and shrubs. Surface soils were powdery dry by late summer and, in these circumstances, sequoias do not seem to produce seedlings at all.

Two other great concerns were the effects of road-building activities, namely, road ballast and pavement placed over sequoia roots, and the cutting of roots from the side of large specimens to accommodate road cuts. Deep cuts made close to a trunk, on occasion, eliminated as much as 35% of the entire root system.

Pavement which covers rather large portions of a tree's entire root system produces growth increases exceeding those mentioned earlier in compacted soils. Not only does impervious pavement eliminate plant competition, but surface evaporative losses are also reduced to a minimum, leaving the "relict" sequoia a greater supply of soil moisture that enables growth to continue beyond the normal growing season. In effect, then, the growing season for such trees extends late into the fall and, in some cases, until freezing weather commences in December. One such specimen, the Sentinel Tree, situated between the Generals Highway and the Giant Forest Village parking lot, has about 75% of its root system covered with pavement, causing great concern until increment borings showed the tree growing nearly 50% faster than before the addition of pavement. Vigor of growth, however, may not be the final criterion of man's influence on such trees. The effects have been measured over a small percentage of the tree's total life, and these changes may eventually prove harmful.

Where roadway construction has cut away roots, annual increment to the trunk has declined significantly immediately after severance because of reduced delivery of soil moisture and nutrients to the crown's photosynthetic factory.

Root removal would seem to reduce proportionately the crown foliage, just as large burn scars do, yet the trees so affected still have healthy crowns. And, curiously enough, the growth patterns developed during the years since the roots' removal show a gradually increasing growth rate even though the total rooting area has not seemed to increase. This may be due to proliferating feeder roots in the reduced root zone, or to greater lateral translocation of photosynthate in the trunk. Here again, no sequoia has apparently fallen or otherwise died because of either of these disturbances by man. However, considering the regulations governing the management of sequoias, this should not be regarded as license to treat them in such a manner.

The most profound change since the advent of western civilization had hitherto not been suspected, although John Muir's observations on the relationships of fire could well have permitted him to recognize it. The change resulted from man's benevolent regard for the great sequoias and his abhorrence of wildfires. His successful program of fire prevention and suppression was more than admirable; yet he had failed to recognize the disadvantage he had prescribed for the sequoia and other early-stage plants whose reproductive success was diminishing in competition with shade-tolerant species. The virtual elimination of sequoia reproduction remains not too serious a problem for species survival. A tree whose life span is 2000-3000 years or more can maintain the species by reproducing under favorable conditions after several centuries of failure. But the circumstances man has created have possibly a more profound effect than he knows, and consequently the studies we have described were undertaken to better understand the relationships of fire to the giant sequoia. Despite considerable knowledge at this time, we can undoubtedly learn much more. Our final section will discuss further these relationships.

The current assessment of changes to sequoia ecosystems by man is considerably different than it was earlier. The direct changes are sometimes expressed as damage to the ecosystem; yet these damages are restricted to relatively small areas and do not seem to affect adversely the larger specimens. The more subtle, indirect effects pose more difficult problems. However, management procedures can control most of those regarded as detrimental to man's interests, and many necessary changes now being implemented will better ensure the future integrity of the species.

7
Man, Fire, and the Future

We have so far written mainly of a single tree species and its interrelation with the other plants and animals within its natural range. A similar treatise for each of the other organisms would also prove of considerable interest and scientific value.

The sequoias included in park reservations were set aside as individuals rather than as communities or ecosystems, most people valuing their uncommon size and age more than their fascinating ecological complexity. Only such rare observers as John Muir valued them as members of a community. Ecology was still in its infancy, its principles hardly formalized by biologists, let alone understandable by the public which viewed them mainly as forest museum pieces.

The attitude of administering agencies was not very different: sequoias were managed as museum pieces, and emotional opportunism more than scientific interest led to their reservation. Stemming from the belief that Mother Nature always knew best, a hands-off policy evolved to attain preservation of the individual trees. It was probably the most logical program that could have come out of the beginnings of park management. Protect the trees from fire and human vandalism and nature would do the rest! But, as we know now, man's objectives and nature's successional plans do not necessarily coincide. The changes took place slowly and either went by unnoticed or were not interpreted as serious until relatively recent times.

Today, in retrospect, we are in an excellent position to comprehend what has happened and why, as is the case with many other ecosystems as well. In the first place, the Act which created the National Park Service in 1916 by no means explicitly directed how man should accomplish its stated goals. Secondly, the magnitude of forest destruction by fire led to such abhorrence of it that its role as a natural environmental factor was all but overlooked.

The phraseology of the Act's first stated goal created a semantic problem. Park management was to guarantee "the maintenance of the scenery and the natural and historical objects in such a manner and by such means as would leave them unimpaired for the enjoyment of future generations." The impreciseness of "unimpaired" reflected the general lack of knowledge regarding biotic communities. Certainly, the word was well intentioned, as were the equally elusive terms "preservation" and "maintenance in a natural condition," both commonly used. On the other hand, interpretations by park administrative personnel varied, and therein lay the trouble.

The vagueness surrounding this terminology permits at least four possible interpretations of the goals for sequoia management in national parks.

1. To preserve the groves as they were first seen by Western man, or at the time of their reservation as parks.
2. To preserve the groves in whatever form natural processes might create without management interference by man.
3. To assure the maintenance of as many sequoia trees as possible.
4. To maintain indefinitely the sequoia plant communities by applying whatever silvicultural practices might be useful toward that goal.

In the earlier years of National Park Service sequoia management there was no definitely stated goal for the species, although the second possibility above was the one seemingly sought. Since then, park administrative personnel have gradually discarded the rather indefinite ideal of preservation of individuals and have accepted in lieu of it the goal of maintaining sequoias' ecosystems on a continuing basis. The transition was not by unanimous consent, and caused occasional sharp differences, especially when persons advanced new ideas based on scientific understanding of the species. In particular, the use of fire as a management tool created understandable differences.

By the time of inception of the National Park Service, the American mind saw fire as something to prevent or to extinguish at the earliest possible opportunity. Little or no compromise was allowed to this philosophy which the forestry profession drilled almost unrelentingly into the public mind in order to remind people to be careful with fire. The earlier literature seldom mentioned fire as a management tool, even though primitive peoples in most parts of the world had so employed it in a rather unsophisticated manner (Reynolds 1959; Stewart 1956). The earlier stages of succession often produced plants valuable for food which were scarce or absent in the later stages.

In the Sierra, early cattlemen would "fire" the hills as they brought their herds in late autumn to lower elevation winter ranges. Where shrubs and trees had once dominated the landscape, more palatable forage crops now grew in their stead. Their fires, however, could scarcely be called "prescribed" and, on occasion, were rather devastating to values important to others. Even John Muir, who appreciated the role of fire in sequoia reproduction, bitterly criticized such burning. With serious concern developing over forest destruction, safety with fire became an almost universal byword. The term "prescription" in conjunction with the use of fire was probably not yet coined, despite burning practiced in the South to aid the growth of long-leaf pine. Almost always, the forestry profession wrote the end products of fire on the debit side of the ledger.

The use of fire as a management tool began to captivate more and more people, some of whom attempted to make public its practicality for certain specific goals. But such visionary persons were to remain a minority for many years, with voices often stilled or subverted by editorial prerogative, public apathy, or utter disbelief. Only recently has this philosophy come into the fruition many would have wanted decades earlier. Even so, it still escapes much of the general public, and even some foresters and biologists are far from agreement upon the subject, however soundly based their concepts may be.

The term "prescription" is used to separate that kind of burning from wild-fire and to indicate that man chooses the conditions under which to burn, thus seeking to realize his goals without creating undue hazards to other forest values.

Prescription burning has two broad goals: (1) reestablishing certain desired vegetation types of earlier stages, and (2) reducing excessive fire hazards that have accumulated in the absence of fire.

In 1955, Herbert Mason of the University of California pointed out that, in the absence of fires in the Sierra Nevada, valuable sugar pine was being replaced by the much less valuable white fir. Some action was necessary to change this ecological trend, or the forest's economic values would be reduced. Although the die was seemingly cast in favor of fire as a management tool, the public and its governmental agencies were not yet ready for such a reversal of an old policy. Admittedly, too, prescription fires might get out of control. Who wanted to shoulder such a responsibility?

Another possible vegetational change resulting from prescription burning is the improvement of forage crops for both wildlife and range animals. With the advance of plant succession, habitats become less suitable for many desirable forms of animal life and the resulting decline in their numbers is a disadvantage to hunters and nature enthusiasts alike. These changes have obvious social and economic implications.

Certainly, man never intended to create conditions under which the giant sequoia could not reproduce itself, but did so inadvertently. Problems demand solutions, and the best solutions are generally derived from a consideration of alternatives. This is especially important where manipulation by fire may provoke adverse reactions from the uninformed public and prejudiced park and forest administrators. Very often, however, the serious weighing of alternatives has led to the realization that fire is the only economically feasible method to attain certain management goals.

The sequoia fire story presented in this book is a good example: our suggestion that experimental burning could teach much about the ecological relationships of sequoian communities met with expected skepticism and opposition by some park officials and public alike. Why not rake up and haul away the ground litter which was preventing sequoia reseeding and also adding to the fire hazard? Some simple arithmetic provides the answer. Leaf litter which is commonly up to 2 inches thick would, if raked up, fill up the equivalent of four railroad gondola cars for every acre of land so cleared! This would not include the limbs, trunks, and cone accumulations that are such serious fire hazards; it would neither open the crown canopy to the penetration of light nor effect the conditioning of the soil referred to earlier. Clearly, this alternative to fire is out of the question.

The accumulation of combustible debris in the absence of periodic fires has, in many areas of sequoia groves, created fire hazards that are perhaps higher now than at any previous time in human history. Biswell (1961) and Hartesveldt (1964) report that fires that prevent such fuel accumulations recurred regularly before man's intervention. In intensive studies in the University of California's Whitaker Forest, Biswell produced convincing evidence that fuel conditions not only were extremely critical but also impaired the sequoia's aesthetic values for the park and forest visitors. Manipulations under his direction showed what could be done to alleviate the situation and solve both problems at the same time. The cost of manipulation is high in the case of dense fuel accumulations.

In some sequoia groves, the fuel build-ups are too great to use prescription burning without considerable preparation. Hand removal of the larger materials is beyond consideration, and the longer no action is taken, the more difficult the solution becomes. Once reduced, fuel can be consumed rather easily by repeated burnings of the pine straw and other ground litter. In this manner, fire hazard could possibly be kept at a minimal level on a continuing basis.

The trend toward fuel reduction by fire has begun through official sanction in Yosemite National Park and in Sequoia and Kings Canyon National Parks, where irreparable damage could result to sequoia groves if raging fires were to enter from outside the boundaries. To date, more than 150 acres of sequoia land have been burned in Kings Canyon National Park and much valuable information is being gleaned from the results. We admit that fire is no panacea for all forest problems, and each situation demands judgment on its merits before any one silvicultural solution is chosen. But the trend has begun, and greater understanding of fire's natural role should continue to favor its use as a tool in the management of various ecosystems.

Although tending toward a hands-off philosophy of management, the older park policy could not be totally regarded in this light. After all, extinguishing wildfires that started by natural means *is* a form of interference by man. But aside from this one notable exception, vegetation management within the parks was largely one of letting nature take her course. Wider recognition of the undesirable changes being induced in natural ecosystems gradually led to the more intensive management of park ecosystems, a change in philosophy that was slow and hardly universal, and a bitter pill for some traditionalists. For them, noninterference management, other than fire control, was akin to the gospel. Amid heated differences of opinion, a Yosemite National Park superintendent in 1934 countered the traditional with the shocking thought that " . . . our flora and fauna have not been primeval for decades."[1] Next, in the text of a talk prepared for the California Academy of Sciences, he stated forthrightly that " . . . the only way the nation can salvage even an aspect of the primeval is through a scientific and prayerful management." While not a scientist, he was somewhat ahead of his time, but his sage advice was diluted in a rather lengthy

[1]Letter to the Director, U.S. National Park Service, from Charles Goff Thompson, Superintendent, Yosemite National Park.

exchange of ideas about the law's intent regarding park management goals (Hartesveldt 1962).

Considering the debate within the National Park Service, we might expect bewilderment in the general public. However, the lack of direct communication has all but precluded their full comprehension of the argument throughout the many years. Only with the announcement that fire was to be used experimentally did a much larger segment of the public become aware of the vaunted sequoia's complex ecosystem. Here was a new and fascinating concept. Ecology was becoming a household word and people were now beginning to see the forest for the trees—all of the trees, and their associated plants and animals. Any fears that the public would reject the management of sequoia parklands, including the use of fire as a management tool, were apparently not well founded. Where logical scientific explanations were offered, the public was seemingly willing to accept drastic changes if they believed it would safeguard their sequoia trees. Many gained much more—an educational revelation, a new way of seeing nature, with principles broadly applicable to other ecosystems as well.

We are gratified that we are able to close by refuting a rather dismal prediction: the giant sequoia's slow but certain demise in the face of a warming climate and the indelicacies of mankind. After 135 million years of developmental history, this tree is not about to make its final exit. Climatic change is slow, and we cannot predict what changes will occur, if any. Mankind did exact a toll from the tree; yet it has responded as if to flaunt man's influence and it is reproducing and growing vigorously where man has apparently damaged both the tree and its environment. Man has assumed the role of benefactor of nature, a role in which he can well expect to perform better than he ever did in the past. We now have the knowledge which, when implemented, will help maintain sequoia communities on a continuous basis, and there is every indication that these magnificent trees will grace the western slope of the Sierra Nevada indefinitely.

And so ends *our* story of the giant sequoias, the greatest of all living things upon this Earth, a story the tree began in the misty Mesozoic age of reptiles. But, is it really the end of the story? We think not. We are merely closing our version of it as we see it at this point in time. And we further suspect that as long as man wonders over the unknown, and as long as there are sequoias reaching for the Sierran skies, curiosity will forever provoke man to probe into that which others have not yet known or have misunderstood. We fully expect, then, that the sequoia story will never be told in all finality, and that its mysteries will provide a continuing fascination for mankind.

Appendix I

Sequoia Relatives

The giant sequoia is a species belonging to the Taxodiaceae, a family of ancient and well-recorded lineage. Today, its range is considerably reduced and it is made up of just 10 genera and 15 species, all of them trees with narrow, linear, or awl-shaped leaves either spirally arranged or appearing two-ranked. The cones are usually globose, either woody or leathery, and usually have persistent cone scales.

Following is a short synopsis of the genera in the family Taxodiaceae as listed in *A Handbook of Coniferae and Ginkogaceae* by Dallimore and Jackson (1967):

Athrotaxis	Tasmanian-cedars. Three species, native only to Tasmania.
Cryptomeria	Japanese-cedar. One species, *C. japonica*. Native to Japan. Many cultivated forms.
Cunninghamia	Chinese-firs. Two species only, in China, Formosa, and other nearby islands.
Glyptostrobus	Chinese deciduous-cypress. One species, only in Canton Province, China.
Metasequoia	Dawn Redwood. One species, *M. glyptostroboides*. Native only to eastern Szechwan and western Hupeh provinces of China. Not discovered until 1941 and first publicized in 1944.
Sciadopitys	Japanese umbrella-pine. One species. Native to Japan.
Sequoia	Coast Redwood. One species, *Sequoia sempervirens*. Native only in coastal California and Southern Oregon.
Sequoiadendron	Giant Sequoia. One species. Native only to west slope of the Sierra Nevada in California.
Taiwania	One species only and native only to Taiwan and China.
Taxodium	Bald-cypress. Three species. Native only to south-eastern United States and Mexico.

Appendix II

COMMON AND SCIENTIFIC NAMES OF PLANTS

Common Name	Scientific Name
Bitter Cherry	*Prunus emarginata*
Bracken Fern	*Pteridium aquilinum*
Bristlecone Pine	*Pinus aristata*
California Black Oak	*Quercus kelloggii*
California Hazelnut	*Corylus rostrata*
Canyon Live Oak	*Quercus chrysolepis*
Chinquapin	*Castanopsis sempervirens*
Coast Redwood	*Sequoia sempervirens*
Cryptantha	*Cryptantha affinis*
Dawn Redwood	*Metasequoia glyptostroboides*
Deer Brush	*Ceanothus integerrimus*
Douglas Fir	*Pseudotsuga menziesii*
Fossil Sequoias	*Sequoia couttsiae*
	Sequoia reichenbachii
	Sequoiadendron chaneyi
Giant Sequoia	*Sequoiadendron giganteum*
Gilia	*Gilia gilioides*
Golden Sequoia	*Sequoiadendron giganteum 'Aureovariegatum'*
	Sequoiadendron giganteum 'Aureum'
Gooseberry	*Ribes roezlii*
Incense Cedar	*Callocedrus decurrens*
Jeffrey Pine	*Pinus jeffreyi*
Lupine	*Lupinus latifolius*
Manzanita (Greenleaf)	*Arctostaphylos patula*
Manzanita (Whiteleaf)	*A. viscida*
Mountain Whitethorn	*Ceanothus cordulatus*
Pacific Dogwood	*Cornus nuttallii*
Phacelia	*Phacelia mutabilis*
Ponderosa Pine	*Pinus ponderosa*
Rattlesnake Plantain	*Goodyera oblongifolia*
Scouler Willow	*Salix scouleriana*
Small-Leaved Ceanothus	*Ceanothus parvifolius*
Sugar Pine	*Pinus lambertiana*
Sweet Cicely	*Osmorhiza chilensis*
Thin-Stemmed Primrose	*Gayophytum nuttallii*
Trail Plant	*Adenocaulon bicolor*
Weeping Sequoia	*Sequoiadendron giganteum 'Pendulum'*
Western Azalea	*Rhododendron occidentale*
Western Yew	*Taxus brevifolia*
White Fir	*Abies concolor*

White Hawkweed	*Hieracium albiflorum*
Wood Violet	*Viola lobata*

Appendix III

COMMON AND SCIENTIFIC NAMES OF ANIMALS

Common Name   Scientific Name

Mammals

Common Name	Scientific Name
Big Brown Bat	*Eptesicus fuscus*
Black Bear	*Ursus americanus*
Botta Pocket Gopher	*Thomomys bottae*
Broad-Handed Mole	*Scapanus latimanus*
California Ground Squirrel	*Otospermophilus beecheyi*
California Myotis	*Myotis californicus*
Chickaree	*Tamiasciurus douglasii*
Coyote	*Canis latrans*
Deer Mouse	*Peromyscus maniculatus*
Douglas Squirrel	See Chickaree
Fringed Myotis	*Myotis thysanodes*
Golden-Mantled Ground Squirrel	*Callospermophilus lateralis*
Hoary Bat	*Lasiurus cinereus*
Little Brown Myotis	*Myotis lucifugus*
Lodgepole Chipmunk	*Eutamias speciosus*
Long-Eared Chipmunk	*Eutamias quadrimaculatus*
Long-Eared Myotis	*Myotis evotis*
Long-Tailed Meadow Mouse	*Microtus longicaudus*
Long-Tailed Weasel	*Mustela frenata*
Marten	*Martes americana*
Mountain Lion (Cougar)	*Felis concolor*
Mountain Meadow Mouse	*Microtus montanus*
Mule Deer	*Odocoileus hemionus*
Raccoon	*Procyon lotor*
Red Bat	*Lasiurus borealis*
Red Squirrel	*Tamiasciurus hudsonicus*
Townsend Chipmunk	*Eutamias townsendii*
Trowbridge Shrew	*Sorex trowbridgii*
Vagrant Shrew	*Sorex vagrans*
Water Shrew	*Sorex palustris*
Western Gray Squirrel	*Sciurus griseus*
Yellow-Pine Chipmunk	*Eutamias amoenus*
Yuma Myotis	*Myotis yumanensis*

Birds

Common Name	Scientific Name
Band-tailed Pigeon	*Columba fasciata*
Black-Headed Grosbeak	*Pheucticus melanocephalus*

Brown Creeper	*Certhia familiaris*
Cassin's Finch	*Carpodacus cassinii*
Common Flicker	*Caloptes auratus*
Dark-Eyed Junco	*Junco hyemalis*
Golden-Crowned Kinglet	*Regulus satrapa*
Goshawk	*Accipiter gentilis*
Hairy Woodpecker	*Dendrocopos villosus*
Hermit Thrush	*Hylocichla guttata*
Mountain Bluebird	*Sialia currucoides*
Mountain Chickadee	*Parus gambeli*
Mountain Quail	*Oreortyx pictus*
Nashville Warbler	*Vermivora ruficapilla*
Olive-Sided Flycatcher	*Nuttallornis borealis*
Pileated Woodpecker	*Dryocopus pileatus*
Purple Finch	*Carpodacus purpureus*
Red-Breasted Nuthatch	*Sitta canadensis*
Red-Tailed Hawk	*Buteo jamaicensis*
Robin	*Turdus migratorius*
Rufous-Sided Towhee	*Pipilo erythrophthalmus*
Solitary Vireo	*Vireo solitarius*
Spotted Owl	*Strix occidentalis*
Steller's Jay	*Cyanocitta stelleri*
Townsend's Solitaire	*Myadestes townsendi*
Warbling Vireo	*Vireo gilvus*
Western Tanager	*Piranga ludoviciana*
Western Wood Peewee	*Contopus sordidulus*
White-Headed Woodpecker	*Dendrocopos albolarvatus*
Winter Wren	*Troglodytes troglodytes*
Yellow-Bellied Sapsucker	*Sphyrapicus varius*
Yellow-Rumped Warbler	*Dendroica coronata*

Amphibians and Reptiles

California Mountain King Snake	*Lampropeltis zonata*
Eshscholtz's Salamander	*Ensatina eshscholtzi*
Gilbert Skink	*Eumeces gilberti*
Mountain Yellow-Legged Frog	*Rana mucosa*
Northern Alligator Lizard	*Gerrhonotus coeruleus*
Ring-Neck Snake	*Diadophis amabilis*
Rubber Boa	*Charina bottae*
Sagebrush Lizard	*Sceloperus graciosus*
Western Aquatic Garter Snake	*Thamnophis couchi*
Western Fence Lizard	*Scheloperus occidentalis*
Western Rattlesnake	*Crotalus viridus*
Western Terrestrial Garter Snake	*Thamnophis elegans*
Western Toad	*Bufo boreas*

COMMON AND SCIENTIFIC NAMES OF INSECTS
AND OTHER ARTHROPODS

Aphid	*Masonaphis* sp.
Bee fly	*Villa* sp.
Book lice	Order: Pscoptera
Carpenter ant	*Campanotus laevigatus*
Crab spider	Family: Thomididae
Gelechiid moth	*Gelechia*
Horntails	*Sirex areolatus*
Horsefly	*Tabanus laticeps*
Long-horned wood-boring beetle	*Phymatodes nitidus*
Lygaeid bug	*Ischnorrhynchus resedae*
Jumping spider	Family: Attidae
Metallic wood-boring beetle	*Trachykele opulenta*
Pseudoscorpion	(not yet identified)
Robberfly	*Neoitamus affinis*
Snakefly	*Aqulla* sp.
Syrphid fly	*Syrphus* sp.

Appendix V

COMMON AND SCIENTIFIC NAMES OF THALLOPHYTES

Gray mould blight	*Botrytus cinerea*
Cubical Brown Rot	*Polyporus* Sp.
Heartrot	*Lenzites saepiaria*
Root rot	*Sclerotium bataticola* Taub.
Soil Bacterium	*Agrobacterium tumefaciens*

Appendix VI

Groves of *Sequoiadendron giganteum* in California

Modified after Rundel (1969)[1]

1. Placer County Grove—also known as American River Grove. Sec. 18, 19, T. 14 N., R. 13 E.; Middle Fork of the American River, Tahoe National Forest, Placer County.

2. North Calaveras Grove—Sec. 14, 15, 22, T. 5 N., R. 15 E.; Calaveras Big Trees State Park, Calaveras County.

3. South Calaveras Grove—Sec. 28, 29, 30, 31, 32, 33, T. 5 N., R. 16 E., plus two groups of outliers just outside of the grove basin; Calaveras Big Trees State Park, Tuolumne County.

4. Tuolumne Grove—Sec. 7, 18, T. 2 S., R. 20 E.; Big Oak Flat Road, 1 mile north of Crane Flat Ranger Station, Yosemite National Park.

5. Merced Grove—Sec. 23, 24, T. 2 S., R. 19 E.; old Coulterville Road, 2 miles southwest of the Tuolumne Grove, Yosemite National Park.

6. Mariposa Grove—Sec. 6, 7, 8, 18, T. 5 S., R. 22 E.; 1.5 miles east of South Entrance to Yosemite National Park, Mariposa County.

7. Nelder Grove—also known as the Fresno Grove. Sec. 5, 6, 8 et al., T. 6 S., R. 22 E.; 4 miles south of Mariposa Grove, Sierra National Forest, Madera County.

8. McKinley Grove—also known as the Dinkey Creek Grove. Sec. 35, T. 10 S., R. 26 E.; 2 miles southeast of Dinkey Creek Ranger Station, Sierra National Forest, Fresno County.

9. Converse Basin Grove—also known as the Kings River Grove. Sec. 4, 5, 7, 8, 17, 18, T. 13 S., R. 28 E., and sec. 12, 13, T. 13 S., R. 27 E.; considered to include the Boole Tree and Cabin Creek groves, which are essentially continuous with the Converse Basin Grove, Sequoia National Forest, Fresno County.

10. Indian Basin Grove—Sec. 4, 8, 9, 16, 17, T. 13 S., R. 28 E.; 2 miles northwest of Hume Lake, Sequoia National Forest.

---

[1] All range figures are calculated from the Mt. Diablo Meridian, California.

11. Lockwood Grove, Sec. 7, 8, 17, T. 13 S., R. 29 E.; head of Lockwood Creek, Sequoia National Forest.

12. Evans Grove—Sec. 15, 16, 17, 20, 21, 22, T. 13 S., R. 29 E.; the Tehipite Dome 15 min quadrangle of the U.S.G.S. shows this as three groves, including what was called the Horseshoe Bend and Windy Gulch groves. Their continuity and the lack of topographic breaks between them indicate that they can best be treated under a single name.

13. Agnew Grove—Sec. 13, T. 13 S., R. 29 E.; Rattlesnake Creek, Sequoia National Forest.

14. Deer Meadow Grove—Sec. 24, T. 13 S., R. 29 E.; immediately south of the Agnew Grove, but separated by a ridge crest so that two names are valid; Sequoia National Forest.

15. Cherry Gap Grove—Sec. 19, 20, T. 13 S., R. 28 E.; just west of state highway 180 at Cherry Gap, Sequoia National Forest.

16. Kennedy Grove—Sec. 21, 22 (?), 27, 28, T. 13 S., R. 29 E.; appears in two units on Tehipite Dome 15 min quadrangle with the smaller portion including small parts of Sec. 21 and 22; Sequoia National Forest.

17. Abbott Creek Grove—Sec. 30, T. 13 S., R. 28 E.; one small grove along and south of Abbott Creek shown on Tehipite Dome 15 min quadrangle; unnamed in the literature, but one unit described by Hartesveldt et al. (1967); Sequoia National Forest.

18. Burton Grove—Sec. 29, T. 13 S., R. 29 E.; between Kennedy Grove and Little Boulder Creek, Sequoia National Forest.

19. Boulder Creek Grove—Sec. 26, 35, T. 13 S., R. 29 E.; along and southwest of Boulder Creek; shown as three tiny unnamed groves on the Tehipite Dome 15 min quadrangle; Sequoia National Forest.

20. Little Boulder Creek Grove—Sec. 27, 34, T. 13 S., R. 29 E.; just south of Little Boulder Creek, Sequoia National Forest.

21. Landslide Grove—Sec. 30, 31, T. 13 S., R. 29 E.; along Landslide Creek. Tehipite Dome 15 min quadrangle shows two units; Sequoia National Forest.

22. Tenmile Grove—Sec. 35, 36; Tenmile Creek, Sequoia National Forest.

23. Bearskin Grove—Sec. 34, 35, T. 13 S., R. 28 E.; Bearskin Creek, Sequoia National Forest.

24. Grant Grove—Sec. 36, T. 13 S., R. 27 E., sec. 31, T. 13 S., R. 28 E.; Kings Canyon National Park and Sequoia National Forest.

25. Sequoia Creek Grove—Sec. 6, T. 14 S., R. 28 E.; Sequoia Creek, Kings Canyon National Park.

26. Big Stump Grove—Sec. 7, 8, 18; Sequoia National Forest and Kings Canyon National Park.

27. Redwood Mountain Grove—Sec. 10, 13, 14, 15, 16, 21, 22, 23, 24, 25, 26, 27, 28, 34. Primarily in Kings Canyon National Park; Whitaker Forest, University of California; The Buena Vista and Big Baldy groves appear to be continuous with this grove; includes three outliers at Big Springs, sec. 2, and one sequoia along Redwood Creek at Cherry Flat, sec. 2 or 11, T. 15 S., R. 28 E.

28. Lost Grove—Sec. 33, 34, T. 14 S., R. 29 E., sec. 3, 4, T. 15 S., R. 29 E.; along General's Highway near west entrance, Sequoia National Park.

29. Muir Grove—Sec. 8, 9, 16, 17; 1.5 miles west of Dorst Campground, Sequoia National Park.

30. Skagway Grove—Sec. 16, 17, 20, T. 15 N., R. 29 E.; 1.5 miles southeast of Muir Grove, Sequoia National Park.

31. Pine Ridge Grove—Sec. 17, 20, T. 15 S., R. 29 E.; 0.5 miles west of Skagway Grove, Sequoia National Park.

32. Suwanee Grove—Sec. 26, T. 15 S., R. 29 E.; 1.5 miles east of Crystal Cave, Sequoia National Park; the Giant Forest quadrangle shows this grove 0.5 mile north of its actual location.

33. Giant Forest—Sec. 36, T. 15 S., R. 29 E., sec. 31, 32, 33, T. 15 S., R. 30 E., sec. 1, 12, T. 16 S., R. 29 E., sec. 4, 5, 6, 7, 8, T. 16 S., R. 30 E.; Sequoia National Park; two small groups of outliers: (1) 0.5 mile northwest of Kaweah Camp in sec. 1, T. 16 S., R. 29 E.; and (2) five trees 0.25 mile south of Marble Fork Bridge along the Crystal Cave Road in sec. 36, T. 15 S., R. 29 E.

34. Redwood Meadow Groves—Sec. 13, T. 16 S., R. 30 E., sec. 16, 17, 18, 19, 20, 21, 29; six separate units were included in this complex by Aley (1963); separate names exist for four of the units although the complex is best represented under the single name; (1) Redwood Meadow Grove is the main grove, including the ranger station, and a single outlier 0.25 mile to the north along the creek; (2) Granite Creek Grove is a small grove along Granite Creek 1.25 miles northeast of the ranger station; (3) Little Redwood Meadow Grove, as used by Fry and White (1938), which apparently applies to a small grove 1.5 miles east of the main grove at a much higher elevation,

and (4) Cliff Creek Grove which includes two small groups of outliers along Cliff Creek, south of the main grove.

35. Castle Creek Groves—Sec. 14, 22, 23, 26, 27, T. 16 S., R. 30 E.; a complex of four groves termed Castle Creek North, South, East, and West by Aley (1963); the north and south groves are extremely small; Sequoia National Park.

36. Atwell Grove—Sec. 1, 2, 10, 11, 12, 14, 15, T. 17 S., R. 30 E.; Sequoia National Park, a single outlier 150 yards above the grove is the highest elevation naturally seeded sequoia known.

37. Oriole Grove—Sec. 4, 5, 8, 9, T. 17 S., R. 30 E.; along upper Squirrel Creek, Sequoia National Park; Fry and White (1938) include this under Squirrel Creek Grove, although they show it as distinct on their map.

38. Squirrel Creek Grove, Sec. 7, T. 17 S., R. 30 E.; along Squirrel Creek, 1 mile west of Oriole Grove, Sequoia National Park.

39. Redwood Creek Grove—Sec. 9, 10, 15, T. 17 S., R. 30 E.; Aley (1963) shows two units along Redwood Creek, Sequoia National Park.

40. East Fork Grove—Sec. 12, 13, 14, 23, 24, T. 17 S., R. 30 E., sec. 7, 8, T. 17 S., R. 31 E.; Sequoia National Park and Sequoia National Forest.

41. New Oriole Grove—Sec. 16, 17, T. 17 S., R. 30 E.; 0.75 mile south of the Oriole Grove, Sequoia National Park.

42. Eden Creek Grove—Sec. 28, 29, 32, 33, T. 17 S., R. 30 E.; along Eden Creek, Sequoia National Park.

43. Cahoon Creek Grove—Sec. 27, T. 17 S., R. 30 E.; 1.5 miles east of Eden Creek Grove on Cahoon Creek, Sequoia National Park.

44. Horse Creek Grove—Sec. 26, 27, T. 17 S., R. 30 E.; 0.25 mile east of Cahoon Creek Grove on Horse Creek, Sequoia National Park.

45. Case Mountain Groves—Sec. 26, 35, 36, T. 17 S., R. 29 E., and possibly sec. 1, T. 18 S., R. 29 E.; two units fall under this name, the larger portion occupying the large basin east of Case Mountain; mostly in private ownership, small part in Sequoia National Park.

46. Coffeepot Canyon Grove—Sec. 31, 32, T. 17 S., R. 30 E.; in Coffeepot Canyon, 1 mile east of Case Mountain Grove, Sequoia National Park.

47. Surprise Grove—Sec. 5, 6, 7, 8, T. 18 S., R. 30 E.; along Bennett Creek near Palmer Cave, Sequoia National Park.

48. Homer's Nose Grove—Sec. 9, T. 18 S., R. 30 E.; located on what is plotted as Cedar Creek on the Mineral King quadrangle sheet, Sequoia National Park.

49. Putnam-Francis Grove—Sec. 10, T. 18 S., R. 30 E.; 0.5 mile east of Homer's Nose Grove, Sequoia National Park.

50. South Fork Grove—Sec. 14, 15, 16, 22, 23, T. 18 S., R. 30 E.; South Fork Kaweah River, Sequoia National Park.

51. Garfield Grove—Sec. 20, 21, 22, 23, 26, 27, 28, 33, 34, 35, T. 18 S., R. 30 E.; Sequoia National Park; several outliers occur along the South Fork of the Kaweah River below the South Fork and Garfield Groves 0.25 mile below the South Fork Ranger Station in Sequoia National Park, and at several points further down the river to 2700 feet (Hartesveldt, 1965).

52. Devil's Canyon Grove—Sec. 31 (?), T. 18 S., R. 30 E.; the exact location is not established; it is variously reported to be within or just outside of Sequoia National Park.

53. Dennison Grove—exact location is not established; T. 18 S., R. 30 E., and/or T. 19 S., R. 30 E.; variously reported as within Sequoia National Park, straddling the park boundary, and just outside of the park.

54. Dillonwood Grove—unsurveyed, T. 18 S., R. 30 E., sec. 2, 3, 4, 9, 10, 11 (?), T. 19 S., R. 30 E.; really an extension of Garfield Grove across Dennison Ridge; Sequoia National Forest.

55. Middle Tule Grove—Sec. 18, 19, 30, T. 19 S., R. 31 E., and sec. 13, T. 19 S., R. 30 E.; North Fork of the Middle Fork of the Tule River, southeast of Moses Mountain; Sequoia National Forest, and Mountain Home State Forest.

56. Maggie Mountain Grove—Sec. 20, T. 19 S., R. 30 E.; 1.5 miles west of Maggie Mountain in the Galena Creek drainage; Sequoia National Forest.

57. Mountain Home Grove—Sec. 25, 26, 27, 35, 36, T. 19 S., R. 30 E., sec. 30, 31, T. 19 S., R. 31 E., sec. 1, 2, 12, T. 20 S., R. 30 E., sec. 6, T. 20 S., R. 31 E.; Mountain Home State Forest and Sequoia National Forest; outliers include two large trees in sec. 34, T. 19 S., R. 30 E., a small group in sec. 2, T. 20 S., R. 30 E., and a larger group in sec. 3, T. 20 S., R. 30 E.

58. Silver Creek Grove—Sec. 29, T. 19 S., R. 31 E.; Silver Creek, 1.5 miles east of Shake Camp Pack Station; Mountain Home State Forest; a small group of outliers lie in sec. 29 near the junction of Silver Creek and the North Fork of the Middle Fork of the Tule River, Sequoia National Forest.

59. Burro Creek Grove—Sec. 32, 33, T. 19 S., R. 31 E., sec. 4, 5, T. 20 S., R. 31 E.; 2 miles east of Balch Park, Sequoia National Forest.

60. Alder Creek Grove—Sec. 9, 15, 16, 17, 21; along Alder Creek, 2 miles east of Camp Wishon; Sequoia National Forest.

61. McIntyre Grove—Sec. 34, 35, 36, T. 20 S., R. 31 E.; South Fork of the Middle Fork of the Tule River, 1 mile east of Camp Nelson; Sequoia National Forest.

62. Belknap Grove—Sec. 34, T. 20 S., R. 31 E., Sec. 2, T. 21 S., R. 31 E.; 1 mile southwest of McIntyre Grove, Sequoia National Forest.

63. Wheel Meadow Grove—Sec. 6, 7, 18, T. 21 S., R. 32 E., sec. 1, T. 20 S., R. 31 E.; South Fork of the Middle Fork of the Tule River, 1 mile southeast of McIntyre Grove, Sequoia National Forest.

64. Freeman Creek Grove—Sec. 27, 28, 29, 32, 33, 34, 35, T. 20 S., R. 32 E.; along Freeman Creek; Sequoia National Forest.

65. Black Mountain Grove—Sec. 6, 7, 8, 9, 16, 17, 18, 20, and unsurveyed land, T. 21 S., R. 30 E., sec. 1, 12 and unsurveyed northeast margin of the Tule River Indian Reservation, and Sequoia National Forest.

66. Red Hill Grove—Sec. 22, 23, 26, 27, and unsurveyed land, T. 21 S., R. 31 E.; 1 mile east of Red Hill summit, Sequoia National Forest.

67. Peyrone Grove—Sec. 34, 35, T. 21 S., R. 31 E., sec. 2, 3, T. 22 S., R. 31 E.; Windy Gap Creek, 1 mile south of the Red Hill Grove, Sequoia National Forest.

68. Parker Peak Grove—unsurveyed land, T. 22 S., R. 31 E.; between Redwood Creek and Eagle Creek, Tule River Indian Reservation.

69. North Cold Spring Grove—unsurveyed land, T. 22 S., R. 30 E.; north of North Cold Spring Peak, Tule Indian Reservation; generally considered to be a part of the Parker Peak Grove.

70. Long Meadow Grove—Sec. 26, 27, 34, 35, 36, T. 22 S., R. 31 E.; west of Long Meadow, Sequoia National Forest.

71. Cunningham Grove—Sec. 30, T. 22 S., R. 32 E.; on ridge south of Long Meadow Creek, 1 mile east of Long Meadow Grove, 1 mile east of Long Meadow; Sequoia National Forest.

72. Starvation Creek Grove—Sec. 9, 10, 15, 16, T. 23 S., R. 31 E., along Starvation Creek, 1 mile west of the Powderhorn Grove, Sequoia National Forest.

73. Powderhorn Grove—Sec. 10, 14, 15, T. 23 S., R. 31 E., 1 mile southwest of Powderhorn Meadow, Sequoia National Forest.

74. Packsaddle Grove—Sec. 12, 13, 14, 24, T. 23 S., R. 31 E.; along Packsaddle Creek, Sequoia National Forest.

75. Deer Creek Grove—Sec. 2, 3, T. 23 S., R. 31 E.; 2 miles east of Pine Flat, Sequoia National Forest.

References

ALEY, T. J. 1963. Final report on the type mapping and regeneration studies in the giant sequoia groves of Kings Canyon and Sequoia National parks. Contract research report for the Western Region, National Park Service. 63 p.

ANDERSON, A. B., R. RIFFER, and A. WONG. 1968. Chemistry of the genus *Sequoia*. *Phytochemistry* **7**(8):1367–1371.

ANDREWS, R. W. 1958. Redwood classic. Superior Publishing Co., Seattle, Wash. 174 p.

ANON. 1853. An immense tree. *Gleason's Pictorial Drawing Room Companion*. **5**(14):217.

———. 1854. Description of the great tree recently felled upon the Sierra Nevada, California. Herald Job Printing Office, New York. 14 p. Reprinted by Francis P. Farquhar, San Francisco, 1960.

———. 1855a. The big tree (*Wellingtonia gigantea*). *Gardener's Chronicle* **15**(1):7–8.

———. 1855b. The Wellingtonia of Lindley. *Am. J. Sci. Ser. 2.* **20**(59):281–282.

———. 1858. (Title unknown), emend. Gordon, *Pinetum 330*. Published in synonymy.

———. 1859. *Wellingtonia gigantea*. *Gardener's Chronicle* **19**(43):850.

———. 1862. (Title unknown) Hort. Am. ex Gordon, *Pinetum* Suppl. 106. Published in synonymy.

———. 1876. Age of the mammoth trees. *Gardener's Monthly* **18**(214):310–311.

———. 1891. (Origin of name of big tree). *Garden and Forest* **4**(164):179.

———. 1903. Save the big trees. *The Outlook* **74**(2):105.

———. 1960. Effects of photoperiod on sequoia. *Argonne National Laboratory annual report*. ANL–6275. (University of Chicago). p 102.

AXELROD, D. I. 1959. Late Tertiary evolution of the Sierran big-tree forest. *Evolution* **13**:9–23.

———. 1962. A Pliocene Sequoiadendron forest from western Nevada. *Univ. Calif. Publ. Geol. Sci.* **39**(3):195–268.

———. 1964. The Miocene Trapper Creek flora of southern Idaho. *Univ. Calif. Publ. Geol. Sci.* **51**:1–148.

BAKER, F. S. 1949. A revised tolerance table. *J. For.* **47**:179–181.

BALOGH, B., and A. B. ANDERSON. 1965. Chemistry of the genus *Sequoia*, II. Isolation of sequirins, new phenolic compounds from the coast redwood, *Sequoia sempervirens*. *Phytochemistry* **4**(4):569–575.

———. 1966. Chemistry of the genus *Sequoia*, III. Structural studies of isosequirin. *Phytochemistry* **5**(3):325–330.

BEETHAM, N. M. 1962. The ecological tolerance range of the seedling stage of *Sequoia gigantea*. Ph.D. Thesis. Duke Univ., 135 p. Univ. Microfilms, Inc., Ann Arbor, Mich.

BEGA, R. V. 1964. Diseases of sequoia. *In* Proc. of FAO/IUFRO symposium on internationally dangerous forest diseases and insects. *FAO/FOREST* **64**:131–139.

BEIDLEMAN, R. G. 1950. Sequoia cones and seeds. *Yosemite Nature Notes* **29**(1):9–11.

BELLUE, A. J. 1930. Origin of the name Sequoia. *Yosemite Nature Notes* **9**(8):75.

BERLAND, O. 1962. Giant Forest's reservation: the legend and the mystery. *Sierra Club Bull.* **47**(9):68–82.

BERRY, J. B. 1924. Western Forest trees. World Book Co., Yonkers-on-Hudson, New York. (Reprinted by Dover Publications, Inc., New York. 1966)

BISWELL, H. H. 1961. Big trees and fire. *Natl. Parks Mag.* **35**(163):11–14.

BLICK, J. D. 1963. The giant sequoia; a study in autecology. Contract report for the Western Region, National Park Service. 93 p. (In Sequoia and Kings Canyon National parks files.)

BLOOMER, H. G. 1868. On the scientific name of the big trees. *Calif. Acad Sci. Proc.* **3**:399.

BROWN, S. 1868. Coning of the Wellingtonia. *Gardener's Chronicle* **28**(33):872.

BUCHHOLZ, J. T. 1938. Cone formation in Sequoia gigantea. *Am. J. Bot.* **25**:296–305.

———. 1939. The generic segregation of the sequoias. *Am. J. Bot.* **26**(7):535–538.

CALIFORNIA, STATE OF. 1924. Big tree measurements, Calaveras Groves of big trees, South Grove. Report from the Evans Cruise, Calaveras Big Trees State Park.

———. 1952. Status of *Sequoia gigantea* in the Sierra Nevada; Senate concurrent resolution No. 44, 1951, general session. Compiled and written by Frederick A. Meyer, Chief Forester, California Div. of Beaches and Parks. State of California Printing Office, Sacramento. 75 p.

CHALLACOMBE, J. R. 1954. When the giants fell. *Pop. Mech. Mag.* **101**(6):65–70, 234–236.

CHANEY, R. W. 1951. A revision of fossil *Sequoia* and *Taxodium* in western North America based on the recent discovery of Metasequoia. *Am. Phil. Soc. Trans.* **40**(3):171–263.

CLARK, G. 1907. Big trees of California. Reflex Publ. Co., Redondo, California. 104 p.

CLARK, S. A. 1937. Golden tapestry of California. Robert McBride and Co., New York.

CLARKE, G. L. 1954. Elements of ecology. John Wiley & Sons, Inc., New York.

COOK, L. F. 1955. The giant sequoias of California. U.S. Government Printing Office, Washington, D.C. 28 p.

DAYTON, W. A. 1943. The names of the giant sequoia. *Leafl. West. Bot.* **3**(10):209–219.

DEBANO, L. F., and J. S. KRAMMES. 1966. Water repellent soils and their relation to wildfire temperatures. *Int. Assoc. Sci. Hydrol.* **11**:14–19.

DECAISNE, J. 1854. Botanical reference to a 'Conifera gigantea of California', probably the *Sequoia gigantea. Soc. Bot. de France Bull.* **1**:70–71.

DEN OUDEN, P., and B. K. BOOM. 1965. Manual of cultivated conifers. Marinus Nijhoff, The Hague.

DIETZ, R. S., and J. C. HOLDEN. 1970. The breakup of Pangaea. *Sci. Am.* **223**(4):30–41.

DONAGHEY, J. L. 1969. The properties of heated soils and their relationships to giant sequoia germination and seedling growth. M.S. Thesis. San Jose State University, San Jose, Calif. 173 p.

DUNBAR, C. O. 1960. Historical geology. John Wiley & Sons, Inc., New York.

ELLSWORTH, R. S. 1924. The giant sequoia. J. D. Berger Press, Oakland. 167 p.

EMBERGER, L. 1968. Les plantes fossiles. Masson et Cie, Paris.

ENDLICHER, S. 1847. Synopsis coniferarum. Scheitlin und Zollikofer, St. Gallen, Switzerland, p. 4.

FRITTS, H. C. 1969. Bristlecone pine in the White Mountains of California: growth and ring-width characteristics. Papers of the Lab. of Tree-ring Research, the Univ. of Ariz., Tucson, 44 p.

FRY, W., and J. R. WHITE. 1930. Big trees. Stanford Univ. Press, Palo Alto, Calif. 114 p. (9th ed. 1948).

GILLETTE, H. P. 1930. Alternate wet and dry periods of 11.2 years shown by California sequoias for 3,125 years. *Water Sewage Works* **77**:14–16.

HARTESVELDT, R. J. 1962. The effects of human impact upon *Sequoia gigantea* and its environment in the Mariposa Grove, Yosemite National Park, California. Ph.D. Thesis. Univ. of Michigan. Univ. Microfilms, Inc., Ann Arbor, Mich. 310 p.

———. 1963. Reconnaissance study of the effects of human impact upon moderately to heavily used sequoia groves in Sequoia and Kings Canyon National Parks. Contract research report to the Regional Director, National Park Service, San Francisco. 46 p.

———. 1964. Sequoia-human impact soil analyses. Report for the Regional Director, National Park Service, San Francisco. 14 p.

———. 1965. An investigation of the effect of direct human impact and of advanced plant succession on *Sequoia gigantea* in Sequoia and Kings Canyon National Parks, California. Contract research report to the Regional Director, Western Region, National Park Service. 82 p.

HARTESVELDT, R. J., and H. T. HARVEY. 1967. The fire ecology of sequoia regeneration. *Tall Timbers Fire Ecology Conf. Proc.* **7**:65–77.

HARTESVELDT, R. J., H. T. HARVEY, and H. S. SHELLHAMMER. 1967. Giant sequoia ecology. Contract report to Regional Director, National Park Service, San Francisco. 55 p.

HARTESVELDT, R. J., H. T. HARVEY, H. S. SHELLHAMMER, and R. E. STECKER. 1968. Giant sequoia. Contract report to Regional Director, National Park Service, San Francisco. 19 p.

HARWELL, C. A. 1947. Little known facts about the big tree. *Audubon* **49**(5):271.

HINDS, J. I. D. 1893. The big trees of California. *Science* **21**(523):76–77.

IRVING, L., H. KROG, and M. MONSON. 1955. The metabolism of some Alaskan animals in winter and summer. *Physiol. Zool.* **28**(3):173–185.

ISE, J. 1961. Our national park policy, a critical history. The Johns Hopkins Press, Baltimore.

JOLY, C. 1883. The Wellingtonia in their natural state. *Revue de L'Horticulture Belge et Etrangere* (Gand, France) **9**(1):190, 201–203.

JOURDAN, J. W. 1932. Accurate surveys determine sizes of rival big trees. *Engineering News-Record* **180**(7):254–255.

KELLOGG, A., and H. BEHR. 1855. *Taxodium giganteum*; or, the Washington cypress. The Pacific, San Francisco. (Reprinted as Calif. Acad. Sci. Proc., 1873 2nd edition, **1**:51–52.)

KILGORE, B. M. 1968. Breeding bird populations in managed and unmanaged stands of *Sequoia gigantea*. Ph.D. Thesis. Univ. Calif. 196 p. Univ. Microfilms, Inc., Ann Arbor, Mich. (Diss. Abstr. **29**(9):3145B).

———. 1971. Response of breeding bird populations to habitat changes in a giant sequoia forest. *Am. Midl. Nat.* **85**(1):135–152.

KOCH, K. H. 1873. Dendrologie, v. 2. F. Enke, Erlangen, Germany.

KRESSMAN, F. W. 1911. Report on sequoia gum. U.S. Forest Products Lab., Madison, Wis. 5 p.

KRUSSMAN, G. 1966. Introduction of Sequoiadendron. *Gardener's Chronicle* **159**(12):279–280.

LAMBERT, A. B. 1828. *Taxodium sempervirens*, Tab. 48. *In* A description of genus Pinus . . . , vol. 2, second edition.

LEONARD, Z. 1839. Narrative of Zenas Leonard, 1831–36. Burrows Bros. Co., Cleveland. (Reprinted in 1904 and 1908).

LEWIS, O. 1955. High Sierra country. Duell, Sloan and Pearce, New York.

LINDLEY, J. T. 1853. (no title). *Gardener's Chronicle* 29 December:819–820, 823.

———. 1855. *Wellingtonia gigantea*. *Hooker's J. Bot. and Kew Misc.* **7**:26.

MARTIN, E. 1957–58. Die Sequoien und ihre Anzucht. Mitt. Deutsch. Dendrol. Ges., Yearbook no. 60. 62 p.

MARTIN, E. J. 1957. Neoplastisches Wachstum bei *Sequoiadendron giganteum* Buchholz. *Phytopathology* **30**(3):342–343. (Neoplastic growth of *Sequoiadendron giganteum* Buchholz.)

MASON, H. L. 1955. Do we want sugar pine? *Sierra Club Bull.* **40**(8):40–44.

MEINECKE, E. P. 1926. Memorandum on the effects of tourist traffic on plant life, particularly big trees, Sequoia National Park, California. Unpubl. 19 p.

———. 1927. Letter regarding the effects of excessive tourist travel in the Mariposa Grove, Yosemite National Park, Cal., to Stephen T. Mather, Director, National Park Service. 4 p.

MENNINGER, E. A. 1967. Fantastic trees. The Viking Press, New York.

METCALF, W. 1948. Youthful years of the big tree. *Pacific Discovery* **1**(3):4–10.

MOONEY, J. 1900. *In* U.S. Bureau of American Ethnology, Nineteenth Annual Report, Part I, p. 108–110, 135–139, 147–148, 219–220, 351, 353–355, 485, and 501. U.S. Government Printing Office, Washington, D.C.

MORRIS, R. 1967. Germination of *Sequoia gigantea* seeds. Unpubl. biology class project, San Jose State University.

MUGGLETON, H. 1859. *Wellingtonia gigantea*. *Gardener's Chronicle* **19**(45):890.

MUIR, J. 1878. The new sequoia forests of California. *Harpers* **57**(342):813–827.

———. 1894. The mountains of California. The Century Co., New York.

———. 1901. Hunting big redwoods. *Atlantic Monthly* **88**(77):304–320.

———. 1911. My first summer in the Sierra. *Atlantic Monthly* **107**(4):521–528.

———. 1912. The Yosemite. The Century Co., New York.

MUNZ, P. A., and D. D. KECK. 1959. A California flora. The University of California Press, Berkeley.

NELMES, W. 1964. The ugliest tree in Britain. *Gardener's Chronicle* **155**(20):457.

NELSON, J. 1866. *Pinaceae*, being a handbook of the firs and pines, by J. Senilis (pseud.). Hatchard and Co., London.

NOYES, W. 1928. Wood and forest. William Noyes, New York. Second Edition.

OLMSTED, F. L. 1952. The Yosemite Valley and Mariposa big trees (1865). *Landscape Architecture* **43**(1):12–25.

PEATTIE, D. C. 1953. A natural history of western trees. Houghton Mifflin Co., Boston 751 p.

POST, T. V., and O KUNTZE. 1904. Lexicon Genarum Phanerogramarum. Stuttgart: Deutsch Verlags–Anstalt. p. 533.

POWERS, S. 1877. Tribes of California. U.S. Government Printing Office, Washington, D.C. 398 p.

PRINCE, W. R. 1854. The giant taxodium of California. *Mag. of Hortic.*, Boston **20**(5):243.

PRESL, K. B. 1838. *In* C. v. Sternberg, Versuch einer geognostich-botanischen darstellung der flora der vorwelt. Fr. Fleischer, Leipzig, Vol. 2, Heft 8.

REMY, J. 1857. Description of gigantic trees of California. *Le Belgique Horticole*, Liege **7**:19–23.

RENFREW, C. 1971. Carbon 14 and the prehistory of Europe. *Sci. Am* **225**(4):63–72.

REYNOLDS, R. D. 1959. Effect of natural fires and aboriginal burning upon the forest of the Central Sierra Nevada. M.A. Thesis. Univ. of Calif., Berkeley. 262 p.

RICKETT, H. W. 1950 Botanical name of the big tree. *J. N. Y. Bot. Gard.* **51**(601):15.

ROBINSON, C. D. 1882. The two redwoods. *The Californian* **5**(30):485–491.

RUNDEL, P. W. 1969. The distribution and ecology of the giant sequoia ecosystem in the Sierra Nevada, California. Ph.D. Thesis. Duke University, Durham, N.C. 204 p.

———. 1971. Community structure and stability in the giant sequoia groves of the Sierra Nevada. *Am. Midl. Nat.* **85**(2):478–492.

———. 1973. The relationship between basal fire scars and crown damage in giant sequoia. *Ecology* **54**(1):210–213.

RUSSELL, C. P. 1957. One hundred years in Yosemite. Yosemite Nat. Hist. Assn., Inc. Yosemite National Park. 195 p.

ST. JOHN, H., and R. W. KRAUSS. 1954. The taxonomic position and the scientific name of the big tree known as *Sequoia gigantea*. *Pac. Sci.* **8**(3):341–358.

SALT, G. W. 1953. An ecological analysis of three California avifaunas. *Condor* **55**(5):258–273.

———. 1957. An analysis of avifaunas in the Teton Mountains and Jackson Hole, Wyo. *Condor* **59**(6):373–393.

SAUNDERS, C. F. 1926. Trees and shrubs of California gardens. Robert McBride and Co., New York.

SCHMECKEBIER, L. F. 1912. The Yosemite. *Natl. Geogr. Mag.* **23**(6):550–556.

SCHUBERT, G. H. 1952. Germination of various coniferous seeds after cold storage. Calif. Forest and Range Experiment Sta. Research Note 83. U.S. Forest Service, Berkeley. 7 p.

———.1957. Silvical characteristics of giant sequoia. Pacific southwest Forest and Range Experiment Sta. Tech. Paper 20. U.S. Forest Service, Berkeley. 13 p.

SCHUBERT, G. H., revised by N. M. Beetham. 1962. Silvical characteristics of giant sequoia. Pacific Southwest Forest and Range Experiment Sta. Tech. Paper No. 20, rev. U.S. Forest Service. 16 p.

SCHWARZ, G. F. 1904. The big trees and forest fires. *Forestry and Irrigation* (Washington, D.C.). **10**(5):213–214.

SEEMAN, B. 1855. Disagreement on bigtree nomenclature. *Bonplandia* (Hanover). **3**(2):27.

SHELLHAMMER, H. S. 1966. Cone-cutting activities of Douglas squirrels in sequoia groves. *J. Mammal*. **47**(3):525–526.

SHINN, C. H. 1889. The great sequoia. *Garden and Forest* **2**:614–615.

SMITH, C. C. 1968. Adaptive nature of the social organization in the genus of tree squirrels *Tamiasciurus*. *Ecol. Monogr.* **38**:31–63.

SPURR, S. H. 1952. Forest inventory. Ronald Press Co., New York. 476 p.

STARK, N. 1968. Seed ecology of *Sequoiadendron giganteum*. *Madrono* **19**(7):267–277.

STARKER, T. J. 1935. Giant growers of the globe. *Am. For.* **41**(6):266–268.

STEBBINS, G. L. 1948. Chromosomes and relationships of Metasequoia and Sequoia. *Science* **108**(2796):95–98.

STECKER, R. E. 1969. Giant sequoia insect ecology. Contract research report to the Western Region, National Park Service. 15 p.

STEELE, R. 1914. Tragedy of a before Christmas tree. *Pioneer Western Lumberman* **62**(7):15, 19, 21.

STEWART, O. C. 1956. Fire as the first great force employed by man. Pages 115–133 *in* W. L. Thomas, Jr., ed. Man's role in changing the face of the earth. Univ. of Chicago Press, Chicago, Ill.

STORER, T. I., and R. L. USINGER. 1963. Sierra Nevada natural history. Univ. of California Press, Berkeley.

SUDWORTH, G. B. 1897. Nomenclature of the arborescent flora of the United States. Division of Forestry Bull. No. 14. U.S. Government Printing Office, Washington, D.C.

———. 1908. Forest trees of the Pacific slope. U.S. Forest Service. U.S. Government Printing Office, Washington, D.C.

SWEENEY, J. R. 1956. Responses of vegetation to fire. *Botany* **28**(4):143–250.

TIEMANN, H. D. 1935. What are the largest trees in the world? *J. For.* **33**(11):903–915.

TODD, J. 1870. The sunset land. Lee and Shepard, Boston.

U.S. DEPARTMENT OF AGRICULTURE. 1948. Woody seed plant manual. Pages 335–336 *in* U.S. Dep. Agric. Misc. Publ. No. 654. U.S. Government Printing Office, Washington.

U.S. Department of the Interior. 1940. Forest conservation on lands administered by the Department of the Interior. U.S. Government Printing Office, Washington. 187 p.

Vankat, J. L. 1970. Vegetation change in Sequoia National Park. Ph.D. Thesis. Univ. of California, Davis. 197 p.

Voss, A. 1908. Coniferen-Nomenclatur-Tabelle. *Mitt. Dtsch. Dendrol. Ges.* **16**(1907):88–95.

White, J. R. 1934. Among the big trees of California. *Natl. Geogr. Mag.* **66**(2):219–232.

Wilson, H. E. 1928. The lore and lure of Sequoia. The Wolder Printing Co., Los Angeles. 132 p.

Winslow, C. F. 1854. Dr. Winslow's letters from the mountains, the big tree. *Calif. Farmer* **2**(8):58.

Wolfe, L. M. 1938. John of the Mountains. Houghton-Mifflin Co., Boston.

Wright, G. M., J. S. Dixon, and B. H. Thompson. 1933. A preliminary survey of faunal relations in national parks. U.S. Dep. Inter. Fauna Series No. 1. U.S. Government Printing Office, Washington, D.C. 157 p.

Wulff, J. V., G. W. Lyons, and E. G. Dudley. 1911. A study of the reproduction of *Sequoia washingtonia*, Sierra Sequoia Stanislaus. Report to the forest supervisor, Stanislaus National Forest. 51 p.

Zinke, P. J., and R. L. Crocker. 1962. The influence of giant sequoia on soil properties. *For. Sci.* **8**:2–11.

Index

Adansonia gregorii F. Muell.

size 63

Aegeriid or clear-winged moth 132

Agrobacterium tumefaciens 62

Ahuehuete 64

Alabama Tree 39, 41

Alaska 67

Aley, T. J. 78, 160, 161

Alitherman hypothesis 79

American Museum of Natural History 8

Amethyst Cliff 67

Anderson, A. B. 55,119

Anderson, R. 115

Andrews, R. W. 9,56

Animal populations 124–126

scientific names, Appendix III 154–155

Anon. 5, 13, 24, 28, 57, 90, 91

Aphid (*Masonaphis* sp.)

biomass 136

Arachnids 136

Argonne National Laboratory 91

Ash Mountain nursery 106

Athenaeum 3

Atwell Grove 116

Austria 77

Axelrod, D. I. 67

Baker, F. S. 105

Balogh, B. 119

Band-tailed pigeon 125

Bark, sequoia 35-38, 40, 41

fire scars 41, 42

flutings and ridges 35, 36, 41

mutation 36, 73

regrown 47

scales 40

thickness 40

Bats 126

Bee flies (*Villa*) 136

Beetham, N. M. 84, 89, 100, 102, 103, 104, 105, 106

Bega, R. V. 55, 62

Behr, H. 24

Beidleman, R. G. 48

Bellue, A. J. 28

Berland, O. 13

Berry, J. B. 66

Bidwell, J. 3

Big Baldy Grove 69

Big brown bat 126

Big Stump Grove 6, 8

"big tree" 25

Big Trees 74

Biomass 84

Biotic community

sequoia forest 83

food webs 83

Bird species 124

classified by feeding habits 125

Biswell, H. H. 149

Bitter cherry 138, 140

Black bear 124

Black Chamber 48, 112, 115, 118

Black-headed grossbeak 125

Black Sea Coast 80

Blick, J. D. 69, 120

Bloomer, H. G. 22

Boabab size 63

Bobcat 125

Bo-tree 65

Boole, F. A. 10

Boole Tree 10, 11, 44

Boom, B. K. 18

Botta pocket gopher 126

Bracken fern (*Pteridium aquilinum*) 123

Bristlecone pine 62

ring count 120

British Museum 8

British nurseries 79

British varieties 18, 19, 20

Broad-handed mole 126

Brown creeper 124, 125

Brown, S. 91

Buchholz, J. T. 24, 88

Buena Vista Grove 69

Bulgaria 80

Calaveras Bigtree National Forest 14

Calaveras Grove 3, 4, 13, 23, 73, 79

Association 14

California Academy of Sciences 22, 149

California black oak

(*Quercus kelloggii*) 122

California ground squirrel 124, 125, 127

California hazelnut

(*Corylus rostrata*) 122

California incense-cedar 140
California mountain king snake 126
California myotis 126
California plant communities
  29 types 121
California State Legislature 10
California, state of 68
California Tree 117
Camel cricket 106
Canada 67
Canadian Zone 125
Canyon live oak
  (*Quercus chrysolepis*) 122
Canyon of the Kings River 10
Carinaria excelsa Casar. 64
Carpenter ant
  (*Camponatus laevigatus*) 134

Carter Ink Company 90
Cassin's finch or purple finch 125
Castanea sativa Mill. 65
Castro, C. 116
Castro Tree 91-94, 95, 97, 134
Central Valley
  bat migration 126
Chalcid wasps 136
Challacombe, J. R. 9
Chaney, R. W. 17, 67
Clark, G. 94
Clark, S. A. 120
Clarke, G. L. 90
Cherokee Indian 25, 26
Cherokee Phoenix 25
Chestnut, sweet or Spanish 65
Chickaree or Douglas squirrel 75, 96, 124, 126
  cone cuttings 97
  metabolic rate 131
  range of 128
  Redwood Mountain variety 131
  reproduction 132
  role of 128-132
  seed dispersal 96, 99
  sequoia cone consumer 83
  territorial defense 129, 130
Chinquapin (*Castanopsis sempervirens*) 122
Chipmunk populations 125, 127
Cieba pentandra (L.). Gaertn. 63
Climatic changes
  post-Pleistocene 77
  Sierra Nevada 16
Climax community 85
  fire climax 86

Coast redwood (*Sequoia*) 15, 23, 119
  adaptation to fire 16
  characteristics 16, 17
  chromosomes 18
  crown gall bacterium 62
  size 63
  sprouting ability 16
  trail plant 122
  wood "unpalatable" 55
Community classification 121, 122
Cone production
  beginning age of 90-92
  England, Europe 91
  in old age 115
  sapling stage 107, 108
  soil moisture correlation 94
  tree tops 95
Cones 88-94
  abundance 91-94
  beetle activity 90, 95, 97-99, 132
  chickaree activity 96
  doubles 133
  foliose lichens 52, 88, 99
  green cones 129
  ink production 90
  insects 133, 134
  pigment 89, 90
  ring counts 89
  scales 48, 49, 52
  staminate 91
  tannin glucoside 90
Conness, J. 12
Continental drift 66
Converse Basin 58, 59, 91
  lumbering, destructive 10
Cook, L. F. 90
Coyote 124, 125
Crab spiders (thomidids) 134
Creepers 127
Cretaceous 67
Crocker, R. L. 48, 83
Czechoslovakia 22, 80

Damping-off effect 105, 106
Dawn redwood (*Metasequoia*)
  characteristics 16, 17
  foliage 16
  fossils 67
  leaves 16
Dayton, W. A. 24
DeBano, L. F. 107
Decaisne, J. 22, 23, 24
Deer 84

Deerbrush   138
Deer Creek Grove   73
Deer mouse   124
Den Ouden, P.   18
Dietz, R. S.   66
Dixon, J. S.   142
Donaghey, J. L.   73, 107
Douglas fir
  (*Pseudotsuga menziessii*)   122, 139
  size   63
Douglas squirrel or chickaree   124
Douglass, A. E.   58
Dowd, A. T.   3, 19, 22
Dracaena draco L.   64
Dragon Tree size   64
Dudley, E. G.   69, 73, 74, 90, 106
Dunbar, C. O.   67

Ellsworth, R. S.   15
Emberger, L.   66, 67
Endlicher, S.   22, 25
Echo du Pacific   3

Ecological concepts
  biotic communities
    competition   139
    succession   141
  giant sequoia   82–86
    biomass   84
    decomposition   83, 84
    fire relationships   141–145
    food webs   83, 127
    tolerance range   85
Egypt   80
Ellsworth Huntington Expedition
  ring count   58
Empidonax flycatchers   125
England   18, 19, 23, 67, 79, 91
Europe   3, 4, 77
  cone production   91
  fossil sequoia   67
  largest specimens   80
  nurseries   18, 19
Eocene   67
Eschscholtz's salamander   126
Eucalyptus regnans F. Muell.
  height   64

"Father of the Forest"   5
Fergusson, G. J.   56
Fibonacci series   49
Ficus religiosa L.   65
Finland   80

Fire prevention   114, 140
  diminishes reproduction   145
  white fir succession   140
Fire-resistance   56
Fire scars   41, 42, 47, 48, 57, 114
  snag-tops   108, 111, 114
  up-hill side   114, 116
Fires
  adaptation to   16
  climax community   85, 86
  coast redwood   16
  debris, duff, litter   9, 104
  desirability of   140
  effect on crowns   42
  fallen trees   116
  germination   123
  giant sequoia's survival   101
  ground-cover after   123
  ground-dwelling birds   123
  leaf litter   141
  management tool   148, 150
  nemesis to insects   134
  plant successions   85, 138, 139
  prescription burning   147–150
  seed dispersal   99
  sequoia regeneration   139
  soil moisture retention   107
  tree tops   116
  wildfire   141, 145, 149
Fitzroya cupressoides
  (molina) Johnston   64
Flycatchers   127
Food webs
  giant sequoia's two   83
  Phytomatodes nitidis beetle   133
  syrphid flies and wasps   136
Forest fires
  incidence and intensity   114
Fossil sequoian ancestors   15, 22, 66
  Cretaceous   67
  Eocene   67
  Idaho community   67
  migration   67, 68
  Miocene   67
  Nevada   67
  North American, eldest   67
  Pleistocene   67, 73, 75
  Pliocene   67, 68
  South American   66
France   18, 22, 80
Fremont, J. C.   4
Fringed myotis   126
Fritts, H. C.   120

Fry, W.   47, 88, 89, 94, 97, 101, 103, 106, 115, 160, 161

Gardener's Chronicle   3, 23, 91
Garfield and Dillon groves   69
Galen Clark Tree   39, 41
Garfield Grove   75, 76
Gelechiid moth (*Gelchia* sp.)   133
General Grant National Park   12
General Grant Tree   6
    age estimates   59
    measurements   44
    rate of growth   115
General Sherman Tree   42, 44, 45, 58, 116
    age estimates   59
    growth rate   44, 115
    measurements   44, 115
Germany   80, 106
Giant Forest   13, 42, 78, 79, 106
    carpenter ants   134
    Circle Meadow area   56
    human impact   143
    leaning trees   119
    lightning strikes   115
    rocky slopes   74
    Senate and House Groups   68, 108
    snag-top sequoias   108
    snow drifts   77
    wet meadows   105, 117
Giant Forest Lodge cabin area   116
Giant sequoia
    alithermal hypothesis   79
    bark   35–38, 40, 41
    brittleness   9, 15, 55
    chickaree, relationship to   128–132
    discovery, claims of   2–4
      early rhetoric   4–6
    distribution   66–75
      Europe   80
      moisture stress   77–79
    earliest close relatives   67
    European horticulture   79, 80
    fire prevention   145
    fossil record   66
    human impact studies   141, 143–150
    insect species utilizing   132–136
    life history   87–120
      regeneration   131, 139
      reproduction   87, 88, 104
       beetle activity   97–99
       chickaree, role of   96, 97, 99, 128–132

      cone production   88–94
      germination   88, 89, 90, 100–102
      green cone retention   89
      pollination   88
      seedlings   100–107
      seeds   88–100, 128
    measurements, early   4, 5
    migration   68
    mutations   36, 69
    northernmost specimen   80
    on slopes   75
    origin   66–68
    root removal   145
    shade-intolerant   139
    soil moisture   73, 74, 77
    specimens downed   5, 6
    See also: sequoia entries; subject entries
Gilbert skink   126
Gilia (*Gilia giliodes*)   123
Gillette, H. P.   58
Gigantea   19
Gleason's Pictorial
    Drawing Room Companion   5, 6
Golden-crowned kinglet   124, 125
Golden-mantled ground squirrel   124, 125, 127
Golden sequoia
    (*S. giganteum* 'Aureum')   19
Gooseberry (*Ribes roezlii*)   123
Goshawk   125
Grant Grove   6
Gray mould blight   106
Gray squirrel   124
Greece and Albania   80
Greenland   67
Grizzly Giant   43, 44, 75
    age-dating   59
    human traffic impact   143
    leaning   117
    lightning bolt   115
Ground-cover plants   122
    prescription burning   123

Hairy woodpecker   125
Harrison, B.   13
Hartesveldt, R. J.   43, 91, 102, 104, 105, 106, 108, 117, 122, 124, 127, 140, 143, 149, 150, 159, 162
Harvey, H. T.   91, 102, 104, 106, 122, 124, 159
Harwell, C. A.   90
Hazelwood Picnic Grounds   119
Hermit thrush   124, 125
Hickey, J.   134

Hinds, J. I. D. 29
Hitchcock, E. 13
Hoary bat 126
Holden, J. C. 66
Hooker, J. 23
Horn tails (Sirex areolatus) 136
Horse flies (Tabanus laticeps) 136
Human impact 142–150
    compacted soil 143, 144
    fire prevention 145
    park management goals 147
    pavement 144
    road building 144
Hungary 57, 77, 80
Huntington, C. P. 8
Huntington, E. 59
    expedition 58

Ichneumonid and braconid wasps 136
Idaho community 67
Incense cedar
    (Libocedrus decurrens) 122
Ink production 90
Insect species
    scientific names, Appendix IV 156
    utilizing giant sequoia 132–136
Ireland 19
Irving, L. 131
Ise, J. 13
Israel 80
Italy 80

Jaquitiba Tree 64
Jeffrey pine 49, 139
Jepson, W. L. 58
Johnson, R. U. 12
Joly, C. 4
Jourdan, J. W. 44
Jumping spider (attids) 134
Jurassic period 66

Kapok size 63
Kauri pines 64
Kaweah Basin 75
Keck, D. D. 121
Kellogg, A. 22, 24
Kilgore, B. M. 124, 125, 127
Kings Canyon National Park 6, 12, 14, 42, 69
    carpenter ants 134
    prescription burns 107, 109, 149
    Sugar Bowl 68
Kings River Forest 58

Kock, K. H. 28
Krammes, J. S. 107
Krauss, R. W. 24
Kressman, F. W. 90
Krog, H. 131
Krussman, G. 4
Kuntze, K. 22
Kuntze, O. 22

Lambert, A. B. 22
Lebanon 80
Legislation landmark 12
Lenzites seapiaria (fungus) 55
Leonard narrative 2, 3
Leonard, Z. 2
Lewis, O. 58
Libby, W. F. 56
Lindley, J. T. 23, 24
Life Zone concept 121
Lightning strikes 113, 115, 116
Lindley, J. 23
Little brown myotis 126
Lobb, W. 22
Lodgepole chipmunk 125
Logging 10–12
    end of 14
Long-eared chipmunk 125
Long-eared myotis 126
Longevity 57–62
    age estimates 58
    fire scars 47
    growth curves, cross-sectional 59
    oldest count on record 58
    radio-carbon dating 56
    ring counts 57, 58
Long-leaf pine 148
Long-tailed meadow mouse 126
Long-tailed weasel 125
Lost Grove 79
Low Countries 80
Lumbering operations 9–12
    felling 9
    fires 9, 10
    log transport 10
    milling 10
    white fir 140
Lygaeid bug (Ischnorrhynchus resedae) 133
Lyons, G. W. 69, 73, 74, 90, 106

McGee Burn experiments 91
Mark Twain Tree 6, 8
Martin, E. 25, 62, 90, 104, 106
Martin, E. J. 66, 67

Mason, H. L. 148
Mammals 124–126
"Mammutbaum" 19
Manzanita 138, 140
Marten 83, 125
Matthew, J. D. 79
Meinecke, E. P. 143
Menninger, E. A. 65
Merced Grove 3, 13
Merriam's Life Zone System 121
Metasequoia (dawn redwood) 16, 66, 151
 fossils 67
 glyptostroboides characteristics 17
Metcalf, W. 90, 95, 105
Meyer, F. A. 10
Mitchell, A. 79
Mites 134
Monson, M. 131
Mooney, J. 25
Morris, R. 102
"Mother of the Forest" 6, 7
Mountain ash size 64
Mountain chickadee 124, 125, 127
Mountain lions 84, 125
Mountain meadow mouse 126
Mountain quail 125, 127
Mountain whitethorn
 (*Ceanothus cordulatus*) 122, 138, 140
Muggleton, H. 91
Muir, J. 6, 9, 12, 41, 42, 56, 57, 58, 69, 73, 74, 75, 90, 100, 119, 145, 147, 156
Muir Grove (Sequoia National Park) 78, 79
Mule deer 124
Munz, P. A. 17, 121

Nashville warbler 125, 127
National Forests
 sequoia acreage 14
National Geographic Society 14
National Park Service 25
 fire as management tool 150
 sequoia management goals 147–150
National Parks
 sequoia acreage owned 14
Nelmes, W. 18
Nelson, J. 24
New Zealand 80
Nomenclature, sequoia 19–25
 common name 25
North Calaveras Grove 58, 122
North Grove 14
Northern alligator lizard 126

Norway 80
Noyes, W. 55
Nuthatches 127

Olive-sided flycatcher 125
Olmstead, F. L. 142
Orchid (*Goodyera oblongifolia*) 141
Oregon junco 124, 125

Pacific dogwood (*Cornus nuttallii*) 122
Payson, L. E. 12, 13
Peattie, D. C. 55, 56
Peepul, or Pipal Tree 65
Peppermint Gum size 64
Pero behrensarius Pack. 106
Phacelia nutabilis 123
Photosynthesis
 ground plants 122
Phymatodes nitidus beetle 90, 129
 role in sequoia regenerations 97–99, 132, 133
Pileated woodpecker 125
Placer County Grove 69
Plant communities
 competition within 137
Plant succession 137–145
 fires, effect of 138, 140, 141
 primary and secondary 137
Plants
 scientific names, Appendix II 152
Poland 77, 80
Polymeric phenolics 55
Ponderosa pine (*Pinus ponderosa*) 49, 122
 dry weight 55
Popcorn flower (*Cryptantha affinis*) 123
Post, T. W. 22
Powderhorn Grove 78
Powers, S. 19
Prescription burning 147–150
 forage crops 148
 ground-cover changes 123
Presl, K. B. 22
Prince, W. R. 4
Pristocauthophilus pacificus Thomas 106
Pseudoscorpions 134
Pseudotsuga menziesii (Mirb.) France 63
Psocids or book lice 133, 134
Pterodactyls 15

Quirk, W. 4

Raccoon 126
Radio-carbon dating 56, 120

Rattlesnake Creek 75
Rattlesnakes, destruction of 125
Red bat 126
Red-breasted muthatch 125
Red fir (*Abies magnifica*) 122
Red-shafted flicker 125
Red-tailed hawk 125
Redwood Canyon 40, 116
Redwood Creek drainage 69, 94
Redwood family
  distribution range 16
Redwood Meadow Grove 68
Redwood Mountain Grove 42, 47, 78, 69
  Castro Tree study 91–94
  chickaree population 129, 131
  ground-cover plants 122
  rocky slopes 94
  seedling survival 104, 106
  Sugar Bowl 68, 108
  vertebrates 124–126
Red squirrels
  high critical temperature 131
Redwood Mountain Grove 14
Remy, J. 5
Renfrew, C. 120
Reptiles 126
Reservations, intent of 12, 13
Reynolds, R. D. 147
Rickett, H. W. 23
Riffer, R. 55, 119
Robberfly (*Neoitamus affinis*) 136
Robin 125, 127
Robinson, C. D. 64
Rockefeller Foundation 14
Romania 80
Roosevelt, T. 13, 14
Roosevelt Tree 42
Root-grafting 47
Root rot 106
Roots 40, 42, 43
Royal Forestry Commission 79
Rubber boa 126
Ruffus-sided towhee 125
Rundel, P. W. 42, 68, 73, 74, 77, 84, 103, 108, 122, 158
Russell, C. P. 117

Sabulodes caberata Gn. 106
Sagebrush lizard 126
Salt, G. W. 125
San Andreas Independent 4
San Jose State University 102

Sapling stage, sequoia's 34, 40
  root system 40
  spire top 34, 40
Sapsucker holes 127
Saunders, C. F. 79
Save-the-Redwoods League 14
Schlobohm, D. F. 12
Schmeckebier, L. F. 58
Schubert, G. H. 72, 77, 119
Schwarz, G. F. 120
Sclerotium bataticola Taub. 106
Scotland
  largest tree 79, 80
Seed cones 16, 48, 52
Seedling stage, sequoia's 30–33
  burned-out logs 107, 109
  cotyledons 30
  crown gall bacterium 62
  damping-off 105
  density 106, 107
  duff and litter 104
  excessive soil moisture 105
  heat canker 104
  insects 106
  leaves 30
  light factor 105, 107
  microenvironmental climate 103
  most vulnerable 80
  optimal growth conditions 104, 105
  optimum site conditions 30
  root rot 106
  root system 103, 104
  shade-intolerant 139
  soil desiccation 103, 104
  survival 101, 103–107
  taproots 30
  winter temperatures 106
Seeds, sequoia 49, 54, 88–100
  animals, effect of 100
  dispersal 73, 88, 95
    role of chickaree 96
  Europe 79
  food value 131
  germination 85, 88–91, 97, 141
    chickaree activity 97, 131
  conditions for 100–102
  experiments 88, 91, 94, 95
  fire, influence of 101, 141
  mineral soil 100
  optimum depth 102
  prescription burning 123
  soil texture 101, 102
  viability 89, 94, 99

after dissemination 100
at various stages 95
rocky slopes 94
Seeman, B. 24
Sempervirens 19
Senate and House Groups 68
Sentinel Tree
effect of pavement 144
Sequirin A and B 55
Sequoia
origin of name 25, 28
Sequoia acreage
distribution by ownership 14
Sequoia age estimates
basal age pattern 59, 60
growth curves 59
increment borings 58
living sequoia 59
oldest known 62
radio-carbon dating 56
ring counts 57, 58, 62
Sequoia couttsiae 67
Sequoiadendron chaneyi 67
Sequoiadendron giganteum
(Lindl.) Buchh. i, 24, 25
characteristics compared 17
closest generic relatives 66
common name 25
synonym 24
varietal forms 18, 19, 20
Sequoiadendron giganteum 'Pendulum' 18
Sequoia forest community 121–128
bird species 124, 125
chickaree, role of 123, 128–132
classification systems 121
decomposition 84
fires 139–145
food chain 126–128
ground cover plants 122, 123
insects 132–136
invertebrates 132–136
mammals 125
moist meadows 126
other tree species 122
plant-animal relationships 123, 124
plant succession 137–145
structure 121–123
Transition Zone 126
vertebrates 123, 124, 127
Sequoia forms
chromosome numbers 17, 18

European varieties 18
horticultural 18, 19
Sequoia gigantea 22, 23, 24
Sequoia giganteum
'Aurevariegatum' 19
Sequoia groves 68-71, 158
biotic community 122
carpenter ants 134
chickaree, role of 128-132
combustible debris 149
cooler climate 73
decadent stage 78
disjunct pattern 68, 70
distribution 61, 69
sequential stages 78
ectotherms 126
fauna characteristics 123-126
feeding habits of birds 125
flooding, effect of 75
food chains 126-128
ground cover plants 122, 123
ground litter removal 148
human impact 143-150
mean altitude 75
mutations 69
prescription burning 149
reproductive fragility 87
reptiles 126
senescence 78
soil moisture 73, 74
stability 79
terminology 68
transpiration, role of 74
white fir 140, 148
winter temperature 77
Sequoia National Forest 69, 91

Sequoia National Park 12, 13, 14, 119
carpenter ants 134
prescription burning 149
Redwood Meadow area 69
Suwanee Grove 127
Tunnel Tree 117
vegetational changes 140
Sequoia reichenbachii 67
Sequoia sempervirens
(coast redwood) 16, 22, 66, 151
decay organisms 55
'Glauca' 22
sempervirens characteristics 17
See also: coast redwood entries
Sequoia sempervirens (Lamb.) Endl.
volume size 63

Sequoia trees
  conical crown   34, 107
  death   116-119
  fire scars   41, 42, 47, 48
  fungus decay   55, 56
  growth rate   114
  in-crown cone studies   94
  leaning   117, 119
  light factor   107
  low branches   81, 108
  maturity
    bottomland trees   42
    crown   41, 42-44
    height   42
    roots   42, 43
    snag-tops   42
    soil moisture   43
    trunks   42, 44
  maximum size   43, 44
  old age   47, 48, 108, 111, 114, 119
    no senescence   115
  sapling stage   107, 108
  sapsucker holes   127
  snag-tops   42, 108, 111, 114
  swollen bases   48, 50
  toppling   116, 117, 118
  trunks   48
  vertical growth   107, 108
  See also: trees, giant sequoia
Sequoia wellingtonia   24
Sequoyah   25, 26
Shellhammer, H. S.   91, 96, 100, 104,
                          106, 122, 124, 159
Shinn, C. H.   69
Sierra Nevada
  absence of fires   148
  climatic changes   16, 77
  climax community   138
  east side   67, 68
  grove distribution map   61, 69
  rise of   68
  sequoia groves   68, 70
  western slope climate   84
"Sierra Redwood"   19, 25
Small-leaved ceanothus
  (Ceanothus parvifolius)   123, 138
Smith, C. C.   128, 131
Snag-tops   42, 108, 111, 114
Snails (Helminthoglypta)   136
Snakefly (Aqulla assimilis)   133
Soil moisture   43, 57, 73, 74
  compaction favorable   144
  cone production correlation   94

damping-off   105, 106
maximum, minimum tolerated   84
moisture stress   77-79
seedling survival   104
  desiccation   103, 104
  optimal growth   104
Soils
  alluvial   77
  compacted by traffic   143, 144
  conditioning by fire   101, 141
  plant succession   138
  podzolic   74
  Sierran soil texture   101
  Spain   77
Solitary vireo   124, 125
Sonora Herald   3
South Calaveras Grove   14, 78, 79
South Fork, Kaweah River   75, 76
South Grove Calaveras Big Tree State Park 42
Southern Hemisphere   80
Spain   77, 80
Spotted owl   125
Spurr, S. H.   59
Stable Tree   47
Starker, T. J.   5
Stark, N.   101, 102
Stebbins, G. L.   17
Stecker, R. E.   90, 97, 106, 124
Steele, R.   9
Stewart, O. C.   147
Steinhauera gigantea   22, 24
Steller's jay   124, 125
St. John, H.   24
Storer, T. I.   121
Sudworth, G. B.   24, 119
Sugar pine (Pinus lambertiana)   122, 140, 148
Sweeney, J. R.   123
Sweet cicely (Osmorhiza chilensis) 122
Sweden   80
Switzerland   18, 80
Synopsis Coniferae   25
Syrphid fly (Syrphus dp.)   136

Tall lupine (Lupinus latifolius)   123
Tanagers   127
Tannin glucoside   90
Taxodiaceae
  genera and species   16, 151
Taxodium (southern and
  pond cypresses)   16, 151
Taxodium giganteum   22, 24
Taxodium mucronatum Ten.   64
Taxodium sempervirens (coast redwood) 22

Taxodium washingtonianum   23, 24
Thin-stemmed primrose
  (*Gayophytum nuttallii*)   123
Thompson, B. H.   142
Thompson, C. G.   149
Tiemann, H. D.   65
Todd, J.   4
Torrey, J.   22
Townsend chipmunk   125
Townsend's solitaire   125
Trachykele opulenta   132
Trail plant (*Adenocaulon bicolor*)   122, 123
Transition Zone   122, 126
Transition and Canadian zones   123
Trapper Creek, Idaho   67
Trees, giant sequoia
  age estimates   58-62
  bark   35-38, 40-42, 47, 73
  decay organisms   55
  fallen decomposers   83
  fire-resistant   57, 58
  fused   47
  old age   47
  ring counts   57, 58
  size and age   44, 57
  total volume   44
  trunks without crowns   47
Trees, other large   63, 64
Trees, world's largest
  measurements   44
  See also: sequoia trees
Trowbridge shrew   125
Tule cypress size   64
Tunnel Tree   19, 21
  removal   117, 118
Tuolumne and Merced groves   3, 13
Turkey   80

U. S. Dept. Agriculture   49, 90
U. S. Dept. Interior   142
U. S. Forest Service   14, 25
Usinger, R. L.   121
USSR   80

Vagrant shrew   126
Vandever, W.   12, 13
Vankat, J. L.   140
Veitch, J.   22, 23
Voss, A.   24

Wagener, W.   119
Walker party's discovery   2, 3, 19

Warblers   127
Warbling vireo   124, 125
Washburn Brothers   117
Washingtonia californica   23, 24
Water shrew   126
"wawona" (big tree)   19
Wawona Tree   117
Wawona Tunnel Tree
  age   62
Weeping sequoia (*Sequoiadendrum
  giganteum* 'Pendulum')   18-20
  U.S. specimens   19
Wellesley, A.   23
Wellingtonia gigantea   23, 24, 25
Western azalea
  (*Rhododendron occidentale*)   123
Western fence lizard   126
Western rattlesnake   126
Western ringneck snake   126
Western robin   124
Western terrestrial garter snake   126
Western tanager   124, 125
Western toad   126
Western whiptail lizard   126
Western wood peewee   125
Western yew (*Taxus brevifolia*)   122
Wet meadows   105, 117
Whitaker's Forest   124, 149
White fir (*Abies concolor*)   122
  canopy   33, 105
  low lumber value   148
  replaced sugar pine   148
White hawkweed
  (*Hieracium albiflorum*)   122, 123
White-headed woodpecker   125, 127
White, J. R.   14, 47, 88, 89, 94, 97, 101, 103, 106, 115, 160, 161
White Mountain Range   120
Wildfires   141, 145, 149
Wild gooseberry   138
Wilson, H. E.   69
Winslow, C. F.   23, 24
Winter temperatures   106
Winter wren   125
Wolfe, L. M.   6, 57
Wong, A.   55, 119
Wood, giant sequoia   55-57
  brittleness   55
  dry weight   55
  durability   55, 56, 120
  fallen trees   119
  fire resistance   56
  heartwood   55, 56

high tannin content 119
radio-carbon dating 56
sapwood 56
soil moisture 59
Woodpeckers 127
Wood violet (*Viola lobata*) 122
Wooster, J. M 4
Wright, G. M. 142
Wulff, J. V. 69, 73, 74, 90, 106

Yellow-bellied sapsucker 125
Yellow-legged frog 126
Yellow Pine Belt 122
Yellow-pine chipmunk 125

Yellow-rumped warbler 124
Yellowstone National Park
    Eocene 67
Yosemite Grant 12, 142
Yosemite National Park 12
    prescription burning 149
Yosemite Valley 12, 13, 142
Yosemite's Mariposa Grove 12, 13,
        39, 41, 44, 75, 105, 115,
        122, 142
    tunneled California Tree 117
    tourist travel 143
    white fir 140
Yugoslavia 80
Yuma myotis 126

Zinke, P. J. 48, 83

☆ U.S. GOVERNMENT PRINTING OFFICE : 1976 O—596—106